KNOW YOUR WOODS

KNOW YOUR WOODS

by

ALBERT CONSTANTINE, JR.

Revised by

HARRY J. HOBBS

CHARLES SCRIBNER'S SONS
New York

Charles Scribner's Sons
Macmillan Publishing Company
866 Third Avenue, New York, N.Y. 10022
Collier Macmillan Canada, Inc.

Library of Congress Cataloging-in-Publication Data

Constantine, Albert.
  Know your woods.

  Bibliography: p.
  Includes indexes.
    1. Trees.   2. Wood.   3. Timber.   4. Trees—
Dictionaries.   5. Wood—Dictionaries.   6. Timber—
Dictionaries.   7. Veneers and veneering.   I. Hobbs,
Harry J.   II. Title.
SD434.C65   1987   674'.1   87-9622
ISBN 0-684-18778-7

Macmillan books are available at special discounts for bulk purchases for sales promotions, premiums, fund-raising, or educational use. For details, contact:

Special Sales Director
Macmillan Publishing Company
866 Third Avenue
New York, N.Y. 10022

First Scribner Paperback Edition 1987

10   9   8

Printed in the United States of America

To the memory of my father

ALBERT CONSTANTINE
1862–1948

who shared his extraordinary knowledge
of woods with me and encouraged me in the
studies that led to the writing of this book

Preface

Every person interested in the broad subject of woods—their identification, characteristics and uses—will find this book a revelation. The information is presented in a clear, nontechnical style for enjoyable and informative reading. So many facts, including some that are unusual or little known, have never before been assembled in a volume of this kind and so skillfully organized for ready reference. In particular, the descriptions of individual woods should be useful to the student as well as to the general reader. This volume will be a much-sought reference by craftsmen engaged in dealing with woods.

William L. Stern

B.S., M.S., Ph.D.

Professor of Botany
College of Agriculture
University of Maryland
College Park, Maryland

A Note About the Illustrations

In addition to photographs from the author's collection and drawings made especially for this book by Howard R. Berry and Arthur Collani, a number of illustrations from other sources are being used by permission. Acknowledgments for the photographs and drawings which have so generously been made available are as follows:

U.S. Forest Service: Frontispiece, Figs. 1, 5, 14E, 54, 62, 63, 65, 66, and the photographs on the following pages: 152, 162 (bottom), 180, 204 (bottom right), 218, 255, 257 (top), 259 (bottom left), 277 (top and bottom left), 299, 305 (left), and 309.

Western Wood Products Association: Figs. 21A–E and the photograph on page 277 (top right).

The Dean Company: Figs. 22, 23, 27A–E, 28, 29, 30, and 31.

Texas Forest Service: Figs. 67 and 69 and the photographs on pages 228 and 268.

The Bettmann Archive, Inc.: Fig. 41.

The American Museum of Natural History: Figures 4 and 14I.

Massachusetts Department of Natural Resources: Photograph on page 191.

Fine Hardwoods/American Walnut Association: Cover, Figs. 10, 11, 35, 36, 52, and the photographs on the following pages: 143, 145, 146, 154, 155 (top right), 157 (right), 163, 168 (top), 176, 179 (top), 189, 190, 199,

200, 204 (bottom left), 209, 210, 219 (bottom), 224, 225, 227 (top), 232 (bottom), 239, (top), 240 (top), 241, 245 (bottom left), 250, 259 (top left and right, bottom right), 264 (top), 267, 269, 284, 285, 286, 287, 301 (bottom), 310, 312 (top), 319, 320 (top), 326, and 328.

Australian News and Information Bureau: Figs. 16 and 51 and the photographs on pages 150 and 164.

United Nations: Figs. 15, 17, 18, 19, 24, 44, 46, 47, 48, 49, 64, 68, and the photographs on pages 147 (bottom), 162 (top), 175 (top), 239 (bottom), and 248.

New Zealand Information Service: Fig. 25 and the photograph on page 215.

U. S. Department of Agriculture: Photographs on the following pages: 147 (top), 157 (left), 165, 166, 175 (bottom left and right), 194, 195, 204 (top left and right), 207, 216 (bottom left and right), 222, 230, 244, 257 (bottom), 272, 277 (bottom right), 283 (left), 301 (top), 305 (right), and 306.

United Brands Company: Photograph on page 234.

Introduction
to the Revised Edition

It has been a privilege and an enjoyable experience for me to revise and bring this useful book up-to-date. On many occasions before the book was first published, I called upon its author, my good friend Albert Constantine, Jr., for personal help in identifying an unfamiliar wood I had come upon, or for his expert advice on selecting wood for a specific use. As an editor and writer in the woodworking craft field, I welcomed the appearance of *Know Your Woods*, and I used it as my chief reference source for facts about woods.

I knew of no other book with so many helpful photographs of wood grain, and I have expanded this feature of the book by including many new closeups of woods not illustrated in the first edition. I have also added a large number of clues to help in identifying the woods we meet and the trees they come from, and I have added sections on new world-wide forestation programs; logging and sawmill operations; latest lumber and veneer manufacturing methods; and other related subjects of interest to anyone who would like to know more about the fascinating life-sequence of fine woods.

A number of associations, state foresters and other persons having special knowledge in this field opened their files of photographs to me. Some took photographs I specially requested. For all of this generous assistance I am sincerely grateful.

Harry Jason Hobbs

Author's
Introduction

Much of the material in this book is based on information gathered during almost forty years of active participation in the fine cabinet-wood business. The Constantine family has been connected with the fine wood trade in New York since 1812— from its early history to the present. For many years, Constantine & Company acted as the official measurers, weighers and inspectors of all foreign timbers entering the port of New York. At an early age, therefore, the author acquired a love for woods which led to many years of research in this field.

Many people find beauty and pleasure in trees and the craft objects which can be produced from their timbers. Because of this, there are no doubt some who would like to know a bit more about these plants to help increase their interest and enjoyment. Wood is pleasant and friendly; it is nice to look at; it is warm in winter, cool in summer and always comfortable to live with. I feel sure that many people share with me this close attachment to wood and will gain from this modest introduction to the study of wood. I have tried to present a general, readable story about trees and woods, their characteristics and uses and some of the fascinating facts not ordinarily encountered by the lover of woods.

Trees producing timber grow in practically all regions of the globe. There is little doubt that wood was one of the earliest materials employed by ancient man in his fabrications. Even today, despite the tremendous emphasis on steel, concrete, glass and plastics in construction and manufacture of all kinds, wood still maintains its importance as an essential commodity. The concrete building is constructed by employing reusable plywood forms; the plastic in radio and television cabinets is strengthened with wood-fiber filler; wood is still most important as a construction material for small homes. More wood is being used today than ever before. Trees also provide us with many intangibles: they improve the appearance of our homes and other buildings, shade us from the hot sun and keep the strong winds from buffeting our dwellings. Trees are effective in flood control, they clothe the watersheds of our reservoirs and rivers and provide refuge for wildlife. Our recreational areas are more useful and enjoyable when surrounded by trees. Briefly then, aside from the material things, the value of trees and tree-covered lands is not measurable in a monetary way.

In order to understand woods and the trees producing them, it is essential that we know something of tree growth, how trees are named and the methods used in collecting and identifying woods. Therefore, I have included sections on these subjects written in nontechnical language. Chapters on medicinal trees, little-known behavior of plants, trees and woods, and woods mentioned in the Bible are also in this volume. The major part of the text is, however, concerned with the woods themselves.

The largest collection of woods in the world is Yale University's Samuel James Record Memorial Collection. Here are housed over 52,000 specimens of wood. More than 240 plant families are represented in this collection, each possessing some woody species. It is certainly beyond the scope of this book to include even a small fraction of this vast array of woods; rather, I have chosen the species described because some are commercially important, others are interesting historically, a number produce valuable fruits and some are of a curious nature. For the most part, however, I have selected trees which are producers of lumber and veneer. The descriptions are brief and for the most part are confined to some of the more interesting facts, including technical information. Among the subjects considered are the appearance of the wood itself, texture, figure, weight, seasoning characteristics and strength data where available. For the craftsman, I have tried to include the working qualities of woods: which can be used with power or hand tools, which finish easily and which require special care. With common trees, a more detailed description of the flowers and leaves is presented; with trees growing in remote areas, descriptions are mostly limited to wood characteristics. Detailed information on the bark has been omitted except where the bark is of striking appearance.

In general, the information given has been selected to provide the craftsman and layman with a broad, practical knowledge of woods. References are cited in the bibliography for those who wish to delve more deeply into a given subject. Illustrations have been liberally employed to provide a vivid, visual supplement to the text. I have tried to approach the subject personally, to convey to readers my own thrill and fascination in this living subject. I hope that I can make woods live for them too.

Albert Constantine, Jr.

Contents

KNOW YOUR WOODS

PART ONE

The Wonderful Story of Woods

Fig. 1. This magnificent stand of virgin eastern hemlock seeded itself, protected itself from its natural enemy—the wind, survived countless centuries as a forest and is now preserved by law. Longfellow Trail, Cook Forest State Park, Pennsylvania.

CHAPTER 1

A Tree Lives

From the seed that chances to lodge in a suitable niche, the seedling emerges. Surely the seed is a thing at which to marvel! When conditions for sprouting are favorable, when the soil is moist and warm, deep changes begin to take place in the dormant seed. The embryo "feeds" upon the stored food in the seed, water is absorbed and the latent plantlet begins to grow. Normally, the embryo grows fast, swelling with vigor and splitting the seed coat. The seedling emerges to greet the sunlight. The upper portion or shoot elongates skyward; the rootlet plumbs the earth to perform its function of anchorage, support, food storage and absorption of water and soil nutrients. Unlike animals, most plants remain stationary throughout their lives.

The seedling tree is tender. Its first leaves may remain within the seed beneath the ground, as in the oak, or they may be carried upward, as in the maple. At the tip of the little shoot, tucked

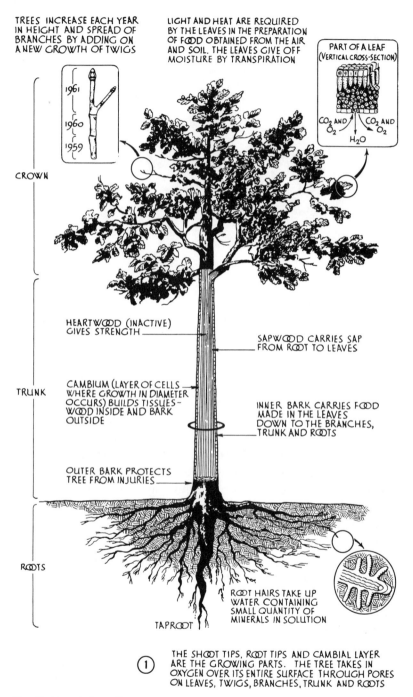

TREES INCREASE EACH YEAR IN HEIGHT AND SPREAD OF BRANCHES BY ADDING ON A NEW GROWTH OF TWIGS

1961
1960
1959

LIGHT AND HEAT ARE REQUIRED BY THE LEAVES IN THE PREPARATION OF FOOD OBTAINED FROM THE AIR AND SOIL. THE LEAVES GIVE OFF MOISTURE BY TRANSPIRATION

PART OF A LEAF (VERTICAL CROSS-SECTION)

CO_2 AND O_2 CO_2 AND O_2
H_2O

CROWN

HEARTWOOD (INACTIVE) GIVES STRENGTH

SAPWOOD CARRIES SAP FROM ROOT TO LEAVES

CAMBIUM (LAYER OF CELLS WHERE GROWTH IN DIAMETER OCCURS) BUILDS TISSUES – WOOD INSIDE AND BARK OUTSIDE

INNER BARK CARRIES FOOD MADE IN THE LEAVES DOWN TO THE BRANCHES, TRUNK AND ROOTS

TRUNK

OUTER BARK PROTECTS TREE FROM INJURIES

ROOTS

ROOT HAIRS TAKE UP WATER CONTAINING SMALL QUANTITY OF MINERALS IN SOLUTION

TAPROOT

① THE SHOOT TIPS, ROOT TIPS AND CAMBIAL LAYER ARE THE GROWING PARTS. THE TREE TAKES IN OXYGEN OVER ITS ENTIRE SURFACE THROUGH PORES ON LEAVES, TWIGS, BRANCHES, TRUNK AND ROOTS

Fig. 2. How a tree lives.

in between the seed leaves, is the terminal bud which contains the growing point (*apical meristem*), which is responsible for the growth in length of the shoot. Theoretically, the tree is capable of indefinite growth, and we know that there are trees now living which are over four thousand years old. Root tips also possess a growing point, the action of which elongates the roots (Fig. 2).

Most trees can be classified into one of two groups, as far as their root systems are concerned: either the fibrous-root system or the taproot. Trees with fibrous-root systems, to which the firs, various types of maples, beeches and many others belong, have many horizontal roots and a maze of smaller rootlets, all close to the level of the ground. Trees with the taproot system have a principal vertical root which in a large tree may go a depth of from 14 to 18 ft., from which smaller separate lateral root systems extend. A few of the more common trees that belong to this group are pines, various hickories and the oaks.

Sometime during its first year of life, another growth tissue is formed as an internal sheath surrounding the stem and root. This sheath is called the *vascular cambium*. It causes the tree to increase in diameter and produces layers of wood toward the inside and layers of bark toward the outside. In regions where growth is interrupted at some time during the year, as in temperate climates, distinguishable layers are produced each growing season in the wood. These layers are called *growth rings*, or *annual rings* where they correspond to yearly increments of wood (Fig. 3). Therefore, by counting these rings, a fairly good estimate of a tree's age can be made. In the tropics, where growth is continuous throughout the year, rings, if formed, are ordinarily not indicative of age. Tree rings can often tell stories: a year of poor rainfall is indicated by narrow annual rings; conversely, years of abundant rainfall are reflected in wide annual rings. Employing this method, scientists can estimate, on a section of an old tree, the climatic conditions of the past. This technique is embodied in the science of dendrochronology.

Using a lens, one can see minute pores on the cross section of a hardwood. These pores are in reality sections of tubes or vessels which transport water and dissolved minerals through the stem and its branches to the leaves. In softwoods, no such vessels are present and the water must move through fiberlike cells. In hardwoods, most of the wood is composed of narrow, elongated cells called fibers. In softwoods, too, the wood is composed almost exclusively of fiberlike cells called *tracheids*. Both the fibers of hardwoods and the fiberlike cells of softwoods serve to strengthen the tree. However, in softwoods the fiberlike cells have the additional function of water conduction.

As stated previously, one of the main functions of roots is anchorage. About 10 percent of the wood mass of a tree is found in the root system. The root system of a large tree is enormous, and the combined length of the roots of a spreading oak amounts to many hundreds of miles. Especially in dry areas, root systems are very well developed; in moister environments, the growth of roots is curtailed. It is important to remember that roots are an integral part of the living organism that is the tree. They require air, food and water for growth and to perform their functions of anchorage, support, storage and absorption.

Like other green plants, trees manufacture food in leaves (*photosynthesis*) in the presence of sunlight, from the carbon dioxide of the air, and the water from the soil (Fig. 2). The simple food thereby produced combines in complex ways with minerals brought up by the water stream, through the trunk from the soil, to produce the living substances of which the tree is built. Most of the solid matter of trees is wood, a chemical compound made up mainly of *cellulose* and *lignin*. It is the latter compound which, in greater or lesser amounts, contributes to the hardness of wood. When wood is burned, the elements of which it is composed are dispersed; the carbon, hydrogen, nitrogen and oxygen are dissipated in the smoke; phosphorus, some carbon and other elements make up the ash. A total of 27 elements, including silver, titanium and nickel, are found in the ashes of white pine wood.

Water is contained in all the tissues of a tree, both dead and alive. Young leaves or tips of roots contain up to 90 percent water. Tree trunks may contain as much as 50 percent. Water is indispensable to the tree, as all living processes take place in this medium. As explained, mineral nutrients are carried from the soil to the top of the tree in a stream of water. In spring, the organic material in the form of sugars and amino acids is rushed

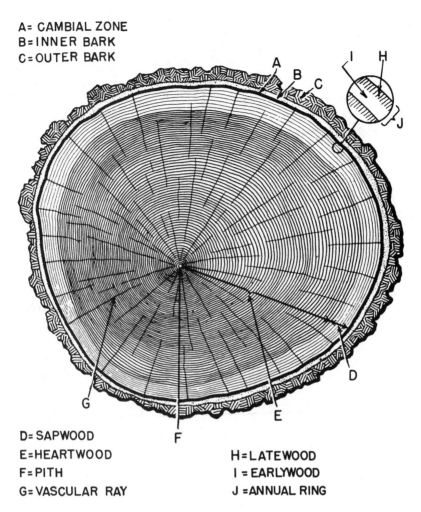

A = CAMBIAL ZONE
B = INNER BARK
C = OUTER BARK

D = SAPWOOD
E = HEARTWOOD
F = PITH
G = VASCULAR RAY

H = LATEWOOD
I = EARLYWOOD
J = ANNUAL RING

Fig. 3. Cross section of tree trunk.

in a stream of water from its place of winter storage to the bursting buds. Water is absorbed by the roots, pushed into the sapwood and then pulled up to the leaves—in redwood, as high as 350 ft. above the ground.

Reproduction occurs when the tree reaches maturity. The sexual reproduction of trees is basically similar to that of animals. In flowering plants, reproduction manifests itself by the appearance of flowers. Male and female reproductive parts may be borne in a single flower or they may occur in separate flowers. Male and female flowers may occur on the same tree or on separate trees as in cottonwood. The male germ cell is carried in

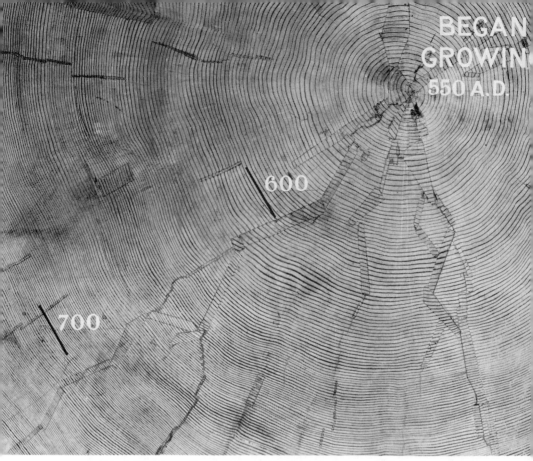

600

700

Fig. 4. This is a cross-section view of a giant sequoia Sequoia washing-tonii. It was 1,341 years old, 332 feet tall, and 90 feet in circumference at the base when felled in Fresno County, California. There were no limbs up to 200 feet. Its fibrous root system spread three acres.

the pollen to the receptive portion of the female sexual apparatus. The sperms fertilize the eggs, which then mature into embryos. The process of reproduction differs in the hardwoods, or flowering plants, from that in the softwoods, or cone-bearing plants.

Sexual reproduction in trees is responsible for the development of diversity. In the germ cells of male and female are located the bearers of hereditary traits, the chromosomes. By combining characters of the pollen parent with those of the seed parent, new combinations may be formed, some of which may be very valuable. But sexual reproduction is not absolutely necessary for the propagation of trees. Many of them can be reproduced by vegetative means such as by cuttings, grafting and budding. These methods enable the grower to maintain stocks of young trees exactly the same as their parents.

Old age comes to trees as to all other living organisms. As noted above, theoretically the life span of a tree is indefinite; however, we find that certain species are longer-lived than others. The gray birch is old at 40; sugar maple lives longer, up to 500 years. Some oaks may live 1,500 years, junipers more than 2,000 years. Some of the giant sequoias (Fig. 4) are believed to have been on earth 1,000 and perhaps 2,000 years before Christ. There are bristlecone pines (*Pinus aristata*) in California over 4,000 years old (Fig. 5). Old trees are like old people. The infirmities of age come upon them. They have difficulty with respiration and their recuperative capacity is impaired; wounds do not heal as easily. The leaves become smaller and their moisture content decreases. It becomes increasingly difficult for the tree to provide water for its vital functions. Soon the tree decays, little by little, until it is entirely consumed. The elements from which it was composed have been released into the environment, to be used again by new life, just developing.

The life a tree has had can be read with a surprising degree of accuracy by examining a cross section. By counting the growth rings and inspecting their condition, experts can pinpoint the year of a forest fire, the years of invasion by insects, a change of lean, and other such occurrences.

The way a forest modifies temperature and humidity has been noticed by all who spend much time in the heavy woods, but the precise effect is realized by few. The changes in temperature vary a great deal in the same forest, depending upon the level between the floor of the forest and the level of the tree tops. The few figures given are of the two extremes—weather at the level of the tree tops and on the ground. These figures are the result of study in an average forest in the northern United States.

Light. On summer afternoons, with bright sunlight, less than 1 percent of the light reaches the floor of the forest, but on overcast, cloudy days, 3 percent of the light measured at the top of the trees reaches the ground.

Wind. In midsummer, trees in full bloom will, at the level of the ground, reduce a wind of fifty miles an hour to approximately 4 miles. Even during the winter, when the trees and branches are bare of foliage, they will reduce the velocity of the air more than 50 percent.

Temperature. During the summer there is practically no variation from the forest floor to the tree tops during the night or on rainy days, but in the hours of bright sunlight, in midsummer, the floor of the forest can be as much as thirty degrees cooler than the top leaves of the trees.

Humidity. There is a similar variation in humidity in the forests from the tree top to the ground. On a hot summer day the variation could be the difference between 28 percent, measured at the top of the trees, and 80 percent on the ground, but on a rainy day or during the night there would be practically no variation in the humidity between the two positions.

Rains and Evaporation. In summer showers, less than half the amount of the rain reaches the level of the ground, but in a continuous steady rain, the percentage is higher. However, each acre of woodland on a summer day returns to the air over two thousand gallons of water through the process known as transpiration.

Insects are extremely important members of the forest community. Their most vital roles are as pollinators of the flowering plants and as scavengers that feed on waste matter and organic remains. The most typical forest insects are those that feed on trees.

The greatest variety of insects is the leaf-chewing type, attracted to the highly nutritious and extremely accessible leaves rather than to any other part of the tree. These are divided into seven broad groups:

Leaf-Mining Insects. The larvae of a number of very small leaf-eating insects feed within the leaf tissues of the leaves.

Gall-Making Insects. Many insects can cause plants to produce abnormal growth called "galls." Most of these gall insects are wasps, flies and sawflies.

Fig. 5. Bristlecone pines are among the oldest known living things in the world. This picturesque sculptured trunk in Patriarch Grove, California's Inyo National Forest, rejects decay. Its neighbors characteristically still have the ability, though parts are dead, to concentrate their vitality on a few branches so that they can survive for centuries.

Twig-Boring Insects. The larvae of a few insects, which are beetles, bore through the tender twigs and small branches of the trees. At times large portions of a tree's crown may be killed. Such damage is especially serious on young trees.

Seed-Eating Insects. The abundant and nutritious food stored in tree seeds presents a lavish feeding and spawning ground for insects.

Cambium-Eating Insects. Many species of insects feed on the highly nutritious cambium and the adjacent layers beneath the bark. Under normal conditions, healthy trees are able to combat the insects by surrounding them with pitch.

Wood-Eating Insects. The woody trunk is the most characteristic organ of the tree. However, the wood is so well protected, so tough and relatively so low in food value that comparatively few insects have become adapted to feeding on it. The majority of wood eaters are attracted to weak or dead trees.

Sap-Sucking Insects. The rich sap of the trees is normally contained beneath the bark or wood to protect the tissues. When these tissues are injured and the sap escapes, a great variety of insects may gather to feed upon it. The injury caused by sap-sucking insects is ordinarily insignificant. Occasionally, a great number of sap suckers remove sufficient volumes of food and water and inject large amounts of poisonous saliva to cause serious injury or even the death of trees.

To most people the surface of dead leaves and the thin layer of top soil that forms the forest floor seem to be a lifeless trash heap. In reality, the floor is the most densely populated stratum of the forest. The number of organisms that live on every square foot may be four times as great as the human population of the world. Most of these organisms are microscopic bacteria, fungi, algae and protozoa. Each year about two tons of leaves, flowers, wood cuttings and twigs fall on every acre of forest floor.

CHAPTER 2

Identification
of Woods

"The Staple of the Stuff is so exquisitely fine, that no Silkworm is able to draw anything near so fine a Thread. So that one who walks about with the meanest stick, holds a piece of Nature's Handicraft, which far surpasses the most elaborate Woof or Needle Work in the World."

Description of wood from Nehemiah Grew, 1682, in his *The Anatomy of Plants Begun,* which contains one of the first treatises on wood structure.

The complexities of wood structure have been recognized for several centuries. Man is a curious creature; he has pondered, investigated and communicated his ideas about the objects of his curiosity. The structure of wood has not been exempt from this inquisitiveness. Indeed, there is hardly a person who has existed on this earth who has not thought to some extent about wood, its kinds, colors, textures and uses.

So that we may know something of how woods are characterized and identified, we must know something about wood itself, of what chemical substances it is composed, how these substances form the ultimate particles of wood (cells) and how the organization of the cells and the compounds they contain impart character to wood.

Our story begins with the *vascular cambium,* that sheath of generative cells which surrounds the tree between the bark and the wood. It is the production of new cells by this sheath that gives rise to wood on the inside and bark on the outside. As mentioned in another chapter, wherever there are climatic periods during the year which are not conducive to growth (cold winters, periodic droughts), the formation of wood is discontinuous. Because of this, successive layers of wood are visible on the cross section of a log. Where the period of growth and production of wood occurs once a year, these layers correspond to the year, so we can call such annual layers *annual rings*. In certain climates, several interrupted periods of growth occur during the year; several layers of wood are produced, and these layers do not correspond to an annual cycle. It is best here to call such layers by the general term *growth rings*. In the tropics, where growth and wood formation are more or less continuous, growth layers are not formed, for the most part, and the wood appears fairly homogeneous from the pith to the bark.

An annual ring is frequently divisible into two layers, one formed during the beginning of the growing season and another toward the end. These are termed *springwood* or *earlywood* and *summerwood* or *latewood*. Cells in springwood are generally larger, and thinner-walled than those in summerwood. The distinctness of these layers is at times important in identification (Fig. 6).

When looking at a cross section of a log, we are frequently impressed by the fact that the wood in the center is of a darker or different color than the wood toward the outside. This inner darker layer is the *heartwood*; the outer layer is the *sapwood*.

The heartwood is physiologically inactive; its cells are dead and frequently clogged with dark-colored waste materials, which give it a characteristic color. Heartwood serves as the main structural element of the trunk. It is more resistant to decay than the sapwood. The sapwood is physiologically active; it contains living cells and is responsible for conducting water and dissolved minerals from the roots to the crown of the tree. Normally, there is less sapwood than heartwood. Heartwood is more valuable commercially and most timbers with which we are familiar come from this colored, denser wood. The characteristic purple-brown of black walnut (*Juglans nigra*) occurs only in the heartwood; the sapwood is almost white. Purpleheart, a beautiful tropical

American timber, exhibits bright purple heartwood; the sapwood is creamy white. The heartwood is commercially valuable; the sapwood is discarded.

Lumber is commonly divided into two main categories: *softwoods* and *hardwoods*. These two groups correspond roughly to conifers or cone-bearing trees and flowering trees. All commercial species of trees belong to one or the other of these groups. This division, based on hardness of wood, has its shortcomings, as there are softwoods (conifers) with harder woods than certain hardwoods (flowering trees). For example, any one of the southern pines (U.S.A.) has harder wood than balsa. Yet, according to this classification, the southern pines are softwoods and balsa is a hardwood. Regardless of the exceptions, this system is in common use and should be understood by the wood enthusiast. There are, however, more fundamental ways of classifying woods, subject to fewer exceptions. These will be considered when we take up wood structure.

Chemically, wood is not a single substance; it is a complex aggregate of compounds, the nature of which is still inadequately understood by wood chemists even today. About 99 percent of the dry weight of wood consists of cellulose and related substances, and of lignin. Cellulose is a carbohydrate, as are sugar and starch; it contains the chemical elements carbon, hydrogen and oxygen, hydrogen and oxygen being present in the same proportions as in water, namely, two of hydrogen for one of oxygen.

The chemical structure of lignin is only partly known. We do know that there are several kinds of lignins in wood, each designated by the name of the chemist who synthesized them, as Braun's lignin, Klason's lignin and Bjorkman's lignin. Since lignin is the substance that makes wood woody (cotton fibers are pure cellulose), the following facts should be noted: (1) Lignin is composed of carbon (61–65) percent, hydrogen (5–6 percent) and oxygen (30 percent). It is the manner in which these three elements are chemically united, and their proportions, that makes lignin differ from cellulose. (2) Lignin is the major constituent remaining in woody tissues after the cellulose has been removed.

Wood also contains minerals, which are present in varying

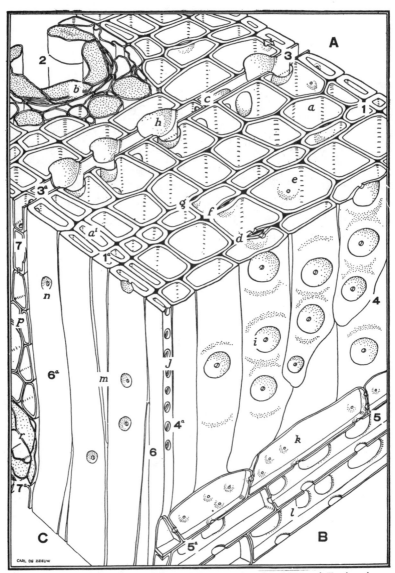

Figs. 6 and 7 schematic drawings from Textbook of Wood Technology by Panshin and DeZeeuw (McGraw-Hill). Above, Fig. 6, three-plane drawing of the wood of eastern white pine or northern white pine (Pinus Strobus).

Surface A. 1-1ᵃ, portion of an annual ring; 2. resin canal; 3-3ᵃ, wood ray; a-a', longitudinal tracheids; b, epithelial cells; c, ray cells; d, pit pair in median sectional view; e, bordered pits in the back walls of longitudinal tracheids, in surface view; f, pit pair in sectional view, showing the margin of the torus, but so cut that the pit apertures are not included in the plane of section; g, pit pair in which neither the pit aperture nor the torus shows; h, window-like pit pairs between longitudinal tracheids and ray parenchyma.

Surface B. 4-4ᵃ, portions of longitudinal tracheids in radial aspect (the ends are blunt); 5-5ᵃ, upper part of uniseriate ray; i, bordered pits on the radial walls of longitudinal spring-wood tracheids (the base of the pit is toward the observer); j, small bordered pits on the radial walls of longitudinal summerwood tracheids, in the same view as in i; k, ray tracheids; l, cells of ray parenchyma.

Surface C. 6-6ᵃ, portions of longitudinal tracheids in tangential aspect; 7-7ᵃ, portion of a xylary ray; m, tapering ends of longitudinal tracheids; n, a small bordered pit on the tangential wall of a longitudinal summerwood tracheid; p, cells of ay parenchyma; r, transverse resin canal.

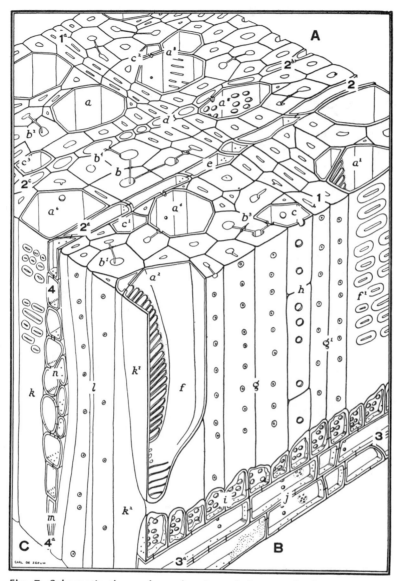

Fig. 7. Schematic three-plane drawing of the wood of sweetgum or redgum (Liquidambar styraciflua).

Surface *A.* 1-1ª, boundary between two annual rings (growth proceeded from right to left); 2-2ª, wood ray consisting of procumbent cells; 2ᵇ-2ᶜ, wood ray consisting of upright cells; a-aᵍ, inclusive, pores (vessels in transverse section); b-b⁴, inclusive, fiber tracheids; c-c³, inclusive, cells of longitudinal parenchyma; e, procumbent ray cell.

Surface *B.* f, f¹, portions of vessel segments; g, g¹, portions of fiber tracheids in lateral surface aspect; h, a strand of longitudinal parenchyma in lateral surface aspect; 3-3ª, upper portion of a heterogeneous wood ray in lateral sectional aspect; i, a marginal row of upright cells; j, two rows of horizontal cells.

Surface *C.* k, portion of a vessel segment in tangential surface aspect; k¹, k², overlapping vessel segments in tangential surface aspect; l, fiber tracheids in tangential surface aspect; 4-4ª, portion of a wood ray intangential sectional view; m, an upright cell in the lower margin; n, procumbent cells in the body of the ray.

amounts and kinds. The principal components of ash (minerals) are calcium, potassium and magnesium; some sodium, manganese, iron and aluminum are also usually present. Other minerals may occur in trace amounts. Numerous other substances may be found in wood; for instance: crystals of calcium oxalate, starch grains, sugars, essential oils (as in camphorwood), fats, fatty oils, resins (in pines), latex, tannins, dyestuffs (in heartwood of fustic) and various alkaloids (such as caffeine).

The identification of woods is based largely on the kinds of cells (Figs. 6 and 7), the arrangement of these cells into tissues, and the gross appearance these tissues present to the eye. Wood cells are microscopic and can be observed on slivers cut so that light will pass through them (about 15/25,000 of an inch thick). Such slivers may need to be dyed to make the cells more easily visible.

In general, wood serves the tree in two ways: it supports the tree (main function of heartwood) and carries water from the roots to the leaves (sapwood). The cells of which wood is composed are specialized to perform these two functions. Thus we have cells which are largely supportive, cells which are supportive and conductive, and cells which are largely conductive. Supportive cells generally have thick, minutely pitted walls, are long, and are sharply tapered at either end. Such cells are classified as *fibers*. Cells which function both in support and conduction have thinner, conspicuously pitted walls, and blunter tips. These cells are called *tracheids*. *Vessels* are tubes composed of short cells which can be called *vessel cells*. The vessel is much like a long pipe made up of shorter lengths of pipe (vessel cells, Fig. 7). Vessel cells are functional largely in conduction. They are thin-walled and open at the ends much as lengths of pipe. A cross section of a vessel is called a pore. All the elements of wood just described are oriented parallel to the axis of the stem. Fibers and vessels are characteristic of hardwoods (flowering trees), the vessels being embedded in a matrix of fibers. Tracheids (Fig. 6) compose most of the wood mass of softwoods (conifers). Thus, based on the wood, the major difference between hardwoods and softwoods is that in the former, vessels (pores) are present. Softwoods do not contain any vessels (pores). Hardwoods are sometimes referred to as *pored* or *por-*

ous timbers and softwoods as *non-pored* or *non-porous* timbers.

In hardwoods, when pores are larger or more abundant in one portion of a growth ring than in another, the wood is *ring porus*. The northern oaks (*Quercus*), ash (*Fraxinus*), and hickory (*Carya*) are examples of ring-porous woods. If the pores, on the other hand, are of fairly even sizes and are well distributed throughout the growth ring, the wood is diffuse porous. The woods of magnolia, maple (*Acer*), birch (*Betula*) and beech (*Fagus*) are diffuse porous. This classification does not apply to softwoods, since they do not have pores.

Other kinds of cells and tissues occur in the woods of hardwoods and softwoods. One category is mostly concerned with the storage of foods. These tissues are the so-called soft tissues, or *parenchyma* (pa-ren'chy-ma). The *vascular rays*, or the tissue which radiates from the pith through the bark, are composed of soft tissue. Vascular rays occur in hardwoods and softwoods. Hardwoods contain vertical strands, grouped in various ways, of soft tissue. Softwoods generally lack such vertical soft tissue. Certain softwoods, as the pines, larches, spruces and Douglas fir, have *resin ducts* (Fig. 6). These are channels in the wood surrounded by special secretory parenchyma cells which exude resin into the canal.

An exhaustive treatment of the kinds of cells and their modifications is beyond the scope of this book, but we should now be able to understand what the trained wood anatomist must consider when identifying woods. He must examine the various facets of wood, the cross section, the tangential-longitudinal and radial-longitudinal sections. He must ascertain the cells present, their relationship to each other, the modifications of their cell walls, their arrangement and their number and distribution. As the external portions of trees differ from species to species, so does the wood differ. However, closely related woods are often so similar that it is impossible to distinguish among them. For example, it is not possible to tell one oak (*Quercus*) from another on the basis of wood structure. Although the wood of eastern white pine is distinguishable from that of the southern pines, woods of the latter group of pine species are not distinguishable from each other. The hard and soft maples are only distinguishable with difficulty; hemlock and true fir are accu-

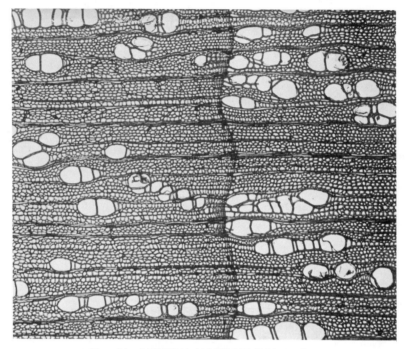

Fig. 8A. EASTERN HOPHORNBEAM (Ostrya virginiana)

Fig. 8. Magnification of the end grains of nine woods 8A-8I on this and following pages. Like a person's fingerprints, there are no two alike in all the 25,000 species of woods. The examination of the end grains, either by magnifying glass or photographs taken through a microscope, is one of the scientist's main helps in identifying wood.

rately distinguishable only with the aid of the microscope. In general practice, nevertheless, it is possible to identify accurately a whole host of commercial timber tree species by the wood alone. Thus, by and large, the best aid in identifying wood is the microstructure of the wood (Fig. 8). This may be observed with the use of a compound microscope, as is done in the laboratory, or by an ordinary 10-power magnifying lens. Many woods are identifiable with such a simple lens. A 20-power wide-field magnifier is shown in Fig. 9.

Many people who are not trained foresters can identify a log section, including a remaining stump come across in the forest, without the help of a lens. Often a brief study of the section together with knowledge of bark characteristics reveals the identity

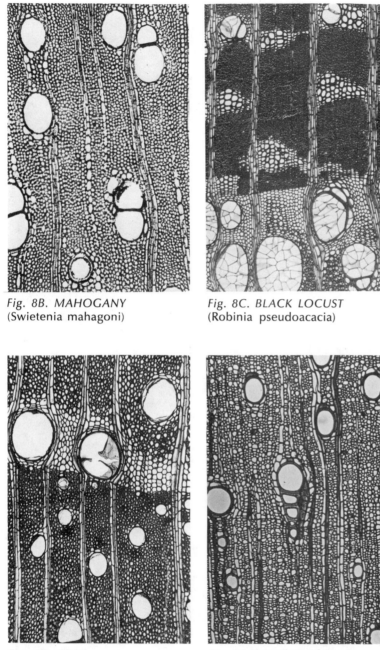

Fig. 8B. MAHOGANY
(Swietenia mahagoni)

Fig. 8C. BLACK LOCUST
(Robinia pseudoacacia)

Fig. 8D. TEAK
(Tectona grandis)

Fig. 8E. YELLOW POPLAR
(Liriodendron tulipifera)

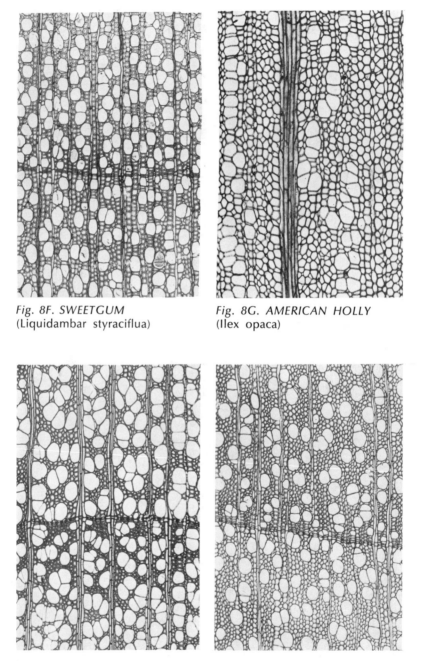

Fig. 8F. SWEETGUM
(Liquidambar styraciflua)

Fig. 8G. AMERICAN HOLLY
(Ilex opaca)

Fig. 8H. PERSIMMON
(Diospyros virginiana)

Fig. 8I. MAGNOLIA
(Magnolia acuminata)

Fig. 9. A convenient 20-power, wide-field, illuminated magnifier manufactured by E. W. Pike & Co., Elizabeth, N.J.

of the specimen. Two log section views are included here, black walnut (Fig. 10) and white ash (Fig. 11).

Other guides to the identification of wood include the color, odor, texture, grain, character of the ash, presence or absence of growth rings, presence or absence of colored heartwood and presence or absence of resin ducts. In short, any stable feature in wood may be employed as a key to identification.

Fig. 10. Black walnut.   *Fig. 11. White ash.*

Closeup views of log sections.

Practically, to identify a timber, the layman needs a sharp knife, a 10- or 12-power magnifying lens and good light. Much can be seen on the cross section and a clean cut will reveal in sharp detail the pattern of cells exposed in this view. Sometimes, by moistening the cut surface, the structural detail will be seen to better advantage. After examining the cut surface, recourse must be made to a "key." A key is a written deductive device by which woods (or plants, or rocks) can be identified by the process of elimination. One examines a statement in the key and either accepts or rejects it. If he accepts a statement, he proceeds to the next closest statement until the wood is identified. Below is a sample of a simple key to woods, based on gross features, extracted from *Trees—The Yearbook of Agriculture, 1949:*

A. Rays comparatively broad and conspicuous
  1. Rays crowded on the end grain .... Sycamore
  2. Rays not crowded on the end grain .... Beech
B. Rays not broad but distinctly visible
  1. Heartwood deep, rich, reddish brown. Annual rings clearly defined .... Black cherry
  2. Heartwood dingy, reddish brown, often streaked darker. Annual rings not sharly defined ... Sweetgum

An example of a more detailed, complex key is as follows:

A. Resin canals present
  1. Resin canals invisible to naked eye
    a. Wood with a somewhat greasy or oily feeling
      ...... Larch
    b. Wood with a dry feeling .... Spruce
  2. Resin canals visible to the naked eye
    a. Ray to tracheid pits pinoid, ray tracheids dentate
      ...... Loblolly pine
    b. Ray to tracheid pits fenestriform, ray tracheids smooth .... Eastern white pine
B. Resin canals absent
  1. Wood aromatic .... Eastern red cedar
  2. Wood odorless
    a. Heartwood red .... Redwood
    b. Heartwood pale brown to dark brown .. Baldcypress

It should be borne in mind that not all woods are identifiable. This is especially true of noncommercial woods and woods collected from remote areas. Such woods may never have been studied and described and probably do not occur in any keys. Another point of interest is that keys to woods are restrictive in some manner, as is indicated in their title: a key to common commercial American woods, a key to Indian woods used for railway ties, a key to coniferous woods of Europe, a key to woods with pores arranged in flamelike fashion, and so on. Therefore, keys, if available, are not the whole answer. The key must fit the lock!

Being able to identify woods by name is more often the result of practical experience than of scientific examination. The person handling and using woods, and even the person attempting to identify the kind of wood a piece of furniture is made of, relies on previous observation. In learning to identify woods words alone are not enough. A photograph is your best aid until you can closely study a piece of the wood. As an example, the wood grain shown in Fig. 12 is primavera. It has distinctive characteristics which defy accurate description.

Fig. 12. Primavera, pale gold, occasional waviness in a striped figure. Sometimes called white mahogany, but is no relation. Primavera comes from Mexico and Central America where it is cut in the dark of the moon when the sap flow is down and better logs can be harvested.

CHAPTER 3

How a Tree
Is Named

*I*n order to deal intelligently with trees, in order to be able to refer to them accurately in writing or in conversation, we must give them names. Generally speaking, there are two classes of names applied to trees: scientific or botanical names, and common names. The botanical name is usually of Latin or Greek derivation, whereas common names may be in many languages. The botanical name for a species is always the same, regardless of the country in which it is used; the common name may vary from place to place. Botanical nomenclature is governed by a strict, international set of rules, the International Code of Botanical Nomenclature. Common names are not subject to international regulation. It is important to remember that every tree (or other plant) has a scientific, botanical name, but it may or may not have a common name. Therefore, the most important name is the scientific name, but common names may have more or less importance, depending upon their standardization, general acceptability and frequency of use. The science of naming trees and other plants is called *taxonomy* or *systematic botany*. One who names plants is a taxonomist or systematic botanist.

A plant is named when, in the opinion of taxonomists, it represents a new species. A species can be defined simply as a kind or sort. In other words, when a newly collected plant is different in certain respects from all other closely related plants, it represents a new kind of plant. So that we may refer to this plant, we need to name it. Not only must we name it, we must also describe it so that others will know to just what kind of plant the name applies. According to the International Code of Botanical Nomenclature, descriptions of new species of flowering plants and conifers must be in Latin. Thus the description will be intelligible to all systematic botanists, regardless of their native tongue. Each new species is given two names (the binomial). It is assigned to a *genus* and allotted a *specific epithet*. Thus we find the red maple is known botanically as *Acer rubrum*; *Acer* is the genus of maples, and *rubrum*, the specific epithet, refers to the red maple. Another example is eastern white pine—*Pinus strobus*; *Pinus* is the genus of pines, and *strobus* pertains to a particular pine, eastern white pine. Scientific names are always set in italic type or underlined when typewritten. The generic name is capitalized; the specific epithet may or may not be capitalized.

When a botanist names a plant, his name is placed after it. It is possible then to know who was responsible for naming and describing a particular species. The individual is known as the author of the name. Frequently authors' names are abbreviated in a set manner. However, extremely well-known taxonomists' names are often represented by only a letter or two. For example: L. for Linnaeus; DC. for de Candolle; H.B.K. for von Humboldt, Bonpland and Kunth; Sieb. & Zucc. for Siebold and Zuccarini; and Benth. for Bentham. Names of one syllable are usually spelled out.

Botanical names at first sight can appear formidable. However, is *Fagus grandifolia* (American beech) any more frightening than "thermonuclear," "hydroelectric" or "superheterodyne"? Words like these appear every day in newspapers and magazines. Furthermore, without knowing it, many of us use common plant names which are identical to the generic names of plants; e.g., chrysanthemum, begonia, geranium, amaryllis, anemone, hydrangea, iris and lotus. Many common names are clearly derived from scientific names or vice versa: the rose is *Rosa,* lavender is *Lavendula,* the violet is *Viola,* the juniper is *Juniperus,* the pine is *Pinus,* the larch is *Larix,* a genus of orchids is *Orchis,* the true laurel is *Laurus* and the true cedar (of Lebanon) is *Cedrus.*

Many times, if we knew the Latin and Greek roots used to make botanical names, we would find that these names are not just gibberish, but actually mean something. Sometimes they are descriptive of the plant, sometimes they honor a man's name, and at other times they note the locality of collection or the native geographic habitat of the species. For example, *Gossweilerodendron balsamiferum* is an African timber tree commonly known as agba. Let us parse this mouthful: Gossweiler/o/ dendron, balsam/i/ferum. "Gossweiler" honors the name of John Gossweiler, a collector in Portuguese West Africa; "dendron" is derived from the Greek for tree; "balsam" from the Latin *balsamum* or the Greek *balsamon* for the gummy substance called balsam; "ferum" from the Latin *fero,* to bear. We can see now that our tonguetwister means Gossweiler's tree, which bears or produces balsam.

Another, more familiar, case is that of the yellow poplar or tulip tree, *Liriodendron tulipifera.* "Lirio" comes from the Greek for lily, *leiron;* "dendron," we already know, means tree; "tulip" refers to the scientific name for the tulip or *Tulipa;* and "ferum" means to bear. Thus we have the lily tree which bears tulips, a reference to the lovely tuliplike flowers of this stately native tree. The name for our eastern hemlock is *Tsuga canadensis.* "Tsuga" is derived from the Japanese name for the local hemlocks of Japan; "canadensis" is Latin for of Canada. Eastern hemlock, then, is the tsuga from Canada. The magnificent redwood of the West is *Sequoia sempervirens.* The generic name "Sequoia" commemorates Sequoyah (also spelled Sequoia), or George Guess (1770?–1843), American Indian inventor of the Cherokee alphabet; "semper" is Latin for forever, ever or always; "virens"

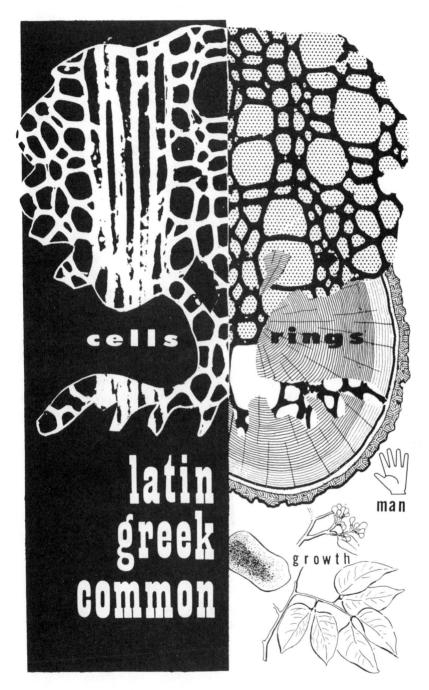

cells

rings

latin
greek
common

man

growth

Fig. 13. How a Tree is Named.

is from the Latin *vireo*, to be green or verdant. The redwood is Sequoyah's (tree) which is always green. We can see from these few examples that the scientific name of a tree is not a thing to be shunned or relegated to specialists. It is usually a meaningful name, full of lore and interest which will help maximize our enjoyment of woods and strengthen our appreciation.

This does not mean that common names are not meaningful or useful. The major objection to their use is their great diversity and general lack of standardization. We find, for instance, that our conception of oak (botanically *Quercus*) is quite different from the Australian idea of oak (*Casuarina*, the silky-oak or *Grevillea*, the turkey oak). Turning to the commonly known name beech, we find that it refers to *Fagus*, our eastern beech; *Nothofagus*, the beech of New Zealand and Australia; *Carpinus*, the blue beech of the eastern United States; *Litsea*, the soft bolly beech of Australia; *Cryptocarya*, the brown beech or jack apple of Australia; and *Myrsine*, the Cape beech of south Africa.

Some outstanding physical characteristics of a wood may prompt the use of a common name descriptive of this feature; ironwood, for instance. A great many woods of above-average hardness are called by this name; however, they may be botanically very diverse: *Krugiodendron ferreum, Syncarpia subargentia, Dialium guianense, Bumelia tenax, Lophira procera, Casuarina* spp., *Eusideroxylon zwageri, Acacia peuce, Backhousia myrtifolia, Ostrya virginiana, Lyonothamnus floribundus, Olneya testosa* and so on. Conversely, we may find a great diversity of vernacular names which apply to a single species. *Swietenia macrophylla* is the species which comprises much of our commercial, New World mahogany. A check shows that the following names apply to this species: caoba, foja pendula, zopilote de mator pescado, ciruela, cirndillo, cedro mondi, caoba mondi, Guatemala mahogany, Mexican mahogany, mahogany, aguano, Central American mahogany, black-veined mahogany, red mahogany, caoba blanca, caoba rosada, large leaf mahogany, Panama mahogany, black mahogany, cedro caoba, caobilla, cedro dulce, yulu, aguna, orura, caoba negra, caobano, sapoton, Brazilian mahogany, Peruvian mahogany, caoba liso, araputango and Honduras mahogany. This example is somewhat extreme, but is representative of the great multiplicity of names sometimes applied to one species of tree. Commercially valuable timbers suffer most from this malady.

Common names can be divided into two broad categories: vernacular and trade. Not all common names are easily placed into one or the other of these classes, and a vernacular name may also be a trade name. Furthermore, as we have seen, a common name may be derived from a scientific name. This in turn may serve as a trade name. In any event, we can define a common name as one which is not a scientific name, i.e., one not Latinized. A vernacular name is one which is in the language of the people inhabiting the region in which a tree grows. A name used in marketing timber can be termed a trade name. *Terminalia superba* is a west African timber tree. Vernacular names are various and include ka-ronko in Sierra Leone, fraké in the Ivory Coast, fram in Ghana, eji in Nigeria and djombe in Cameroons. A popular trade name for this wood is Korina. *Afrormosia elata,* a west African commercial species, is known in the trade as kokrodua. However, kokrodua is also the native Ashanti name in Ghana. In the trade, *Alstonia congensis* is called by its scientific name alstonia. Native or vernacular names are various and include bantang foro in Senegal, kaiwi in Sierra Leone, emien on the Ivory Coast, sindru in Ghana, abun in Nigeria and bokuk in Cameroons. A more common example is *Liquidambar styraciflua*. Known in the eastern United States as sweetgum or bilsted, on the market it is sold as redgum or sapgum. A good instance of duplicity of names is afforded by *Taxodium distichum,* usually called baldcypress. In the trade it may be listed as red cypress, white cypress or yellow cypress. Other names also applied are common baldcypress, gulf cypress, southern cypress, tidewater red cypress and cypress. An interesting sidelight is that this species is not even a true cypress; these belong to the genus *Cupressus*.

It is evident from the common names applied to trees and timbers that they are usually descriptive or comparative. Certain trade names are fabricated to glorify a wood and charm prospective buyers. Less desirable woods are compared with more desirable—Philippine mahogany basks in glory reflected from the well-known and much used New World mahoganies, although in certain respects it is inferior. Common names have an attractiveness all their own; they frequently reflect the peoples who have named them, or are quaint and graceful: *Amelanchier*, the shadbush (it blooms when the shad are spawning); *Amyris balsamifera*, the torchwood (its gum-containing wood burns as a torch); *Symphonia globulifera*, doctor gum (probably a reference to the local medicinal use of its gum); *Populus deltoides*, eastern cottonwood (the fruits bear a cottony mass which is freed at maturity); *Chionanthus virginica*, fringetree (refers to the fringelike aspect of the drooping, narrow-petaled flowers); *Cliftonia monophylla*, buckwheat-tree (a reference to the clusters of fruits resembling buckwheat cereal grains); and *Coccoloba uvifera*, the seagrape (an allusion to the grapelike clusters of edible fruits borne by this seaside tree).

"What's in a name?" Shakespeare knew that a rose by any other name would smell as sweet, but without our system of botanical names, we could not keep tree families and relatives in an orderly relationship.

CHAPTER 4

Knowing Trees By Name

*E*veryone knows the common names of the trees he lives with, often because someone long ago told him the names. Recognizing strange trees in the woods and along the country roads calls for more knowledge of tree characteristics. And while tree identification is beyond the scope of this book, and not essential to a study of woods, we do offer a few suggestions. Most of us have a natural curiosity for facts, and knowing a few trees by sight is a satisfying experience.

The best aid to identifying a tree is to know its flower. All trees do have flowers, although they do last only a short time. Next comes familiarity with leaf, twig, fruit and bark. Manuals on botany illustrate thirty-five or more shapes of tree leaves. Remembering even a few basic leaf shapes will help. Twigs are not such a simple key. Fruit is a helpful key, but like flowers, is seasonal. Learning tree shapes created by characteristic branching tendencies is useful but tricky because many trees have similar tendencies. Bark characteristics remain as the best year-round supplementary aid.

Bark becomes an essential aid when identifying leafless deciduous trees in winter, as well as fallen logs and log sections wherever you find them. Bark characteristics such as color, texture and especially pattern are important clues. A few examples of bark are given to illustrate marked differences and to emphasize the value of more extensive study.

[33

Fig. 14A. American elm. Dark, ashy gray, deeply furrowed. Broad, forking, flat ridges tending to scale on older trees.

Fig. 14B. Black birch. Distinctive dark, reddish brown, smooth, shiny. Accented horizontal pores increasing with age as bark becomes scaly.

Fig. 14C. Black locust. Brown, with a bold pattern of thick, deep furrows and rough, forked edges.

Fig. 14D. Black walnut. Dark brown, deep furrows with rounded, usually criss-crossed ridges.

Fig. 14E. Eastern hemlock. Dark brown to purplish, deeply furrowed into broad, scaly ridges.

Fig. 14F. Norway spruce. Dark reddish brown to chocolate brown. Thin, irregular, wavy scales, partly lifted around edges.

Fig. 14G. Ponderosa pine. Reddish brown to black in young trees, changing to yellowish brown in trees 100 to 300 hundred years old. Irregular fissures; large, flat, scaly plates.

Fig. 14H. Red maple. Gray, thin, scaly, varying with age from light gray to dark gray and from smooth to rough with shaggy scales on large trunks.

Fig. 14l. Redwood. Reddish brown, thick, deeply furrowed with a fluted appearance; fibrous, jagged.

Fig. 14J. Shagbark hickory. Bark of young trees is light gray, smooth, tight. With age it becomes darker, very shaggy with long, thin plates attached at middle, loose at each end.

Fig. 14K. Sugar maple. Dark gray. Smooth and close on young trees. Furrowed into long, rough, irregular scales on older trees.

Fig. 14L. Tuliptree. Color varies from gray to dark brown. Thick, tight, often straight, deep furrows and ridges formed with distinctive regularity.

Fig. 14M. White ash. Dark gray becoming ashy gray with age. Deep fissures and narrow, forking ridges looking somewhat braided. Fissures are diamond-shaped, an important identifying characteristic.

Fig. 15. Thailand. Where even the bulldozers find no safe path in the forest and elephants rule supreme, doing four hours daily work moving logs for men.

CHAPTER 5

Out of the Forest
Into Logs
and Lumber

*H*ave you ever stopped and given a moment of thought when you held a small piece of fine cabinet wood in your hand as to where the original tree came from—how it traveled over thousands of miles of land and water finally to reach you in its present form? It is difficult perhaps to conceive that men faced hardships of primitive living, dangers of wild animals, poisonous snakes and tropical fevers in a far-distant tropical forest or jungle so that you finally might be able to have this finished product. To appreciate fully the hardships and romance of logging, let us consider the first step in producing a fine piece of wood—logging trees.

Before a tree can be harvested, several generations of men have watched it grow. On an average a hardwood tree useful for sawlog timber has been growing for 100 to 120 years before it is ready for market. Selection of size and species calls for

Fig. 16. Australia. Cables and tongs move monstrous Eucalyptus log onto railroad flatcar for trip to mill.

knowledgeable loggers and often a preliminary search by an experienced forester who marks the trees to be felled.

Locating suitable trees, regardless of what kind they may be or in what country, and the process of felling trees, converting them into logs and transporting the logs to sawmills or to marketplaces, is all a part of what is known as logging. The problems met, the methods used, vary greatly according to the species and the part of the world from which the trees come.

It is an enterprise that requires skill and often the ability to endure hardships. The importance of this has long been recognized, as in early biblical times, when it was recorded Solomon, in a message to the King of Tyre, said, ''Command thou that they hew me cedar trees out of Lebanon; . . . for thou knowest that there is not among us any that can skill to hew timber like unto the Sidonians.''

Since then the known world has grown and the number of new trees known to man has multiplied many times. There has been a complete evolution and improvement in the way man lives and works, but in many countries—perhaps the one from which came the piece of wood that you hold in your hand—

Fig. 17. Gabon. The economy of this heavily-forested part of Africa is based on its lumber exports. Okoume logs brought out of the dense forest partway by truck now are being skillfully maneuvered into position to start their final downstream journey to the coastal port.

the method of living and conditions of working are as primitive as ever.

Books could be devoted to methods and ways of logging. For example, a piece of teak from India has perhaps taken six years to reach you. These trees are so very large and heavy that, before being felled, they are girdled as they stand in the forest and left to die so their weight will be greatly decreased. The elephant has been, and will be for many years to come, the principal means of transporting teak logs. An elephant with an average working lifetime of fifty years can drag a log weighing up to four tons over rough, mountainous land.

If your piece of wood has come from Australia or tropical America, oxen power most likely started the tree on its journey to you. In some cases as many as ten yoke of oxen are used to draw a single log out to the nearest waterway. Some of the logs are so heavy they will sink in water, and in these cases, other, much lighter, logs are lashed alongside heavy ones to prevent them from sinking as they are floated to the port where they are to be loaded on the steamer.

Fig. 18. Amsterdam. Logs for export are piled high outside one of Europe's largest lumber ports. An additional 50,000 tons of logs can be stored in warehouses not fully in view.

Moving logs down waterways is essential in many densely forested regions. In log form the wood is not damaged by water immersion. In fact, water curbs insect and fungus attacks, prevents rotting and greatly reduces splitting.

If it is a piece of tamo you are holding in your hand, it probably grew in the mountainous regions of Japan and was carried down through rugged terrain to the point of transportation on the shoulders of men.

On the west coast of Africa, large logs were felled by hand and, after being squared up with axes, were pulled to the nearest stream—sometimes by hundreds of men for a single log. The logs were laid alongside streams until the rainy season came, and the waters carried them down to the harbors where they were put on rafts, towed out to steamers and loaded. In seasons when the rains failed, logs could not be brought out of the forest. Today, mechanized power is gradually replacing hand operations in various places of the world, but it will be a long time before it replaces primitive methods in many far-distant places.

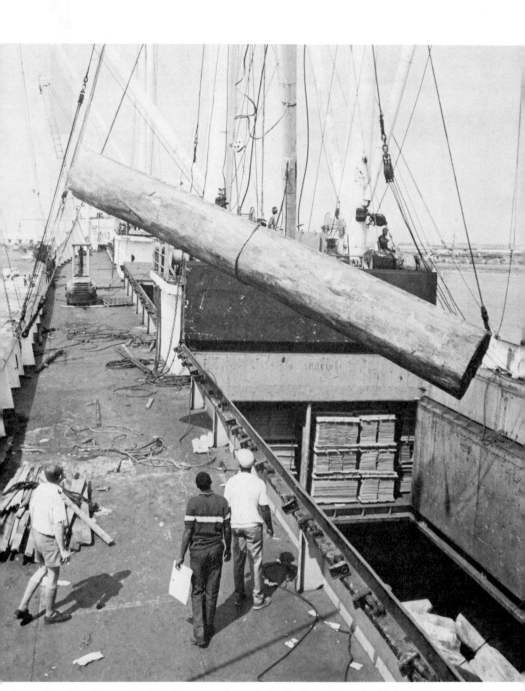

Fig. 19. Congo. Ship's boom swings de-barked log into hold below another compartment where cut lumber on skids is lashed for travel.

Fig. 20. Inspection yards of Constantine & Company, sixth to eighth streets on the East River, New York City. There were six million feet of mahogany logs in the yard when this photograph was taken, October 18, 1884.

After logs and lumber reach the port of embarkation, there is a long way to go before reaching the final market. The final port often depends upon the species of wood and whether or not it is of prime quality. Different ports of the world specialize in different woods and also in different qualities of wood.

For many years New York City was considered the leading market in the United States for the importation of mahogany and other woods from all parts of the world. On the East River there were the large storage yards of Constantine & Company to which foreign shippers in different ports of the world sent their logs. Going into the yard, the logs would be either measured or weighed and a measurement certificate issued. Importers in this country also brought logs and had them stored in the yards of Constantine & Company, where they would be inspected by manufacturers of lumber and veneers from various parts of the United States. When the logs were sold, they were shipped to the respective mills.

Adjoining Constantine & Company were the log yards of Willard Hawes & Co., for years probably the country's largest importers of practically all the rare and exotic woods of the world, including mahogany. Today, these two yards are gone. Both were taken away to form part of the Franklin D. Roosevelt Drive, along the East River, in New York City. However, Constantine & Company, in a limited way, still issues inspection returns on cargoes when requested. Some logs are still brought into New York, some go into Boston, a few into Philadelphia, some into Pensacola and New Orleans. What is probably the leading port of arrival in this country today is Norfolk, Virginia, where the logs are inspected prior to purchase.

In Europe, England still maintains the position that it had for many years. Both Liverpool, which specializes in African mahogany and other African woods, and London, which has the African mahogany and woods from the East, have public storage yards. At regular periods, auction sales are held where all the logs are put up in separate parcels and auctioned off to the highest bidder. Buyers attend these sales from many countries of the world, and there are wood brokers, like the stock brokers in Wall Street, who execute purchase orders from clients in many different countries, using their judgment on the value of the different lots of logs offered.

At one time in New York similar public auction sales were conducted in the offices of Constantine & Company at their log yard at Seventh Street and the East River.

In France, the log markets are Le Havre, Bordeaux, which specializes in African wood, and Marseilles, which specializes in wood from the East. Paris is a manufacturing market for veneers and lumbers. Logs are brought into Paris, manufactured by the mills, then offered to buyers from many places in the form of veneers and lumber.

Hamburg and Bremen in Germany are large log markets. In the Netherlands, Rotterdam and Amsterdam are the markets where logs are shipped; in Belgium, Antwerp is the large log market. From these various markets, dealers in logs and manufacturers of veneers and lumber procure much of their timber.

Some of the other larger organizations will send their buyers directly to those countries throughout the world in which the various timbers are grown and there will make local contracts to buy directly from native shippers. All this is a fascinating business. Like the diamond business, with its headquarters in Holland, it is a lifetime study for those who deal in timbers from far countries.

Aside from being able to recognize and identify the various species of logs, which is relatively simple to these people, the great science lies in determining the value of the logs. In highly figured logs, each log is carefully studied on the outside and the signs are read, indicating what the interior of the log will look like after it has been opened up and cut into choice veneers. What will the color be in the logs? Will there be any extraneous strain going in from the ends of logs, which some wood is subject to? Will there be any defects in the logs—such as ring checks, gum pockets or cross-breaks—which could make a valuable log almost worthless?

What type of figure will the log contain? Will it have a stripe —a broad stripe or a fine pronounced stripe? Will it have a mottle figure or a roe figure, and how strong will be the figure? Will it go through the entire log or only part of the log? The appraisal of logs of this kind is one that requires a highly specialized knowledge of woods, and most individuals more or less work with just one type of wood. One dealer may be a specialist in African mahogany, another in Honduras mahogany, another in Peruvian mahogany. One may specialize in woods from the East or only certain woods that come from the East; another may be a specialist in woods coming from the Philippines.

We recall an instance some years ago in New York in which great interest was shown in a log of Ceylon satinwood. It was a fine, large log containing about 1,000 ft., and interest was very keen among all the log buyers because the log showed signs of having a finer quality bee's-wing figure than any log that had been shown. Many bids were received for this log and it was finally sold to a firm which offered $5 per foot, or approximately $5,000 for the log.

When the log was prepared for manufacturing into sliced veneers, it was found that the figure was so strong and presented such a quantity of what is called "end wood" in the log that it was impossible to cut the wood into veneers. Because of this it had very little value—almost a total loss to the buyer. On the other hand, logs are often found which have very little indication of value on the outside but when opened prove highly valuable.

Large sums of money can be made by the wood expert who can detect figures and things that escape the eye of the other people, and who can obtain the logs at a fair price. A great gamble, equal to that of horseracing (but the stakes are often higher!), this is another phase of the log business which makes it so interesting to people who have lived with it, and the reason they find they are never able to get the love of it out of their blood.

Formerly, logs would be sold by board measure, by a type of measurement called Liverpool sales measure, by Constantine measurement or by Scribner & Doyle measurement, but some would be sold by weight. Today, practically all are sold by weight.

Following is a picture story based on logging and lumbering practices in the United States. Pine is one of the country's principal woods.

Fig. 21A. U.S.A. Logging for pine. Loggers make final severing cuts with axes to release this superb ponderosa pine tree, felling it skillfully where it does the least damage to other valuable trees.

Fig. 21B. Hydraulic tongs on truck's shovel attachment lift heavy sections of ponderosa pine onto truck for trip to mill.

Fig. 21C. At the saw-mill, machine operator controls headrig which now saws ponderosa log into manageable, squared timber or cants.

Fig. 21D. Pine cants come to gang saws and feed through two at a time, coming out as eight boards from each cant.

Fig. 21E. Pine boards from the gang saws go through molding-headed planer which then molds, tongues, grooves, and surfaces in one pass.

CHAPTER 6

From Logs to Veneers

M ost of the woods that we talk about are, at some time or other and in some form or other, converted into veneers. A few veneer mills have been erected in various tropical and other distant places where the wood grows, but most of the logs are transported overseas by boat, or in our own country by rail or truck to the sawmill.

Many logs, when they arrive at the mill, are dumped overboard into a log pond, where they are usually kept until wanted. Immersion in the water protects the logs from insects and fungus attacks and prevents rotting and splitting. African mahogany logs, measuring as much as 6 ft. after being squared and weighing from 10 to 15 tons, are sometimes handled by large sawmills.

SAWING THE LOG

Hoisted from the pond into the mill, the log is mounted on a car, resembling a flat railroad car, which runs on a track. The sawyer controls the powerful machinery which moves the log to the carriage, as well as the carriage itself. This is now moved slowly against a large band saw having wheels 8 ft. or more in diameter and a blade as much as 50 ft. long and 14 in. or more wide. This blade travels as a rule at the speed of from 7,500 to 8,000 ft. per minute. The first cut is generally made near the center of the log for the purpose of "opening" it and examining the wood of the interior.

I spent many hours of my early life in sawmills watching mahogany and other logs being opened and have always been fascinated by the big saws, running at a speed of a mile and a half a minute. Occasionally one of the bandsaw blades will break and do thousands of dollars of damage. Such accidents have at times taken the lives of sawyers, who have to stand within two or three feet of the saw.

Only a small percentage of the logs has a highly figured grain suitable for veneers. Those having straight or narrow grain are sawed into flitches, which are smaller timbers, squared on all four sides. Their thickness, width and length depends upon the size of the log and the extent of the figured grain. There are four generally accepted methods of cutting veneers: sawing, slicing, rotary cutting and half-rounding.

SAWED VENEERS

Sawed veneers are cut from flitches mounted on a movable carriage. The type of saw used is usually the segmental circular saw, the blade of which is built up of many parts or segments molded to a cast-iron hub. Although these segments are very thin, the saw wastes as much veneer as is cut in sawing veneers of, generally, 1/24 in. thickness. Thicker veneers may also be sawed, in which case the waste is proportionately less.

In practice, the saw is used very little, because in terms of modern technology, it is a slow and wasteful method. When it is used, it is used for cutting veneers thicker than the present common standard, which is usually 1/28 in., and the trend appears to be toward even thinner veneers. Those brought in from other countries are likely to measure only 1/40 or 1/42 of an inch in thickness.

Fig. 22. Cherry log, clutched by the dragon, is about to take its turn in the pre-soaking vat before it goes to veneer slicer.

SLICED VENEERS

Sliced veneers are cut with a knife. In this case the flitch must first be softened by steaming or "cooking" in boiling water for several hours (Fig. 22). The *veneer slicer* is a very heavy machine consisting of two main parts: a movable bed to which the flitch is bolted, and a knife supported in a rigid frame. The bed moves up and down while the knife remains stationary (Fig. 23). The veneer is sliced with a shearing cut as it moves against the knife. After each cut, the knife is given a slight sideways movement corresponding to the thickness of the veneer so that all sheets are exactly of the same thickness. The *standard thickness* of 1/28th in. is the veneer thickness you see on fine pianos, television cabinets, furniture and paneling in rooms. Veneers can be cut much thinner—as thin as 1/100 in. A great deal of thin veneer is used in laminating plywood for special purposes. As in sawed veneers, the sheets are kept and piled in the order in which they were cut. Sheets cut from the same flitch are always kept together, because only veneer cut from the same log can be matched for perfect uniformity and in such ways that the grain and figure will form a decorative pattern.

ROTARY-CUT VENEERS

Rotary-cut veneers are also cut with a knife, but from a whole round log instead of a flitch (Fig. 24). Slicing can produce veneer

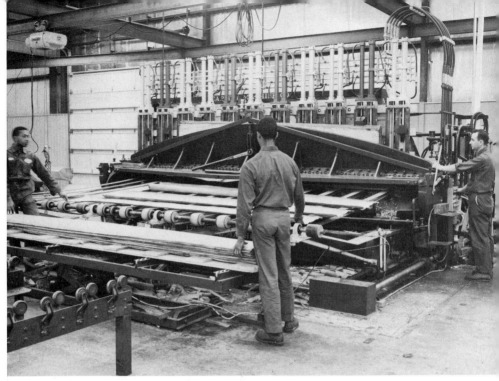

Fig. 23. This 17-foot veneer slicer with a heated knife and pressure bar slices off very thin sheets of cherry veneer of uniform thickness and stacks them with the aid of operators.

Fig. 24. Huge log of gaboon wood turns against stationary knife in rotary veneer slicer to produce wide sheets of veneer for facing plywood panels, Gabon, Africa.

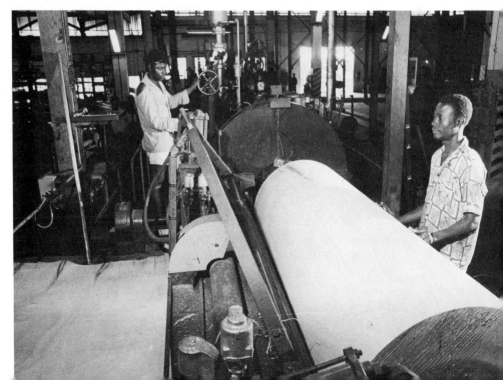

sheets only as wide as the log size permits. Rotary cutting produces veneers of wider dimension than the diameter of the log or any flitch cut from the log.

Bark must be removed before cutting the log into veneer. This can be done with an automatic lathe, which replaces the adze, an old-time hand tool. But even the lathe has its successors now, and before a log enters a sawmill it travels over a debarker. Because logs are cut with a knife, they must first be softened by steaming or boiling. After that, the log is mounted in a lathe and rotated against the knife, which is held rigidly. By giving the knife a slight sideways movement in the direction of the center of the log, a continuous sheet or peeling of uniform thickness results. This is cut into suitable widths on a clipper machine. The center of the log is cut up for crating lumber. Knives as long as 10 ft. are used for the rotary cutting of veneers, and knives as long as 17 ft. are used for slicing veneers. These knives weigh several hundred pounds and require the constant attention of an expert to keep the edge in proper shape at all times. Some woods require a very sharp knife; others require a duller edge. Some woods need a great amount of steaming or boiling beforehand; others very little. Acquiring the skill to judge the necessary steps to slice each and every log to obtain the finest results is a task which demands constant and methodical study.

HALF-ROUND VENEERS

Half-round veneers are also cut on a veneer lathe. In this case half the log is bolted to the lathe and revolved against the knife. The sheets of veneers cut in this manner are slightly rounded. Walnut stumps and bird's-eye maple are examples. In cutting wood this way, an entirely different figure effect is obtained than when the log is sliced.

An advanced technique utilizes a vertical vacuum bed to hold a half-round flitch while a slicer knife cuts thin veneers down to the last sliver of log.

DRYING VENEERS

All types of veneers are dried after they are cut. This is done in various ways. Nowadays most veneers are placed in a machine

Fig. 25. Large sheets of white pine veneer are fed into driers by workers in New Zealand factory.

(Fig. 25) which consists of a series of heated plates which move up and down like bellows, alternately squeezing and releasing the sheets of veneers placed between them. After drying, the veneers cut from the same flitch are placed in numerical order, measured and crated for shipment. Veneers keep well after manufacturing, and will remain in good shape indefinitely if they are laid flat on some flat platform with a slight weight on top of them. If veneers in the home workshop should become dry and buckled, they may be flattened just by sprinkling the sheets with water. A good way to do this is to use a whisk broom dipped into a pail. The damp veneers should then have a heavy weight placed on them. Soon they become perfectly flat and ready for use again.

Manufacturing methods in other parts of the world also reflect advanced technology in veneer production and usage.

THE ADVANTAGES OF VENEERING

It would be impossible to construct a piece of furniture of many of the highly figured woods, such as walnut burl, because the grain of such wood as produced is structurally weak and would split and warp all out of shape. Many of the types of figures shown in this book could not be obtained in the manufacture of lumber. Other woods, particularly tropical varieties, such as ebony, are so dense that if a piece of furniture were constructed from the solid wood, it would be so heavy as to be practically immovable.

The art of veneering has been practiced for many years, though the scientific way of utilizing veneers was not developed until the beginning of this century. The plywood industry is now a large and important one. In the furniture industry the scientific knowledge of veneering, combined with its older decorative values, has enabled the manufacturer to create a product that is greatly superior to solid wood, both structurally and artistically.

Some of the lumbers of the rare, exotic, figured woods might cost up to ten dollars per foot in the lumber form, whereas produced in the veneer form they can be converted into plywood, if desired, by gluing them on straight-grain lumber of the same kind of wood. By that means not only is strength obtained, but costs are kept within permissible limits.

CHAPTER 7

The Physical Appearance of Wood

*T*he general, gross physical properties of wood are of prime importance to the craftsman and woodworker. No two human beings are absolutely identical. Twins appear alike but there is usually some distinguishing characteristic. Similarly, no two pieces of wood are exactly alike or have precisely the same figure. There are differences in grain, figure, texture, color and other physical properties. It is these characteristics of wood that will largely govern a woodworker's choice. Features such as color, grain, figure and texture enter into the appearance of the finished product. Colored woods are desirable for period furniture, but not for some modern pieces; a decorative figure need not be used for a bookcase backing, but it is highly beneficial to the appearance of a table top; the wood turner will select a fine-textured wood for his work rather than one of coarse texture. In brief, the worker in wood, like any artist, should carefully choose his medium in order to achieve the best results for his efforts. Below are some of the general characteristics of wood which will be of interest to the craftsman.

As an initial guide to selection of wood on the basis of amount of figure, without regard for color, this summary is helpful: woods relatively high in figure include white ash, black ash, chestnut, Douglas fir, rock elm, soft elm, hackberry, western larch, black locust, red oak and white oak.

The terms grain, figure and texture are frequently misused. An inaccurate application of these terms can detract from their value. Such misuse often involves the direction of sawing. Timber that is cut parallel to the rays as shown at A, Fig. 26, is termed

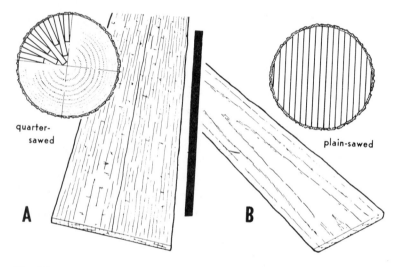

Fig. 26.

quarter-sawed. That cut perpendicular to the rays (B, Fig. 26) is termed flat-sawed or plain-sawed. In quarter-sawed timber the rays are viewed en face, and the growth rings appear as roughly parallel vertical lines. In flat-sawed timber, the rays are viewed on end and growth rings appear as inverted V's.

Veneers, regarded as the most beautiful wood form, can be cut in more ways than are practical for solid wood. To illustrate the variety, Fig. 27 shows the major ways of cutting cherry veneer.

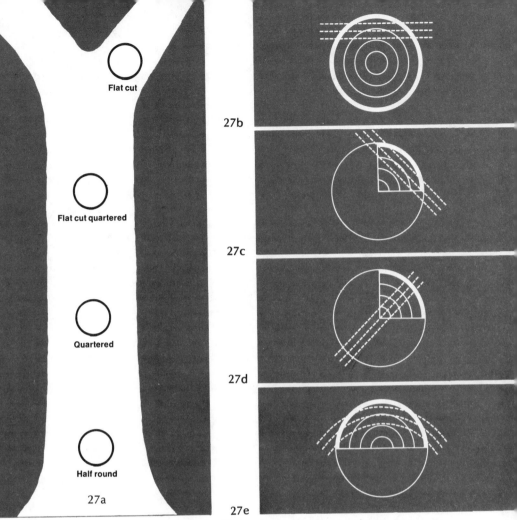

Flat cut

27b

Flat cut quartered

27c

Quartered

27d

Half round

27a

27e

Fig. 27A. Customary method of utilizing logs cut from a cherry tree. When logs are reasonably straight and uniform, they yield veneers of best figure if cut in this manner.

Fig. 27B. Log in cross-section view. To be flat cut the log is first sawed in half. Each half, or flitch, in turn is mounted so that it moves up and down against a knife. Slicing is parallel to the center line and at a tangent to the growth rings in the tree.

Fig. 27C. Flat cut quartered. The technique here is to slice the quartered log along a line parallel to the growth rings.

Fig. 27D. Quartered. Log has been sawed into quarters. Slicing knife cuts at right angles to the growth rings.

Fig. 27E. Half round. The log is rotary cut. A half log is rotated against the cutting knife so there is a gradual cutting across growth rings. This method produces a more pronounced, leafier figure.

Fig. 28. Flat-cut cherry, figured.

Fig. 29. Flat-cut cherry, rope figured.

Fig. 30. Flat-cut cherry, burly.

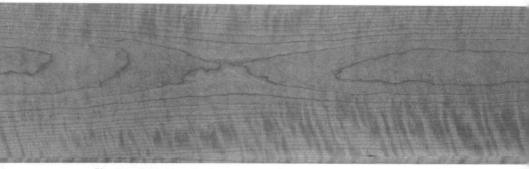

Fig. 31. Quarter-cut cherry, figured.

Cutting methods strongly influence the resulting figure, but the way a log is cut, even from the same species, cannot be counted on to produce the same figure characteristics.

To show the wide differences in the same wood species, cut by the same method, examples of figure variation in cherry are grouped here in Figs. 28 to 31.

GRAIN

Grain, used in the restricted, technical sense, is the direction or orientation of wood cells, particularly the fibrous elements. There are six general types of grain: (1) *Straight grain:* In such timber, the fibers and other longitudinally oriented elements are more or less parallel to the vertical axis of the stem (Fig. 32). (2) *Irregular grain:* This kind of grain is produced in timber where the fibers are at varying and irregular inclinations to the vertical axis of a log. It is frequently restricted to limited areas in the region of knots or swollen butts. (3) *Diagonal grain* is a mill-

Fig. 32. Straight-grain walnut, plain sawed.

ing defect and results when otherwise straight-grained timbers are not sawed parallel to the vertical axis of the log. (4) *Spiral grain* is produced when the fibers follow a spiral or helical course in the living tree. The twist may be right- or left-handed. (5) *Interlocked grain* results from the fibers in successive growth layers being inclined or spiraled in opposite directions. Interlocked grain is relatively uncommon in timbers from the temperate zone but is characteristic of many tropical timbers. (6) *Wavy grain* is produced when the direction of the fibers is constantly changing so that a line drawn parallel with them appears as a wavy line on a longitudinal surface.

FIGURE

The term "grain" is frequently misused in referring to the natural design or pattern seen on the surface of wood. This pattern is not the grain of the wood, but the *figure*. Figure frequently results from the interaction of several features present in the wood—for example: the presence, absence, abundance and/or conspicuousness of growth rings; the prominence and abundance of the vascular rays; the type of grain and its modification in the vicinity of knots, burls, crotches, buttresses and swollen butts; local variations in color due to uneven deposition of coloring substances in wood. The grain in wood is particularly important in its effect on figure. Different kinds of irregular grain may give rise to *blister* or *quilted figure*; interlocked grain produces *ribbon* or *striped figure*; wavy grain shows as *fiddleback figure*; and a combination of wavy grain and interlocked grain produces a broken ripple on quartered surfaces called *rope figure*. The names given to figure variations are many. Some are narrowly applied to increase the sale of a given lot of veneer; others truly reflect or characterize the pattern. Among the more popular figures we find silver "grain," mottle figure, snail figure, finger-roll figure, plum-pudding figure, bird's-eye figure, curly figure, swirl figure, swirly knots, burl figure, crotch figure, feather-crotch figure, moonshine crotch, stump-wood figure and pigment figure.

Among the most strikingly beautiful patterns are those exhibited in wood from the vicinity of crotches. A crotch is that place in a tree where the main stem (or large branch) forks to

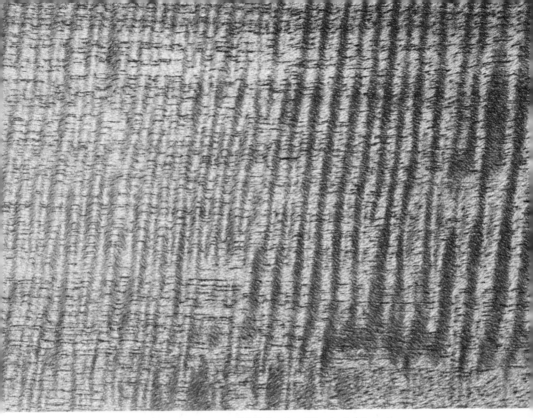

Fig. 33. African mahogany, strong fiddleback with straight grain.

Fig. 34. American black walnut, crotch.

produce two smaller stems. Crotch figure is obtained from wood below the bifurcation and is the result of stem division.

Burls are responsible for the formation of a number of interesting natural designs. A burl is an abnormal, wartlike excrescence on the trunk or branches of a tree. Examined closely, it may appear to consist of a great mass of "eyes" or dormant buds. The surface of such a bulge may be smooth or rough. In either case the alignment of the fibers is very irregular and the burl is thus gnarled. Because of this many bizarre figures are derived from veneers cut from burls. Causes of burls are imperfectly understood and the following reasons have been advanced to explain this unusual growth: injury from frost, fire or mechanical contact; and irritation of the cambium by bacteria, fungi and possibly viruses. A legend states that wounds inflicted by woodpeckers cause burls. However, this is easily discredited in that trees produce burls in regions where woodpeckers do not exist. Burls can and do grow on all species of trees; however, they are found more commonly on certain trees, as for example, the redwood (*Sequoia sempervirens*).

Records show that at the height of the Roman Empire, decorative burls were in demand for table tops and other articles of furniture. Wealthy Romans paid high prices for particularly fancy or unusual burl patterns. Even today good burl wood commands top prices, for the percentage of trees in which burls develop is small, and in many of these burls the wood is defective. Burl veneer has high decorative value for inlays and overlays and for matching into four- or eight-piece combinations.

BIRD'S-EYE FIGURE

The figure in a bird's-eye maple log resembles somewhat the figure in a burl. It contains a small eye like that of a burl, but it is more distinct. In a burl, the eye is surrounded by a series of clusters, but in bird's-eye maple each eye stands out separately. This is one of the few woods which is laid face side down in veneering, because of the conical shape of the eye. When laid face side down, the eyes will never chip out. This maple is very popular in the musical-instrument trade because of its wonderful sounding qualities. It is also a favorite in seating stock for its durability and toughness.

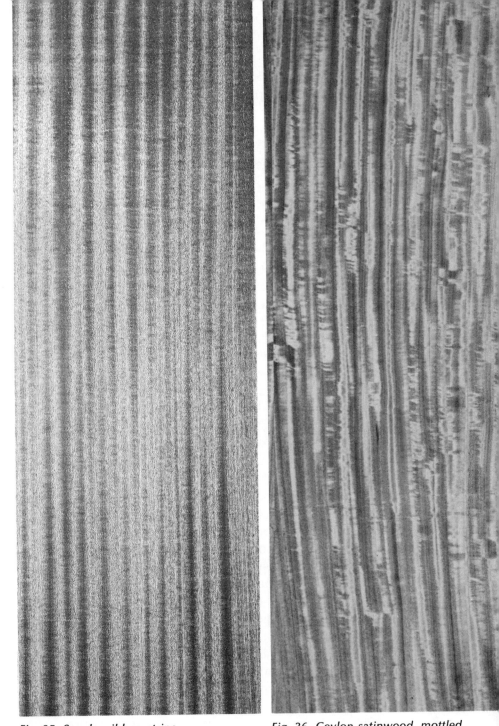

Fig. 35. Sapele, ribbon-stripe.　　　　*Fig. 36. Ceylon satinwood, mottled.*

There has long been a discussion as to what causes the bird's-eye figure in maple. The accepted belief today is that it is caused by a stunted growth. It is found in trees where the growth has been the slowest—always on the northeast slopes of hills and in trees that have been hemmed in on all sides in the forest, where the tree has had little light and air. Careful studies made over a period of many years in marking trees have shown that when a tree that had been among a large number of trees has been left to stand alone after the clearing away of the other trees, and when, after twenty years or more, this tree was cut down and brought into the veneer mill and manufactured, it would yield plain veneer for the number of years it was out in the open, but had developed the bird's-eye figure during the years that it lacked space and sunshine.

The part of the log from which the butt figure is obtained is the buttressed or swollen part of the tree, just above the ground. It usually shows a crinkly, curly figure, obtainable only in relatively few woods and more commonly associated with walnut, in this country. To preserve this figure as much as possible, a walnut tree is not sawed down, but dug out, the main roots cut, and then pulled over. Logs are sent in this condition to the mill.

TEXTURE

Another important physical aspect of wood is the *texture*. Texture pertains to the relative size and the amount of variation in the size of wood cells. It refers, if you will, to the "feel" of the wood. Texture is described as coarse, fine, and even and uneven. The differentiation between coarse and fine texture is based on the dimensions of the pores and the width and abundance of the rays. Timbers in which the vessels are wide, or rays broad, are said to be of *coarse texture*. When vessels are narrow, and rays thin, the timber is of *fine texture*. Many intermediate grades also exist. For example, oak (*Quercus*) is coarse-textured; walnut (*Juglans nigra*) and mahogany (*Swietenia* spp.) are moderately coarse-textured; sycamore (*Platanus* spp.) is fine-textured, and European boxwood (*Buxus sempervirens*) is very fine-textured. Strictly speaking, all softwoods are fine- or at most only moderately coarse-textured, as their cells are of relatively small diameter. The texture of softwoods is frequently influenced

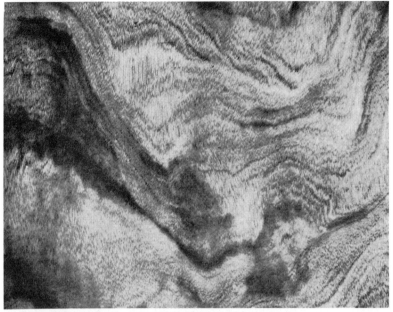

Fig. 37. African mahogany, moonshine swirl.

Fig. 38. Carpathian elm burl.

by the alternation of the zones of spring- and summer-wood. When the contrast between the zones is strongly marked, as in pitch pine (*Pinus rigida*), Douglas fir (*Pseudotsuga menziesii*) or larch (*Larix* spp.), the wood is said to be of *uneven* texture. In eastern white pine (*Pinus strobus*), the true firs (*Abies* spp.) and spruces (*Picea* spp.), the wood shows little or no contrast between spring- and summer-wood. Consequently, we can say these woods are *even-textured*. The same terminology can be applied to hardwoods—diffuse porous woods being even-textured, ring porous woods being uneven-textured.

THE COLOR OF WOOD

From the practical viewpoint, color is important in wood because it may enhance or detract from the decorative value of the timber. Ebony (*Diospyros* spp.), mahogany (*Swietenia* spp.) and walnut (*Juglans* spp.) owe their desirability at least in part to their decorative color. On the other hand, wood for toothpicks and wooden spoons is more desirable if it is uncolored.

We know that color is caused largely by various infiltrates in the cell wall. Some of the infiltrates, as in logwood (*Haematoxylon* spp.), are extracted and used as dyes. Some undergo changes when timber is exposed to light, air or heat, with the result that many timbers darken with age and others fade. Mahogany fades under strong sunlight but darkens under moderate light. African mahogany coming from one port on the west coast of Africa will have an entirely different color than mahogany coming from another port, relatively only a short distance away. A specialist can generally tell by the color of the logs which port they come from, whether Grand Bassam, Half Assinee or Axim.

Different species of walnut will also vary greatly according to the country it comes from, whether Italy, France or the United States, and with the latter it will also vary according to the section or state it comes from. This is easily explained, because color is caused by the presence of extraneous materials in the walls of the wood and the color is dependent upon the type of soil and its content. Also, in many of the woods there are distinct differences in color between the sapwood and the heartwood.

Several timbers, such as teak (*Tectona*) and Borneo white seraya (*Parashorea* spp.), exhibit quite a range of color when

Fig. 39. American black walnut butt.

Fig. 40. Bird's-eye maple.

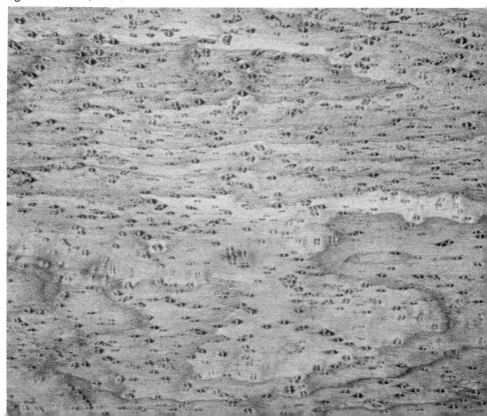

freshly planed, but after a short exposure to daylight the colors even out considerably. The moist heat that is employed during kiln-seasoning darkens many woods—so much so that some are steamed purposely to alter the color, as beech (*Fagus*) and walnut (*Juglans*) sapwood. Color changes are also effected by chemical means; liming lightens color and fuming with ammonia gas darkens it, removing the pink or red shades. Bleaching of wood is also feasible and produces attractive finishes.

ODOR AND TASTE IN WOOD

Many timbers have a characteristic odor, which is apparent when they are worked in a fairly fresh condition but which usually disappears as the wood dries out. Perhaps the most outstanding examples are the characteristic resinous odors of pines, the spicy aroma of sandalwood (*Santalum album*) and Spanish cedar (*Cedrela* spp.), and the camphorlike odor of Formosan camphorwood (*Cinnamomum camphora*). Certain Australian woods of the *Acacia* group possess an odor not unlike violets. Coachwood (*Ceratopetalum apetalum*) is reminiscent of newly cut hay. Some woods, e.g., *Viburnum lentago*, have a fetid odor.

The taste of wood is closely related to odor and can probably be traced to the same constituents. Both properties influence the utilization of timber. The choice of woods for food containers is restricted to those without pronounced odor or taste. The flavor of tobacco on the other hand is alleged to be improved when stored in boxes made of Spanish cedar (*Cedrela* spp.). Camphorwood and eastern red cedar are used to make boxes in which clothes are stored because of their reputed repellent effect on insects.

LUSTER IN WOOD

Luster depends on the ability of the cell walls to reflect light. Some timbers have this property to a high degree; others are comparatively dull. As a general rule, quarter-sawed surfaces are more lustrous than are flat-sawed ones. If stripe, fiddleback or roe figures are present, the figure is considerably enhanced in timbers having natural luster. Although luster is an asset in a cabinet wood, the capacity for taking a good polish is just as important from a practical viewpoint, and the two do not necessarily occur together.

CHAPTER 8

Woods of the Bible

*T*he Bible is a source of many interesting references concerning trees and woods, some of which are familiar to us today. The tree and its fruit have always been symbolic of strength and fertility.

Perhaps the most famous Bible tree in this regard is the cedar of Lebanon, *Cedrus libani*. In Psalms 92:12 we read, "The righteous shall flourish like the palm tree: he shall grow like a cedar in Lebanon." Further, it is stated in Ezekiel 31:3–18, "Behold the Assyrian was a cedar in Lebanon with fair branches . . . and his top was among the thick boughs." There are almost fifty references in the Bible traceable to the cedar of Lebanon. This is most likely because these trees were the grandest trees with which the Israelites were acquainted. They grow rapidly and attain heights of 120 ft. and trunk diameters up to 8 ft. Such magnificent specimens must have induced feelings of awe and reverence in biblical times.

Today only a pitifully small remnant of this once-proud forest remains. What has become of this remnant? Lebanon has created the Cedars of Lebanon National Park and protects it as a "national treasure." It is still known by the French name "Les Cedres." The park is near the village of Basharri or Becherre, eighty-four miles north of Beirut in the Lebanon Mountains. It is an easy three-hour drive from Beirut. No woodsman can now deplete these celebrated trees, because of a strictly enforced national law. The grove numbers around four hundred trees and a few smaller groves are known to exist elsewhere in Lebanon. The Lebanese revere the tree and have made it the national tree and the official emblem of the nation. It is used on everything from the flag to a postage stamp. Efforts are being made to propagate the tree from seeds, although it has been in cultivation for some time. Europe and America have many specimens. One of the most magnificent is in Portland, Oregon. This tree has a straight bole 2 ft. in diameter with a height of approximately 100 ft., and is free of limbs for about half that distance.

Many other trees mentioned in the Bible were symbolic as well as practical. Among these is the myrtle (*Myrtus communis*). Besides its use as a spice, myrtle is representative of fertility and life, as in Isaiah 41:19. Isaiah, restoring the dry, barren desert and wilderness with the life-giving tree, declares, "I will plant in the wilderness the cedar, the shittah tree and the myrtle, and the oil tree; I will set in the desert the fir tree and the pine, and the box tree together." These trees can all be found today, providing the same life-giving shade for which they were noted in biblical times.

The olive (*Olea europea*) is mentioned in Genesis 8:11: "And the dove came in to him in the evening; and lo, in her mouth was an olive leaf pluckt off; so Noah knew that the waters were abated from off the earth." Perhaps this was the beginning of the olive branch as symbolizing peace. The same branch, which signified God's peace with Noah, has been used throughout history as a reminder of peace between nations, and can be seen today as a symbol on the flag of the United Nations.

The wood provided by trees has been turned into many decorative and useful articles. The cabinetmakers of today follow a long tradition of a handicraft which was practiced by car-

Fig. 41. The famous cedar-of-Lebanon tree, shown here in a compact stand, is said to have provided the beautiful wood used in King Solomon's Temple. In the Near East it is now protected by law from lumbermen. In warm coastal areas of the United States it is being planted for its rare beauty and to guard against extinction of the species.

penters centuries ago. Men searched the world over for rare and useful woods during biblical times, even as they do today. It is said in Ezekiel 27:15, "The men of Dedan were thy merchants; many isles were the merchandise of thine hand; they brought thee for a present horns of ivory and ebony" (*Diospyros* spp.).

Other trees, including the cedar of Lebanon, were used during biblical times for construction purposes. The builder and craftsman of today is no doubt interested in timbers used in those days. The ark of Noah was of gopher wood (gopher being in the Hebrew). The Lord said to Noah, "Make thee an ark of gopher wood" (Genesis 6:14). The gopher wood of the Bible

Fig. 42. The Bible, in Exodus 26, refers to shittim wood used to build the tabernacle.

most likely is one of the true cypresses, *Cupressus sempervirens* var. *horizontalis*. Although the walnut (*Juglans regia*) is not mentioned in the Bible as sought for timber, the ancient Hebrews were acquainted with its fruit (Song 6:11). Probably they also used its wood in construction of some sort.

Pinus halepensis, though referred to in the Bible as a fir, enters as a building material in Song 1:17, "The beams of our house are cedar, and our rafters of fir," and in Ezekiel 27:5, "They have made all thy ship boards of fir trees of Senir." Reference in the Bible to almug trees has been traced to *Pterocarpus santalinus.* We read in I Kings 10:11–12 that "the king made of the almug trees pillars for the house of the Lord, and for the king's house, harps also and psalteries for the singers."

The oak (*Quercus* spp.) is mentioned by a variety of names in the Bible. Several species now grow in the Holy Land which may have been employed in biblical days. A statement in Isaiah 44:14 refers to the logging of oaks: "He heweth him down cedars, and taketh the cypress and the oak."

Acacia wood is known as shittim in the Bible and was commonly used in construction: Exodus 26:15–16, 26, 32, 37, "And thou shalt make boards for the tabernacle of shittim wood standing up . . . and thou shalt make bars of shittim wood . . .

Fig. 43. The sacred chest, the Ark of the Covenant, was made of acacia wood.

and thou shalt hang it upon four pillars of shittim wood . . . and thou shalt make for the hanging five pillars of shittim wood."

The Ark of the Covenant, which the Lord ordered Moses and the Hebrews to construct, was a sacred chest made of *Acacia* wood overlaid with gold, the lid of which constituted the "mercy seat," or place of propitiation, over which two cherubim extended their wings. This is described in Exodus 25:10, when the Lord said to Moses: "And they shall make an ark of shittim wood: two cubits and a half shall be the length thereof and a cubit and a half the breadth thereof, and a cubit and a half the height thereof." This was placed in the tabernacle, which was also built of shittim wood; so were most of the furnishings as mentioned above. Citations of shittim wood occur in large numbers in the Old Testament. Apparently it was a favored building material.

Incense and spices were in wide use during biblical times. They appealed to the senses and the spirit and are often mentioned in both testaments. Some of these aromatic materials were derived from trees. The aloes of the Old Testament supposedly refer to *Santalum album*, or sandalwood. In Psalms 45:8 we read, "All thy garments smell of myrrh, and aloes, and cassia," and in Song 4:14, "myrrh and aloes, with all chief spices." Aloe was probably mixed with myrrh when wrapped among the burying garments in embalming.

The incense or frankincense of the Bible was derived from a species of *Boswellia*, a tree related to the gumbo limbo of the Florida Keys and West Indies. Among the many, many references to frankincense in the Old and New Testaments is Jeremiah 6:20, "To what purpose cometh there to me incense from Sheba, and the sweet cane from a far country?" Perhaps the most famous reference is in part of the Christmas story from Matthew 2:11, "And when they were come into the house, they saw the young child with Mary his mother, and fell down, and worshipped him: and when they had opened their treasures, they presented unto him gifts; gold, and frankincense, and myrrh."

At least two species of *Cinnamomum* entered into the spice cabinets of Bible cooks and into the boudoirs of maidens: *C. cassia* and *C. zeylanicum*. In Exodus 30:23–24 we find, "Take thou also unto thee principal spices . . . and of cassia five hundred shekels." The cinnamon of the Bible is directly translatable from the Hebrew "kinamôn"—thus, in Proverbs 7:17, "I have perfumed my bed with myrrh, aloes, and cinnamon." That often mentioned scent, myrrh, is derived from *Commiophora myrrh*. References to the use of myrrh are legion and it must have been a valuable article of commerce in ancient times. Myrrh is also a symbol of sensuousness, for it is mentioned in this way in the Song of Solomon, for example, 1:13: "A bundle of myrrh is my well-beloved unto me." Many other examples of aromatic tree products occur throughout the Books.

There are a number of fruit trees in the Holy Land, and the ancients made wide use of those available. There is no doubt that the fruit of the date palm (*Phoenix dactylifera*) was exceedingly important—important as a comestible and as a symbol of fertility. The palm tree of the Bible almost surely refers to the date palm. At one time it was as common in Palestine as it is now in Egypt. In Psalms 92:12–14 it is stated: "The righteous shall flourish like a palm tree" and in Jeremiah 10:5: "They are upright as the palm tree." The Hebrew word for the date palm is "tamar." This palm became the Jews' symbol of grace and elegance and was often bestowed by them upon women, as, for instance, to the sister of Absalom. In Genesis 38:6 we find that "Judah took a wife for Er his firstborn, whose name was Tamar." In II Samuel 13:1 is the reference to Absalom's sister: "Absalom . . . had a fair sister, whose name was Tamar."

Other fruit-bearing trees mentioned in the Bible are the almond (*Amygdalus communis*); the "husks" in Jesus' parable of the prodigal son were—no doubt the pods of the carob tree (*Ceratonia siliqua*); the fig (*Ficus carica*)—mentioned abundantly in both testaments; the sycamore of Amos—also a fig (*Ficus sycamorus*); the fruit of the olive (*Olea europea*)—the source of anointing oil, cooking oil, oil for lamps and medicinal oils; the fruit or nut of the pistachio (*Pistacia vera*); the apple of the Bible—probably a plum or near relative (*Prunus armeniaca*); *Punica granatum*, the pomegranate, known to the ancient Israelites; and the grape (*Vitus vinifera*), although not a tree, which should be included here if only for its overwhelming importance.

Trees have always been used for the shade which their leafy branches have provided. Man, through the ages, has sought relief from the scorching rays of the sun under the shelter of trees. "The shady trees cover him with their shadow; the willows (*Salix* spp.) of the brook compass him about," is in Job 40:22. Hosea 4:13 also gives reference to the shade provided by trees: "They sacrifice upon the tops of the mountains, and burn incense upon the hills, under oaks (*Quercus* spp.) and poplars (*Populus alba*) and elms (*Pistacia terebinthus* var. *palaestina*), because the shadow thereof is good."

One of the oldest ways in which the tree has served man is as a source of fuel for warmth and cooking. Man might not have survived without this protection of his life, and its importance is even mentioned in Proverbs 26:20: "Where no wood is, there the fire goeth out."

One of the questions very often asked concerning the woods of the Bible is, "What kind of wood was the cross made of?" Although there is no definite answer to this given in the Bible, the legend of the flowering dogwood has often been told. This legend, although very beautiful, is entirely fallacious. As the legend goes, at the time of the crucifixion, the dogwood tree was the size of the oak and other forest trees. This tree was so sturdy that it was chosen as the timber for the cross. It is said that "To be thus used for such a cruel purpose distressed the tree so greatly, that Jesus who was nailed upon it, sensed this, and in His gentle pity for all sorrow and suffering, said to it: 'Because of your regret and pity for my suffering, never again shall the dogwood tree grow large enough to be used as a cross. Henceforth it shall be slender and bent and twisted, and its blossoms shall be in the form of a cross—two long and two short petals. And in the center of the outer edge of each petal there will be nail prints, brown with rust and stained with red, and in the center of the flower will be a crown of thorns and all who see it will remember.'" The flowering dogwood (*Cornus florida*), to which this quotation refers, occurs in eastern North America, where it is native. It was completely unknown in biblical days. The "petals" in the story above are not petals but colored bracts, while the actual flowers of the tree compose the central "crown of thorns." Other, similar legends revolve about the wood used for the cross. Early Christian legendry states that the aspen (*Populus*) was so used. At the time of the crucifixion, aspen trees everywhere shuddered when the nails were driven into the wood and the holy blood gushed forth upon the cross. This may be an allusion to the European trembling aspen, *Populus tremula*.

Another often-told legend concerns a tree which, while not mentioned in the Bible, is often associated with it. The redbud has long been called the "Judas tree," because of the legend which tells how Judas Iscariot, after betraying Jesus, hanged himself on a Near East cousin of the redbud, *Cercis siliquastrum*. It is said that the white flowers of this tree blushed red with shame and have remained so ever since. Just how it was that tradition selected this tree of all the Palestinian trees as the one on which Judas committed suicide, is not clear. In any event, it has been known as the Judas tree for much over two hundred years. The poplar (*Populus*) is another of the trees on which ancient legend says that Judas hanged himself.

CHAPTER 9

Planting Trees Around the World

Only in the last two decades have there been significant gains in forestation around the world. The United Nations and its affiliated agencies have been in great part responsible for the new emphasis on establishing forests. In many places United Nations funds have been provided to outside foresters to introduce scientific methods in an effort to accelerate wise and purposeful forestation. Aggressive tree-planting programs are now a vital part of nearly every country's economic program. The following pictures give some indication of the work going on in many countries.

Fig. 44. Making seedling pots for the nursery. To carry out the mammoth plan for cultivating saplings needed to reduce erosion, halt desert encroachment, and provide lumber and lumber products for construction, Algeria has the help of the United Nations. Here an Algerian native encases prepared soil in a wrapping of clear plastic to make a simple, quick, and cheap seedling pot.

Fig. 45. On the barren mountain side of Lebanon the famous cedar-of-Lebanon appears in cultivated rows and soon will be planted in contoured, terraced levels of the steep slopes. This government's afforestation program, aided by the United Nations, is aimed at stopping land erosion and creating a potentially productive timber resource to help the nation's economy.

Fig. 46. In eastern Africa where rich forests were overcut and not replanted after World War II, an intensive reforestation program has gotten under way. Here in the Sudan a forestry expert from India directs natives where to take tiny, potted seedlings for transplanting. When grown, the trees will become lumber for home use and export.

Fig. 47. A camel caravan bears trees for conquering the desert. Baskets on the ladened camels contain mimosa seedlings. Holes in the foreground sand are ready for the transplanting operation. The yellow-flowered mimosa was chosen not for beauty but for its rapid growth and bushy shape. In as little as three years these mimosa plants will broaden into green thickets to stabilize the shifting sands of the Gasa desert.

Fig. 48. Nursery lot, lote vivero, in Colombia, South America, is planted with eucalyptus. An expanding program of afforestation is rapidly making this country self-sufficient in lumber and lumber products. It was started less than ten years ago to curb imports of more than twenty million dollars annually.

Fig. 49. Little more than a decade ago the Tunisian government embarked on an extensive forestry program with three objectives: to protect the soil from erosion, to conserve water supplies, and to develop wood production. Now long rows of thriving eucalyptus trees and acacia are halting the desert. The Reforestation Institute claims the most varied collection of forest trees in the Mediterranean.

CHAPTER 10

State Trees

*R*esearch shows that tree species now growing in North America existed long before the country was inhabited by man: maples as long ago as sixty million years; and poplars, oaks, pines, elms and possibly other trees grew here during the Ice Age. Greenland is named because of its trees, to differentiate it from Iceland, which is almost without trees.

The commercial forest lands of the United States consist of about 488 million acres. Old-growth saw timber covers 50 million acres; second-growth timber, 133 million. There are 120 million acres in the cordwood areas, 102 million acres in fair-to-satisfactory restocking areas and 83 million acres in poor-to-nonrestocking areas.

There are about 180 different species of trees in the United States that may be ranked as commercially important, although only relatively few species of wood are ordinarily readily available except in large cities. Forest regions and principal types of forests are shown on the accompanying map, Fig. 50.

The individual states of the United States have long recognized the importance of trees, and each state has selected a particular tree with which to identify itself. This has been done by acts of the state legislatures, by garden clubs, by vote of the people, or, in some cases, because it is the most prominent or most valuable tree growing in that state. New York State took the lead in 1889 in selecting the sugar maple as its official tree, and was followed by the other states.

Below the states are listed alphabetically with the common name of the tree. The botanical name and individual description of the wood may be found by referring to each of the individual woods described in this book.

STATE	COMMON NAME
Alabama	Longleaf pine
Alaska	Sitka spruce
Arizona	Blue paloverde
Arkansas	Shortleaf pine
California	California redwood
Colorado	Blue spruce
Connecticut	White oak
Delaware	American holly
District of Columbia	None (although American sycamore and black cherry are mentioned on some lists)
Florida	Cabbage palmetto (cabbage palm)
Georgia	Live oak
Hawaii	Kukui (candlenut)
Idaho	Western white pine
Illinois	Bur oak

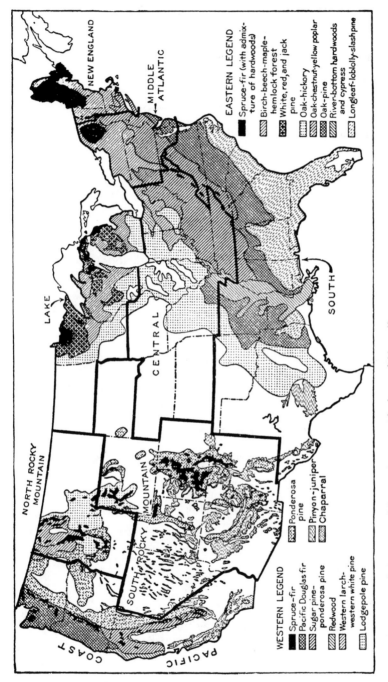

Fig. 50. Forests of the United States (except Alaska and Hawaii).

STATE	COMMON NAME
Indiana	Tulip tree (yellow poplar)
Iowa	American black walnut
Kansas	Cottonwood
Kentucky	Tulip tree (yellow poplar)
Louisiana	Southern magnolia
Maine	Eastern white pine
Maryland	White oak
Massachusetts	American elm
Michigan	Apple
Minnesota	Red pine (also called Norway pine)
Mississippi	Southern magnolia
Missouri	Dogwood
Montana	Ponderosa pine
Nebraska	American elm
Nevada	Singleleaf pinyon pine (aspen also is sometimes referred to as the state tree)
New Hampshire	White birch
New Jersey	Northern red oak
New Mexico	Pinyon pine
New York	Sugar maple
North Carolina	None (although yellow poplar is sometimes mentioned)
North Dakota	American elm
Ohio	Buckeye
Oklahoma	Eastern redbud
Oregon	Douglas fir

STATE	COMMON NAME
Pennsylvania	Eastern hemlock
Rhode Island	Red maple
South Carolina	Cabbage palmetto
South Dakota	Black Hills spruce
Tennessee	Tulip tree (yellow poplar)
Texas	Pecan
Utah	Blue spruce
Vermont	Sugar maple
Virginia	Dogwood
Washington	Western hemlock
West Virginia	Sugar maple
Wisconsin	Sugar maple
Wyoming	Balsam poplar (sometimes referred to by the general name "cottonwood")

CHAPTER 11

Drugs from Trees

*T*rees are often thought of primarily as producers of timbers and of edible fruit. Less commonly known is that
some of our important medicinal constituents are tree products.
Although many drugs previously acquired from natural sources
are now prepared synthetically, others are still in wide use.

As with all drugs, drugs derived from trees have been replaced with more potent preparations. On the other hand, new
drugs secured from trees become evident from time to time.
Pharmaceutical companies are still eager to support botanical
expeditions with the hope that some previously unknown drug
product may result from new collections. Most United States
drug houses employ botanical hunters who ship many of their
newly found specimens to the Department of Agriculture's
Plant Introduction Gardens in Glendale, Maryland, where some
must undergo quarantine.

Aboriginal tribes are still found employing tree products as drugs of which we have had no previous knowledge. Drugs of this nature were employed from the earliest times. It is known, for example, that an extract from the juniper tree was used as a cancer "curative" by the ancient Greeks and Romans.

It is not possible here to list and describe all the known trees that produce drugs. A few of the more common medicinal products obtained from trees are described below:

ACACIA (*Acacia senegal*) The gum of *Acacia senegal* is the gum arabic of present-day commerce and is that referred to as Sudan gum and Somali gum, among others. It is a characteristic tree throughout the drier parts of the Sudan and southern Sahara. The gum, it is said, is yielded only when the tree is unhealthy, and efforts to improve its condition are followed by a reduction in yield. Gum arabic is an exudation from the tree, used as a base for many mucilages, as an emulsifying agent in pharmacy and in tannic acid, which is used in the treatment of burns.

ALLSPICE (*Pimenta officinalis*) A fragrant tree sometimes 40 ft. high, the allspice is native to Jamaica, Cuba, southern Mexico and parts of Central America. The berries, while still green, are gathered and dried for export. Although used chiefly in cookery, allspice is employed as a carminative and stimulant in drug preparations.

ARECA (*Areca catechu*) This is a tall palm tree, from 30 to 50 ft., indigenous to the Malay Archipelago. The seed, or betel "nut" of commercial and native use, is chewed by the natives to produce the garish red mouth and black teeth considered in good fashion. It is rarely used in human medicine, but frequently employed by veterinarians as a vermifuge because of its active principal, the alkaloid arecoline.

BALM OF GILEAD (*Populus candicans* and other species) The dried winter buds of this species possess a natural resinous substance which imparts a tendency to prevent rancidity in ointments. Applied externally, the resin is useful in healing wounds. Internally it is a stimulating expectorant in the treatment of bronchitis.

BALSAM OF PERU (*Myroxylon balsamum* var. *pereirae*) The range of this variety extends from southern Mexico southward through Central America, mostly on the Pacific side. Its principal value is in its vanilla-scented resin, which is known as balsam of Peru. The drug was introduced into Europe by the Spaniards in the sixteenth century. Its source has been the Balsam Coast, originally a part of Guatemala, now of Salvador, and the misleading name is derived from the fact that in colonial days the product was frequently sent to Callao, Peru, for transshipment to Spain. To obtain the balsam, the trees are beaten until the bark falls off. The resulting gummy exudation is collected on rags, which are then boiled to remove the gum, packed in bladders and taken to market. It is used in medicine as a stimulant dressing for indolent ulcers, for tuberculosis of the bone and skin and as a dressing for wounds.

The South American trees also yield oleoresin, sometimes called "balsamum tolutanum" or balsam tolu. It is considered inferior to the Salvador product. Its main use is in the preparation of syrup tolu—a feeble stimulant-expectorant of pleasant taste—and as a vehicle for cough mixture.

BENJAMIN TREE (*Styrax benzoin*) This tall tree, a native of Sumatra and Java, is covered with whitish, downy bark. Once a year the bark is wounded in the vicinity of the lower branches to permit exudation of sap, which hardens on exposure to air and produces gum benzoin, a white, fragrant gum used in medicine as a stimulating expectorant. Tincture of benzoin compound, universally used and known, is made with this product and is employed in steam inhalators for the relief of bronchitis and laryngitis. In the East Indies, the gum is burned by the Hindus as a perfume in their places of worship.

BOLDO (*Boldea boldus*) The leaves of this strongly aromatic tree, native to the dry sunny hillsides of Chile, are used as a seasoning for foods and as an antispasmatic and hepatic stimulant. The bark is a source of tannin.

CACAO (*Theobroma cacao*) This is a small, handsome evergreen tree, indigenous to Mexico, the West Indies and South America. The pods (fruits) of this tree produce numerous large seeds, which when roasted and ground, give us our cocoa or chocolate of commerce. Cocoa butter is used in many food substitutes and medicinally as a base for emollients and suppositories. At one time, it was practically the major treatment for sunburn.

CAMPHOR TREE (*Cinnamomum camphora*) This evergreen tree sometimes attains a great size and is native to Formosa, Japan and some parts of China. It grows so slowly that fifty years or more usually elapses before the drug, camphor, is removed from the bark by the process of sublimation. Camphor was used for many years by "old wives" as a charm and as a cure for many illnesses, and hung in bags around the neck to ward off plagues. It is used in medicine mainly as a local remedy and counter-irritant, and as an ingredient in many ointments for relieving muscle pains. A derivative is also used hypodermically as an emergency stimulant in some cases of heart failure.

CANELLA BARK or WHITE CINNAMON (*Canella winterana*) The white cinnamon is native to the Florida Keys and West Indies. Its yellowish inner bark is cinnamon-scented and is employed as an aromatic stimulant and tonic.

CASCARA (*Rhamnus purshiana*) This small tree grows in the northwestern United States and British Columbia. Because of the large demand for the wood, the trees have been depleted in Oregon and Washington but are more readily available in Canada. The wood, which is yellow, orange-brown or orange, is easy to work and takes a good finish, but has little or no commercial value because of the small size of the timber. The inside of freshly cut bark is bright yellow, turning to brown when exposed to the sun, and has a bitter taste. The bark is the source of the drug known as cascara sagrada, used in medicine as a laxative and cathartic. An average tree will yield about 10 lbs. of dried bark. The bark is stripped from the tree during the dry season, hung on wires to dry in the shade and shipped in 100-lb. bales or bags to dealers. The bark must age for a year or more before being used medicinally. Cascara is also known under a number of different names, such as brittle wood, buckthorn, yellow wood, polecat tree, bitter bark and wild coffee.

CASSIA (*Cassia fistula*) Cassia is a large tree which may reach 45 ft. in height. It is native to India and has a hard, heavy wood. The trunk is covered with a smooth, ash-colored bark. It is now distributed throughout the world tropics under the name "golden shower" and is used as an ornamental shade tree. The crushed fruit of this tree is officially known as cassia pulp and is used as an aromatic flavoring and mild laxative.

CASTANEA (*Castanea dentata*) The American chestnut is a large, spreading deciduous tree often reaching 100 ft. in height but now almost extinct, owing to a pernicious fungus-caused blight. There have been attempts to obtain disease-resistant varieties. The leaves were used in medicine as a treatment for whooping cough; however, modern pharmacology attributes to them no other properties than that of a mild astringent.

CHALMOOGRA (*Hydnocarpus kurzii* or *Taraktogenos kurzii*) For centuries leprosy has been one of the most dreaded diseases of mankind and it was long thought to be incurable. It was known, however, that the natives of Burma and other parts of Southeast Asia used the seeds and oil obtained from the chalmoogra tree in the treatment of skin diseases. In experiments carried on at the University of Hawaii this oil was used in the development of a successful treatment for leprosy.

CINCHONA (*Cinchona succiruba*) The Peruvian bark tree is native to the high mountains of Peru and Ecuador. It is also widely cultivated throughout the tropics in Java, Sumatra and elsewhere. The bark from this tree has been used since the seventeenth century in the treatment of malaria. There are many official drugs obtained from the bark of this tree: mainly, quinine, quinidine, cinchonine and cinchonidine. Quinidine is much depended upon in treating some forms of heart failure. Modern synthetic drugs such as chloroquine and primaquine have proven superior to quinine in the treatment of malaria.

CINNAMON (*Cinnamomum loureiri* or *Cinnamomum zeylanicum*) The cinnamon tree is native to China and Japan but is now cultivated in India and other tropical lands. Several species are used in the production of the cinnamon of commerce. Cinnamon is among the most delightful of aromatics, efficient as a flavoring in candies and in cooking. It is warm and cordial to the stomach, flavorful in medicine and efficient as a carminative.

CLOVE TREE (*Eugenia caryophyllata*) It is a small evergreen tree, indigenous to the Moluccas and perhaps the southern Philippine Islands. Throughout the year it is covered with a succession of beautiful, rosy flowers. The dried flower buds give us our commercial cloves, an aromatic spice much prized by chefs. An aromatic oil expressed from these cloves is used in many forms of pharmaceutical preparations, the most familiar of which is the oil of cloves, used to control toothaches.

COCA (*Erythroxylon coca*) This shrub or small tree is native to the eastern slopes of the Andes from Colombia to Bolivia but is grown throughout tropical South America and in Java and the surrounding islands. The leaves of this and other species are the source of cocaine and its component alkaloids. Natives chew the leaves for their stimulating effects. During the reign of the Incas, athletic prowess was attributed in part to the strength and sustaining power derived from masticating dried coca leaves. The drug cocaine acts internally as a circulatory and respiratory stimulant. Externally it is used mainly as a local anesthetic to deaden pain quickly. It takes over 100 lbs. of the leaves of this tree to make 1 lb. of cocaine.

CURARE (*Strychnos toxifera* and others) This tree produces one of the most violent poisons known. The Indians of northern South America have long used curare as an arrow poison. In preparing curare, portions of the bark and roots are boiled down, the impurities skimmed off and the residue filtered. Catalytic agents are added and the whole mass is boiled to a syrup. This is exposed to the sun and dried to a paste, which is kept in tightly covered gourds or bamboo tubes. The paste, if introduced into the circulation in minute quantities, paralyzes the motor nerves almost instantly and soon causes death by cardiac failure. The lethal effects are due to certain alkaloids. One of these, curarine, has now been made available to medicine for use in shock therapy and is an ideal muscle relaxant.

EASTERN WHITE PINE (*Pinus strobus*) The bark of this tree, which grows throughout the whole eastern portion of the

United States and Canada, is used as an ingredient in cough syrups and in the treatment of bronchial afflictions.

EUCALYPTUS (*Eucalyptus globulus* and other species) The genus *Eucalyptus* comprises large evergreen trees, sometimes 300 to 350 ft. in height. *E. globulus* grows in Tasmania, where it is called blue gum. Medically, oil of eucalyptus, which is distilled from the leaves, is an active germicide and is used locally in infections of the upper respiratory tract. It is also used as an astringent.

GUAIACUM (*Guaiacum officinale*) Guaiacum or gum guaiac is a hard resin that exudes naturally from the stems of lignum vitae trees. It is obtained commercially from incisions in the bark or from the cut ends of logs. Gum guaiac is used as a stimulant and laxative.

JAMAICA DOGWOOD (*Piscidia piscipula*) These medium-sized trees occur in countries bounded by the Gulf of Mexico and the Caribbean Sea. The bark is used medicinally as an anodyne and hypnotic. Natives use the bark to stupefy fish—hence the name fishfuddle tree.

KOLA (*Cola nitida* and *C. acuminata*) These large trees are native to Guinea and western tropical Africa. They are also cultivated in the West Indies and South America for their seeds, which when dried are used commercially in some medicines as a stimulant. The nuts contain much caffeine and when chewed help to overcome fatigue. They form a staple in the diet of natives (cf. coca). Kola is also used as an ingredient in some of the carbonated drinks commonly used, like Coca-Cola.

MANNA or EUROPEAN FLOWERING ASH (*Fraxinus ornus*) A native of southern Europe, this ash is widely cultivated in Italy and Sicily, where it grows to 20 or 25 ft. in height. Incisions are made in the lower portions of the tree to permit the flow of a sugary substance which dries naturally on the trees in small globules. Manna is a gentle demulcent laxative usually prescribed with other laxative agents.

NUTMEG (*Myristica fragrans*) This is a small tree, somewhat resembling an orange, native to the Mollucas. Grown from seed, it

Fig. 51. Eucalyptus trees flourish in Australia and Tasmania. This typical forest stand consists of shaggy-bark giants reaching a height of nearly 300 feet. Leaves are used for drugs; timber is converted into lumber and veneer.

flowers and fruits after the ninth year. The dried kernel of the nut, commonly known as nutmeg, is a valuable flavoring and cooking agent. Mace, another food flavoring, is obtained from the fleshy covering of the seed (the aril). Nutmeg owes its medicinal properties purely to the volatile oil. It has stimulant and carminative properties, but in large doses nutmegs are highly toxic and produce convulsions.

NUX VOMICA (*Strychnos nux-vomica*) Nux vomica or the strychnine tree grows in India, parts of China, and Ceylon and provides from its seeds strychnine, a deadly poison. This powerful drug is used as a heart stimulant and tonic, either alone or in conjunction with other drugs.

QUASSIA (*Quassia amara*) This bitter-tasting species has a natural range extending from northern South America through the West Indies, Central America and southern Mexico. The wood has been an item of commerce from Surinam since about the middle of the eighteenth century, called quassia or bitterwood in Surinam. It was introduced into the London Pharmacopoeia in 1788, but in the 1809 edition was superseded by Jamaica bitterwood (*Aeschrion*), which was obtainable in larger sizes. The bitter principle of both kinds of wood (quassin) is readily soluble in cold water and for many years there was a demand for cups, called bitter cups, turned from the wood. The drug is used as a tonic and vermifuge and formerly was a febrifuge. It is also used as an insecticide and as an ingredient of certain proprietary medicines.

QUERCUS (*Quercus alba*) A large, handsome tree native to North America, it is one of the more than fifty species of oaks in the United States. The dried inner bark is used externally in medicine because of its astringent properties. Tannic acid is probably the active ingredient.

RAUWOLFIA (*Rauwolfia serpentina* and other species) Extracts from the roots of these shrubs have been used in India for the treatment of nervous disorders for many centuries. Records show that roots and leaves of *R. serpentina* were used in Ayruvedic medicine as antidotes for bites of reptiles and the stings of insects and as a remedy for diarrhea. Only recently was the dried

Fig. 52. Group of ornamental sassafras trees. When harvested, the roots and bark of sassafras are turned into drug products and confections. Sassafras lumber is usually mixed and marketed with black ash.

and powdered root of *R. serpentina* introduced into clinical medicine here for the treatment of hypertension and nervous troubles, including mental illness. Various drugs (e.g., serpentine, rauwolfinine, reserpinine and reserpine) derived from the powdered root constitute a general class of tranquilizers commonly used today.

SASSAFRAS (*Sassafras albidum*) A delightful tree of eastern North America, all parts of which are aromatic. The bark of the roots is the source of the commercial oil of sassafras. Small roots in asparaguslike bunches are a common article of local commerce and are used in making sassafras tea, a beverage of reputed medicinal virtues, particularly as a "spring tonic." Root bark is also active as a diuretic.

SENNA (*Cassia acutifolia* and other species) This ancient drug is obtained from the dried leaflets, and also the pods, of several species of *Cassia* which are indigenous to the arid regions of Egypt and Arabia. Wild plants are still used as a source of the drug in Egypt. Medicinally, senna acts as a purgative.

STAR ANISE (*Illicium verum*) Although not the true anise (*Pimpinella anisum*), the star anise is also used as a flavoring and is active medicinally as a carminative. The Chinese prepare a medicinal tea from the fruits and regard it as good for colic and constipation. Interestingly enough, all other species of *Illicium* except *I. verum* are poisonous.

WILD BLACK CHERRY (*Prunus virginiana* and *P. serotina*) This tree from North America furnishes a bark which upon infusion yields hydrocyanic acid and is used in the treatment of bronchitis. "Cherry stalks" act as a mild stomachic and bitter tonic.

CHAPTER 12

Little-Known Behavior of Trees and Woods

Most plants and animals attain a form which is considered typical for their kind. They attract little attention and therefore are not of particular interest in this regard. Those animals that are distinctive for one reason or another usually draw a great deal of attention. The kangaroo with its ponderous tail, bipedal form of locomotion and abdominal pouch (marsupium) in which the normally premature young are carried is a good example of an unusual animal. The elephant and its trunk; the ostrich, a flightless bird; aquatic mammals such as whales and seals; a flying mammal, the bat—all are of extraordinary interest because of some unique anatomical structure or mode of life.

Certain woody plants and trees are the kangaroos and bats of the vegetable kingdom and are important for the same reasons: they differ in some outstanding respect from their relatives.

Fig. 53. Interior of mangrove swamp on Plantation Key, Florida, showing the tangled mass of aerial roots. This forest is periodically inundated by the Atlantic Ocean.

Some of the more exciting of these unusual woody plants will be described and illustrated below. Some are trees; some, woody vines; some, shrubs. In some cases the shape of the trunk is noteworthy; in others the wood itself is unusual. It is apparent that not all peculiar woody plants can be included in this short chapter. Our purpose is merely to introduce the kinds of peculiar woody plants in which the peculiarity is normal to the species.

In some trees a portion of the root system is aerial and extends above the surface of the ground. The red mangrove (*Rhizophora mangle*) is a common tropical tree which inhabits the margins of muddy salt flats. The trunk, strangely enough, is borne aloft on a network of stiltlike aerial roots (Fig. 53). Forests of red mangrove form impenetrable masses along certain seacoasts because of these interwoven stilt roots.

Aerial roots are frequently formed by the baldcypress (*Taxodium distichum*) of the southeastern United States (Fig. 54). In this tree the aerial roots are referred to as "knees" because of their resemblance to human knees. The baldcypress commonly grows in swamps; the knees, which are really branches of the underground root system, project above the surface of the

Fig. 54. The baldcypress found in swamp areas and often seen standing in water sends up stumps, called aerial roots, through which the tree can breathe. Roots are sold as cypress knees. This thick stand follows Wadboo Creek, Francis Marion National Park, South Carolina.

water. Craftsmen often fashion these knees into novelties, lamp bases being a favorite.

One of the most curious trees is the papaya (*Carica papaya*) of tropical lands. A close examination of the structure of the main stem often prompts the question "When is a tree not a tree?" In the papaya we have a treelike plant which may attain a height of 30 ft. or more. It has an unbranched trunk bearing a crown of long-stalked leaves. If we cut the trunk apart and examine the structure microscopically, we find that the only "woody" material present is confined to strands embedded in a matrix of an almost pulpy, pithlike material. The main supportive material in the stem is a network of thick-walled fibers in the bark! Many a wood collector has found, to his dismay, that on being dried, the trunk of the papaya reverts to a soupy mass. After complete drying, the only solid material remaining is the meshwork of bark fibers. The papaya is really an arborescent herb!

Fig. 55. Cross section of fronds of arborescent fern.

Most of us are familiar with members of the lily family. We know that these are, in general, low-growing herbaceous plants. However, some of the tropical members are anything but low-growing and herbaceous. *Cordyline australis* is a tree lily which exhibits a slender woody trunk surmounted by a crown of strap-shaped, lilylike leaves. At this point it is well to mention that many plant families, which in the temperate zone are represented only by herbs, have tropical members which are treelike and have decidedly woody stems. The lobelias become arborescent and woody in the tropics; members of the sunflower family (*Compositae*) reach tree proportions in the Andes; the forget-me-not family (*Boraginaceae*) in the tropics is represented by commercially important timber trees (e.g., *Cordia* spp.). In a sense, these tree representatives of plant families commonly considered as herbaceous are noteworthy.

Along the same line, most of us are acquainted with ferns merely as lowly, though attractive, plants of the woods and fields. The breath of the tropics must invigorate certain of the ferns, for there they reach majestic proportions (for ferns, that

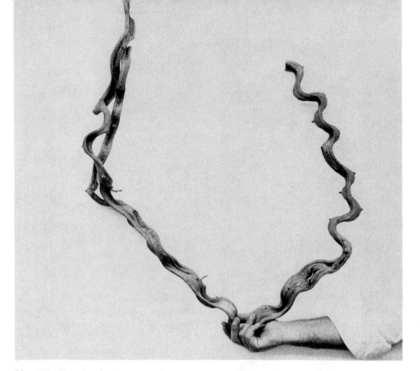

Fig. 56. Tropical vine (escalera de mono or monkey ladder).

is). They "get up on their hind legs," as it were. The normally underground horizontal stem becomes vertical and increases in diameter to support a massive crown of leaves. The fronds on some tropical, arborescent ferns may exceed 10 ft. in length (Fig. 55). These tree ferns are a far cry from the potted Boston fern which stood in Grandmother's window.

Tropical vines often assume bizarre forms both externally and internally. Certain species of *Bauhinia* (legume family) are called *escalera de mono* or monkey ladder, an allusion to the sinuate nature of the vine, which supposedly enables monkeys to use them as ladders (Fig. 56). A cross section of the stem of a native passion flower (*Passiflora multiflora*) reveals wood which is almost unbelievably complex in outline. Instead of a cylindrical woody body, we are confronted with a highly convoluted and dissected mass (Fig. 57). Many vines exhibit curiously lobed and parted xylem masses; these may occur even when the stem is cylindrical externally!

Certain species of mylady (*Aspidosperma* spp.) from the Guianas have trunks which are actually deeply lobed in cross

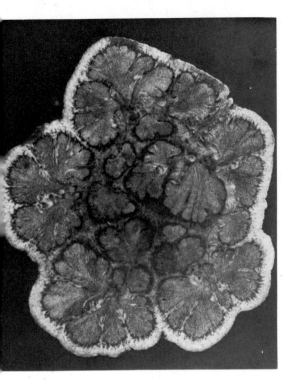

Fig. 57. Cross section of the anomalous stem of the many-flowered passion flower (Passiflora multiflora). Notice the numerous convoluted masses in the stem—each a portion of the wood axis. The actual size is approximately that of a silver dollar.

Fig. 58. Cross section of trunk of Aspidosperma.

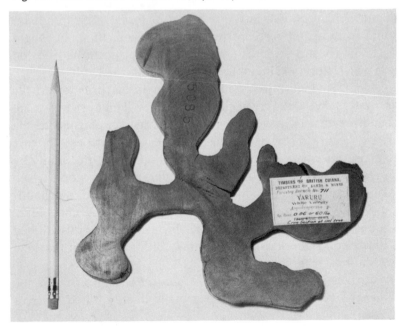

Fig. 60. Fruit from the cannon-ball tree.

Fig. 61. The tropical Aspidosperma *has flattened fruits of leg-of-mutton* shape.

section (Fig. 58). Flanges taken from these trunks are fashioned into paddles by the natives of British Guiana. This practice has given rise to the common name paddlewood for this tree. Similar lobing also occurs in other tree species of different families.

The baobab tree (*Adansonia digitata*) of Africa is the elephant of the plant kingdom. It is elephantine from its thickly folded bark to its greatly distorted massive trunk. Perhaps the most curious feature of this tree is the sharply tapered trunk, which in the extreme is almost pear-shaped. Occasionally these trees will have several main stems and this heightens the outlandish appearance. Imagine, if you will, three pear-shaped trunks of immense girth, united at the base, each with thickly folded bark, tapered abruptly at the apex and bearing a ridiculous crown of short, stubby branches which are leafless during part of the year.

Many tropical timber trees, although of normal structure, bear fruits which are truly unsurpassed in form. The winged fruit of *Centrolobium* (a legume) is far different from the pod of the pea, which belongs to the same family (Fig. 59). The candle tree (*Parmentiera cerifera*) bears quantities of smooth, yellow, hanging fruits which greatly resemble long wax candles. Supposedly these "candles" provide excellent feed for cattle. The cannon-ball tree (*Couroupita guianensis*), (Fig. 60), of the Brazil nut family, is noted for its huge, hard cannon-ball-like fruits. Other members of this family also have large woody fruits which may open with a lid, as a teapot. The sausagelike, drooping fruits of *Kigelia pinnata* have, no doubt, given rise to the common name sausage tree for this species. The underside of a sausage tree bearing fruit reminds one of standing in the cooler of a delicatessen amid the hanging salami and Bologna sausages. The tree is a fairly common ornamental in the tropics and subtropics and is cultivated in Florida. *Aspidosperma*, a tropical relative of the milkweed, bears flattened fruits of leg-of-mutton shape. The most interesting feature here is the thin, waferlike seeds stacked like pancakes within. The wind can no doubt blow these seeds for many miles (Fig. 61).

Another peculiar tree is the banyan (*Ficus bengalensis*), growing principally in India and Burma. It is considered sacred by the Hindus and little of the wood is available commercially.

Fig. 62. Bristlecone pine survives the rigors of the mountain top be-cause part dies off in order that other parts may be sustained on the limited food supply.

Fig. 63. Seven elms were determined to grow in a crowded clump in the middle of an open field in Nebraska.

Fig. 64. The roots of rubber trees outlast trunk and branches. Saplings are grafted to old stumps to renew productivity on this Malaysian plantation.

Fig. 65. This thriving yellow birch in New Hampshire started as a seed on an old stump and clung to life by sending aerial roots to the ground.

Fig. 66. Live oak, three times wider than high, sheds leaves and grows new ones year-round. This ancient tree stands in Audubon Park, New Orleans.

However, it is not particularly suitable for general use. The tree is very large and throws down numerous aerial roots from the branches. These root in the ground and grow into separate trunks. A banyan tree has been recorded with a spread of 2,000 ft. around the branches.

More than eleven thousand feet above sea level in the Inyo National Forest life is difficult to sustain. An unusual tree known as bristlecone pine survives because of its peculiar habits. It is one of the oldest living things in the world; yet, in many trees, only a part is alive. The bristlecone usually has gnarled and grotesquely twisted branches. Some are dead, lessening the demand on the declining root system, so that at least a small part of the tree may live on in equilibrium with its harsh environment.

The determination to survive is indeed deep-seated. In an open field in Nebraska, seven elm trees chose to grow in a crowded clump where their seeds landed by chance. Twin elms are so common the name has been applied to hundreds of country restaurants. Multigrowth of birches is common. But seven elms in one clump make for a unique example of nature's strange behavior.

In Malaya, where half the world's natural rubber is produced by trees, the hard-worked older trees are destroyed by chemical poisoning. Roots remain alive, and young trees are grafted on the old stump to renew productivity.

The seed of a yellow birch landed by chance on an old stump deep in a forest area in the White Mountains, in New Hampshire. Seeking essential nourishment, some of the roots reached outward, beyond the stump, and grew in the surrounding ground. They remain as live, stilt roots even now, after the old stump has rotted away.

The live oak grows along the south Atlantic and Gulf coast regions. This tree, praised for its spreading branches festooned with picturesque Spanish moss streamers flowing in the breeze, rates mention for two unusual habits. First, it may extend twisting lateral branches so low and so long that it becomes three times as broad as it is high. Second, although green all year, it constantly sheds its leaves and grows new ones in an almost endless cycle, little noticed except by homeowners who are forever raking them.

Fig. 67. It took a thousand years for this live oak to develop an artistic entanglement of branches that few trees will ever match. It grows in Texas and is known as the Goose Island Oak.

Fig. 68. The unknown tree. Giant of the African jungle, whose wood is now somewhere in lumber, remains unnamed.

Another live oak, said to be one thousand years old, stands in Goose Island State Park, in Texas. If not the largest, measuring 35 ft. around its trunk, it appears to have the most contorted tangle of massive branches ever photographed.

The unknown tree! Although the giant tree in Fig. 68 does not rank with the largest sequoias, it is estimated to measure nearly 15 ft. in diameter. When last seen by the photographer the African Congo natives were preparing it for harvest. Local names for trees in foreign jungles frequently have no relation to our nomenclature, and since five American experts have declined to name it, this tree remains only in this photographic reproduction, and is truly the unknown tree.

Is Fig. 69 the Garden of Eden? No, this old longleaf pine grows in Sabine County, Texas. In spite of its strange companion, a large projecting root with an evil snake eye menacing onlookers, this forked and twisted specimen has become National Champion Longleaf Pine. Pines of this species do well to grow much over 100 ft., but this champion, stripped of most lower bark, stretched up to 134 ft. and is still growing, making a strange sight to behold.

These few examples have been drawn from a vast number of tree curiosa and only serve to illustrate that trees are not all "run-of-the-mill." A little study will uncover many more such oddities for the interested woodworker. As mentioned previously, tree peculiarities can often be put to practical use in the construction of craft objects.

Fig. 69. National Champion Longleaf Pine, Sabine County, Texas.

CHAPTER 13

Collecting Woods
of the World
As a Hobby

HOW TO COLLECT WOODS

One of the most fascinating and intriguing of all occupations is the collection of woods. As in other fields of pursuit, there is a correct, scientific way in which to collect woods, and incorrect, careless methods. For a sample of wood to be scientifically valuable, it must be correlated with a specimen of the leaves, twigs and flowers (herbarium specimen) gathered from the same tree from which the wood was extracted. The manner in which woods with herbarium vouchers are collected is discussed in this chapter.

Let us imagine that we, as wood enthusiasts, have undertaken to collect wood samples in the tropics, say in the Republic of Panama. In the tropics we find the greatest diversity of woody plants, and we know our collecting should yield commendable results. However, without the proper equipment and know-how, no expedition can be successful. What then, shall we take?

114]

Remember, the material will depend in large part on the duration of the trip, facilities available in the field such as lodging, transportation and food, the terrain, climate, and so forth. Panama is a tropical area, with generally high rainfall, high temperatures, and relative humidity. The western portion, at least on the Pacific side, is fairly well inhabited. Food and lodging of a kind are available, and we can obtain a vehicle with which we can travel the Inter-American Highway. Here is an actual, though greatly abridged, list of equipment taken by members of Yale's Samuel James Record Memorial Collection on a wood-collecting expedition to Panama:

String tags, 1,000	Saw, hand
Compass	Saw, chain
Paper bags, 100	Axes, felling
First-aid supplies	Camera, 35mm. single-lens
Leather-palmed gloves	reflex
Film, color and black-and-	Camera, 120, double-lens
white	reflex
Light meter	Pencils, graphite
Machetes	Pencils, indelible
Presses, botanical	Diameter tape
Driers, botanical	Flashlights and batteries
Ventilators, botanical	Pruning shears
Twine, butcher's	Stove, gasoline
Pliers with cutter	Lamp, gasoline
Rope, 3/4 in. hemp	Altimeter
Files, mill bastard	Preserving fluids and jars
Field notebooks	Shotgun with ammunition
Binoculars	
Botanical literature (manuals,	
etc.)	

You will notice that camping equipment, drugs, food, fuel and other necessaries have been omitted. Even so, the list is quite extensive. A trip to a more remote area would require many more pieces of gear.

The wood sample should be obtained from the main stem or trunk of the tree. Because the latest-formed wood is anatomically most mature, the collector should attempt to include some in his sample. To extract the sample, the tree may be felled, or a piece of wood may be split from the trunk, as illustrated in Fig. 70.

PATH OF AX
TO SPLIT SECTION
FROM TREE

Fig. 70. How to split wood samples from the trunk of a tree.

The latter method is by far the easier, but requires more skill, if less brawn, than the former. A sample split out in this way will be acceptable, and if the cuts are deep enough, both heartwood and sapwood will be represented. A note of caution: samples should not be cut from buttresses, which frequently have an entirely different wood structure from the remainder of the trunk. Wood from small trees and shrubs can be best obtained by the use of a saw. In this case select a small segment of the trunk of a small tree or a few sections from the main stems of a shrub.

After wood samples have been taken, voucher specimens should be gathered from the same plant. Voucher specimens comprise leafy twigs bearing flowers and fruits, if possible. When collecting in remote or poorly known areas, it is almost imperative that flowers be collected. Identification is largely based on floral structure and it is frequently impossible to determine a species from a botanically poorly known region without flowers. It is, therefore, the practice of many collectors, when in remote areas, to gather specimens only from plants which are in flower or at least have fruits.

One should select representative material in abundance to aid in identification. Voucher material may be collected by climbing the tree, felling it, or shooting down branches with a shotgun. The latter method is frequently easiest, though with certain extremely tall trees it is not too successful.

We now have our wood sample and corresponding herbarium material. Both kinds of samples are numbered identically; the wood with an indelible pencil or numbers impressed with steel dies, the herbarium vouchers with a numbered string tag. Notes regarding the collection are entered into our field book under a number corresponding to that on the samples. Such data as the height and diameter of the tree, characteristics of the bark, whether buttresses are present, flower color, flower aroma, peculiarities of the leaves and fruits, habitat of the tree, exposure, soil, geographic locality, altitude, date of collection, and other information are among those recorded in the field book.

In moist tropical lands it is essential that we care for our specimens immediately to prevent deterioration by fungi. Woods season best when stored in an airy, shaded location. Large pieces should be split to facilitate drying.

Herbarium specimens require more care. These must be pressed flat and dried, no mean task in the tropics. To perform these operations a botanical press and a heat source must be used. A botanical press is a simple affair consisting of two lattices of wooden strips fastened at joints with copper rivets (Fig. 71). Ash or hickory is best for this use, as presses so made will stand a great deal of abuse.

Plants to be dried are placed carefully into a folded half sheet of newsprint. This is then placed between two blotters

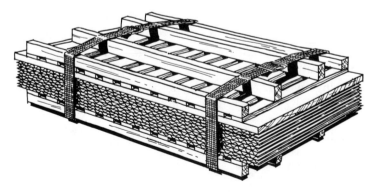

Fig. 71. Simply-made press for herbarium specimens.

(driers), which, in turn, are placed between two pieces of corrugated cardboards (ventilators), as shown in the illustration. The sandwich is built up within the press; ventilator, drier, plant in newsprint, drier, ventilator and so on. After a convenient-sized sandwich has been made, the press is closed, and pressure is applied by straps, as illustrated. In the field, the press is supported over some heat source—gasoline or kerosene stove, auto engine, cooking fire—so that the corrugations act as flues for the hot air. Specimens are examined periodically, the dried ones removed, others rearranged for better drying, and the press restrapped and set over the heat source again. Dried specimens should be so stored as to prevent their again becoming moist. Polyethylene bags containing a desiccant are useful for this purpose. Specimens can be shipped, suitably wrapped, in these containers.

Herbarium vouchers may be sent for identification to several botanical institutes in this country.[1] It is customary that those who identify material are privileged to keep the specimens in return for the identifications. The herbarium voucher, thus retained by a botanical institution and bearing the collector's name and number (the same as is on the wood sample), provides a means whereby the identification can be verified in the future. It is an indispensable record and makes a wood sample scientifically valuable. The identification of woods may be open to serious question when not substantiated with a herbarium voucher stored in a botanical institution.

COLLECTIONS OF WOODS

Collections of woods may be divided into two categories: institutional collections and private collections. Presently there are over 65 institutional wood collections in the world, the largest containing over 52,000 samples and maintaining its own her-

---

[1] Identifications may be requested from The New York Botanical Garden, Bronx Park, New York, N.Y.; The U.S. National Herbarium, Smithsonian Institution, Washington, D.C.; Chicago Natural History Museum, Chicago, Ill.; Harvard University Herbarium, Cambridge, Mass.; Samuel James Record Memorial Collection, Yale School of Forestry, New Haven, Conn., and other institutions. Wood samples may be identified by writing the Director, Forest Products Laboratory, Madison, Wis. It is always best to write first and ask the curators if they would be willing to accept material for identification.

barium of voucher specimens. Some of the more important of these collections are located as follows: Forest Research Institute, Bogor, Indonesia (32,000 specimens); Harvard University Herbarium, Cambridge, Massachusetts (25,000 specimens); Chicago Natural History Museum, Chicago (18,000 specimens); Forest Products Research Institute, College, Laguna, Philippines (10,526 specimens); Forest Research Institute, P.O. New Forest, Dehra Dun, India (14,337 specimens); Forest Research Institute, Kepong, Malaya (7,000 specimens); Museums of Economic Botany, Royal Botanic Gardens, Kew, England (between 16,000 and 20,000 specimens); V. L. Komarov Botanical Institute of The Academy of Sciences of the U.S.S.R., Leningrad, U.S.S.R. (8,000 specimens); Forest Products Laboratory, Madison, Wisconsin (17,330 specimens); The Samuel James Record Memorial Collection, School of Forestry, Yale University, New Haven, Connecticut (52,500 specimens); Centre Technique Forestier Tropical, Nogent-sur-Marne, France (10,117 specimens); The Imperial Forestry Institute Wood Collection, Department of Forestry, University of Oxford, Oxford, England (18,700 specimens); Forest Products Research Laboratory, Princes Risborough, England (23,000 specimens); Division of Forest Products, C.S.I.R.O., South Melbourne, Australia (17,000 specimens); and Harry Philip Brown Wood Collection, College of Forestry, State University of New York, Syracuse, New York (25,000 specimens).

Most of these collections perform several functions, the major one of which is to act as a repository of specimens. Research in wood structure, plant anatomy and taxonomy are carried on in many wood collections and associated laboratories. Wood samples are made available to reputable scientists for their own studies. Exchanges are carried out whereby duplicates from one collection are transferred to another. In short, the wood collection is like a library with wood samples for books— always available for research and study.

Many private collections of woods are maintained throughout the world. Private collections are kept for various reasons, the uppermost, I suppose, being the love of the collector for woods. Some collectors pride themselves in keeping botanically accurate records on collections and identifications; others are interested in the woods from the craftsman's point of view, and still others hold both motives. Frequently the amateur collector of woods is instrumental in providing needed samples for study to scientists. At other times they help to acquaint the lay public with the beauty of wood and the need for protecting forest resources. A large number of these nonprofessional collectors have banded together to form the International Wood Collectors Society, "A non-profit organization of scientists, botanists, dendrologists, technologists, wood collectors, hobbyists and craftsmen for mutual reciprocation and assistance."

CHAPTER 14

Modern Craftsmen Use a Wide Variety of Woods

*I*f you were asked to name the most popular furniture woods, you would have no hesitation in saying mahogany, walnut, maple and oak, but beyond that, you might begin to wonder which woods to list next. To what extent is white pine now used in furniture? How about cherry? Does anyone use teak for furniture these days? "Of course teak is used," you would answer, because you would recollect the advertisements you had seen for modern Scandinavian furniture made of teak—and beech, too.

By the time you were through considering all aspects of this subject, you would probably have quite a list of furniture woods. And if you stopped to compare it with the woods associated with the great periods of furniture design, you would begin to suspect that probably more different woods and veneers are being used for furniture in the twentieth century than at any time in the past.

If a cabinetmaker wanted to reproduce a chest of drawers or a gateleg table of the Jacobean period, there would be no question about the wood to use; it would be oak. We associate oak with the Jacobean and Cromwellian styles, and nowadays would not think of using anything else in a reproduction, although oak was not, by any means, the only wood used. Much common furniture built in that period of English history was made of less expensive woods such as deal, chestnut and beech.

With the development of the William-and-Mary style, walnut became popular. In early colonial days in America, native woods were largely used—pine, oak, maple, birch, walnut, cherry and others. After the middle of the eighteenth century, a good deal of mahogany was imported for the more expensive types of furniture.

Mahogany, of course, was the principal wood in Chippendale and Hepplewhite furniture. Much satinwood and other fine veneers were used in veneering Hepplewhite pieces. Sheraton-style furniture also was mainly made of mahogany; many surfaces were veneered with mahogany and other veneers, and inlays often embellished the cabinetwork. Furniture of the Louis XIV, XV and XVI periods made use of oak and walnut, linden (basswood) *Tilia* spp., pear and other so-called "fruit woods."

Duncan Phyfe, the New York cabinetmaker who set the highest standards of American cabinetmaking, was especially particular about the woods he used. He gained a reputation for purchasing only the finest available mahogany and figured mahogany veneers. Choice mahogany logs were highly prized—and correspondingly expensive.

Thomas Constantine, one of the author's ancestors, was a cabinetmaker who must have known Duncan Phyfe quite well, because they were neighbors for some time. Thomas Constantine was so interested in the importation of mahogany that in 1812 he became one of the founders of Constantine & Company, which for many years dealt principally in the distribution of mahogany.

In a somewhat later period rosewood became the favorite wood for the more expensive types of hand-carved Victorian pieces. The strength, hardness and density of that rich, dark-colored wood made it possible for furniture makers to let their imaginations run wild in designing curved and ornately carved members.

All the cabinet woods of the classical furniture periods, as well as an extraordinary variety of veneers, are now available to every woodworker—even those in localities far distant from any of the principal woodworking centers. And these woods and veneers are being used with taste and skill by both professionals and amateurs. This was well demonstrated in connection with the 1958 Constantine Woodworking Awards, presented to amateur craftsmen, in a contest which drew entries from all over the United States, as well as Canada, England, Scotland, Germany, Japan and Africa. The most spectacular use of rare and beautifully grained woods was found, of course, among the entries in which the use of veneers was featured. Entries showed that craftsmen are using a great variety of woods and veneers—and doing it with great skill and ingenuity. They are displaying boldness and originality. Even when they follow traditional designs and build reproductions of period furniture, they show a creative spirit. They must, indeed, gain much of their inspiration from the beauty and infinite variety of the woods and veneers with which they work.

CHAPTER 15

Test Your Knowledge: Wood Quiz

*T*here is no better or more pleasant way to review one's knowledge of a subject than by the question-and-answer method. This chapter has therefore been written in the form of a quiz. Since many will read right through these pages for general information rather than to test their grasp of various details about woods, the answer will be given directly after each question. Another reason for adopting this style of treatment is that some facts are presented in this chapter which have not been mentioned elsewhere in the book. However, those who wish to use the quiz for review purposes—to check on what they already know about woods—may do so readily by using a card to cover the answer in each instance until they have considered the question and tried to answer.

Ques. 1   What American tree produces a sap from which a well-known syrup and candy are obtained?
Ans. Sugar maple.

Ques. 2   What wood is the favorite for butchers' blocks?
Ans. American sycamore, because of its toughness.

Ques. 3   What is the species of tree referred to in the book *A Tree Grows in Brooklyn*?
Ans. Ailanthus.

Ques. 4   What wood gives a sticky feeling to the touch which remains noticeable even after a great many years of exposure to weather?
Ans. Pyinkado, known as the ironwood of Burma.

Ques. 5   What native wood is considered one of the best for arrows?
Ans. Port Orford white cedar.

Ques. 6   What wood is the most satisfactory—and is used in large quantities—for storage-battery separators?
Ans. Port Orford white cedar.

Ques. 7   What is the wood most preferred in the manufacture of artificial limbs?
Ans. Black willow and Ohio buckeye.

Ques. 8   What woods are often used in the manufacture of wood excelsior?
Ans. Balm of Gilead poplar and black willow.

Ques. 9   What wood is the most desirable for manufacturing containers for liquids?
Ans. White oak, because the pores are filled with tyloses which do not permit liquids to penetrate.

Ques. 10   What native wood is used in the manufacture of fly rods?
Ans. Lancewood or the downy serviceberry.

Ques. 11   What tree has a red sap which exudes like blood from wounds on a body?
Ans. Banak.

Ques. 12   What wood when freshly cut has an odor resembling that of Fuller's earth?
Ans. Alstonia.

Ques. 13   What tree has gum, white in color and resembling wax, which is used for candles and which burns freely?
Ans. Canarium.

Ques. 14   How was the town of Flagstaff, Arizona, named, and what tree was involved?
Ans. On July 4, 1876, lumberjacks stripped the tallest ponderosa pine of all its branches to fly the American flag.

Ques. 15   What is the only American wood whose name has been reviewed by the U.S. Supreme Court?
Ans. Ponderosa pine.

Ques. 16   What wood growing in Malaya has its principal value in the latex used in the manufacture of chewing gum?
Ans. Jĕlutong.

Ques. 17   What tree has aerial roots?
Ans. Baldcypress.

Ques. 18   Which tropical American wood is it that, when the leaves are bruised, has a strong odor like that of garlic?
Ans. Salmwood.

Ques. 19   What is probably the largest hardwood tree in the world?

Ans. The mountain ash from Tasmania. Some trees have been reported in excess of 326 ft. in height.

Ques. 20   What wood is used for the making of manicure sticks?

Ans. Sour orange.

Ques. 21   What wood has been called rarer than diamonds?

Ans. Pink ivory.

Ques. 22   What wood is used in the manufacture of the famous Hawaiian ukuleles?

Ans. Koa.

Ques. 23   What is the hardest, heaviest and closest-grained wood known?

Ans. Lignum vitae, from Central America.

Ques. 24   What wood is often referred to and sold under the name white mahogany?

Ans. Prima vera.

Ques. 25   What type of pine furnishes a figure similar to that seen in bird's-eye maple and is sometimes referred to as bird's-eye pine?

Ans. Lodgepole pine.

Ques. 26   What wood is generally used in the manufacture of toothpicks?

Ans. Paper birch.

Ques. 27   What tree did the Indians believe to be a manifestation of the Great Spirit?

Ans. Pecan.

Ques. 28   What spruce was first discovered on Pikes Peak?

Ans. Blue spruce (in 1862).

Ques. 29   What American tree in the Southwest was one of the foremost reasons for the shedding of blood between the early white settlers and the Indians?

Ans. Single-leaf pinyon, as the Indians strongly objected to the destruction of this tree.

Ques. 30   What trees did the Indians consider to be immortal?

Ans. Redwood trees, because of their long life.

Ques. 31   What trees have leaves so rough and tough that the natives use them for sandpapering?

Ans. Teak.

Ques. 32   What pink-colored wood has the same figure as bird's-eye maple?

Ans. Medang tabak, from Borneo.

Ques. 33   What wood is known as the "ebony of America"?

Ans. Persimmon.

Ques. 34   What is the principal wood used in the manufacture of high-grade heads for golf clubs?

Ans. Persimmon.

Ques. 35   What wood is known as Australian mahogany?

Ans. Rose mahogany, from Malaya.

Ques. 36   What is the wood known in England as Borneo teak?

Ans. Ipil.

Ques. 37   What wood is known as Persian lilac?

Ans. Chinaberry, from Texas.

Ques. 38   What wood could be used as a substitute for balsa because of its texture and characteristics?

Ans. Erima, from New Guinea.

Ques. 39   What wood is used in Japan for cutting into thin veneers to line small articles, and for business cards?
Ans. Empress tree.

Ques. 40   What wood is generally known abroad as "red wood"?
Ans. Danzig or Scotch pine.

Ques. 41   What is the hardest and heaviest wood produced in Japan?
Ans. Japanese oak.

Ques. 42   What American wood is particularly suitable for food containers?
Ans. American beech, because it does not impart taste or odor.

Ques. 43   What wood is used for violin bows?
Ans. Beefwood is sometimes used for the manufacture of the cheaper violin bows, but the more expensive bows are made of Pernambuco wood or brazilwood (Caesalpinia echinata). Growing in eastern Brazil, this wood is a rich bright red color and mainly used as a dyewood, but the best pieces are selected for turning and for making violin bows. Many violinists will use no other kind for their bows because of the peculiarly strong, resilient spring which is found only in this wood. When planed, it has a bright, metallic, lustrous surface and shows a fine snakelike ripple.

Ques. 44   What wood resembles American black walnut but is much lighter in color?
Ans. Butternut.

Ques. 45   What wood is principally used in printing for the backing blocks on which engravings and electrotype plates are mounted?
Ans. Black cherry.

Ques. 46   What woods are particularly adaptable for bending?
Ans. American beech and white ash.

Ques. 47   Nearly 80 percent of what wood is used in the manufacture of wooden tool handles?
Ans. Hickory.

Ques. 48   What is the most desirable wood for making excelsior?
Ans. Quaking aspen.

Ques. 49   What wood is used in making matches?
Ans. Quaking aspen.

Ques. 50   How many different kinds of forest trees are there in the United States?
Ans. The number usually given is 1,182.

Ques. 51   What state has the largest number of different kinds of trees?
Ans. Florida—314 species of native and naturalized trees. Texas, Georgia and California follow in that order.

Ques. 52   What state has the least number of different kinds of trees?
Ans. North Dakota is almost treeless except for the cottonwoods and willows that grow along the streams. That is no aspersion, however, against the beautiful, happy state of North Dakota as a grass region. And it does, in fact, have an official tree —the American elm.

Ques. 53   What is the world's tallest known standing tree?
Ans. Founders Tree, a redwood in the Humboldt State Redwood Park, near Dyerville, in California. It was recently reported to be over 368 ft. tall.

Ques. 54 How large do pine cones grow?

Ans. The sugar pine of the Pacific coast produces the longest, some exceeding 20 in. in length. The Mugho pine of Europe produces cones from less than 1 to 2 in. long.

Ques. 55 How many Christmas trees are produced in the U.S. each year?

Ans. About 21 million trees, of which 87 percent are produced in private forest lands. About a million are harvested in the national forests. About 100,000 acres of woodland, most of them owned by farmers, are devoted solely to growing Christmas trees.

Ques. 56 How much wood is used for fuel?

Ans. It is estimated that 63,-000,000 cords of wood are used annually for fuel—about one-eighth of all the wood used in the U.S.

Ques. 57 How many crossties are required for a mile of railway track?

Ans. About 3,000 crossties are used in a mile of track.

Ques. 58 How many crossties are there in railway track throughout the U.S.?

Ans. More than one billion.

Ques. 59 How many wooden fence posts do American farmers use?

Ans. About 500 million a year.

Ques. 60 What is the hardest American wood in terms of density?

Ans. Black ironwood, of a little known species found in southern Florida. It has a specific gravity of 1.04 and is so heavy it sinks in water.

Ques. 61 What is the softest American wood in terms of density?

Ans. Corkbark, found in parts of Arizona and New Mexico— gravity 0.28.

Ques. 62 How much pulpwood does a newspaper use?

Ans. The N.Y. Times, Sunday edition, has a consumption of 800 cords of pulpwood—a product of 800 acres.

Ques. 63 What wood was the Constitution ("Old Ironsides") made of?

Ans. Live oak.

Ques. 64 What wood was used by the South Carolinians to build the stockade on Sullivan Island where the British fleet was defeated in 1776?

Ans. The trunks of the cabbage palmetto.

Ques. 65 What southern tree of the U.S. has no heartwood until it is eighteen years of age or over?

Ans. Longleaf pine.

Ques. 66 What American wood in the early 1700's was proclaimed by Great Britain as belonging to the British Crown for the masts of the Royal Navy?

Ans. Shortleaf pine.

Ques. 67 How did the eastern cottonwood receive its name?

Ans. From the cottony fluff that is on the seeds.

Ques. 68 The buds of what tree were preserved by the ancient Chinese to use for seasoning their rice?

Ans. Magnolia.

Ques. 69 What tree did Andrew Jackson plant on the grounds of the White House in memory of his wife, Rachel?

Ans. Southern magnolia.

Ques. 70 What product other than wood does the blue gum tree of New South Wales produce?

Ans. Oil of eucalyptus, obtained from the distillation of the oil in the leaves of this tree and other species of eucalyptus.

Ques. 71 What two woods in the Far East are known as particularly good for fire-resistant qualities?

Ans. Burma teak and blue gum.

Ques. 72 What wood grows in Queensland and is used largely for the manufacture of electrical equipment because of its high insulating value?

Ans. Queensland walnut.

Ques. 73 What English tree at times has been sold as a substitute for lacewood?

Ans. London plane tree.

Ques. 74 How was partridge wood, which comes from Venezuela, named?

Ans. Because the figure it produces has a resemblance to the markings on a partridge wing.

Ques. 75 What is the wood in which the sapwood is of much greater value than the heartwood?

Ans. American persimmon.

Ques. 76 What tree provides us with the product to control toothaches?

Ans. The clove tree, with the oil of cloves.

Ques. 77 What tree provides us with a base for many mucilages?

Ans. The acacia or the shittim wood of the Bible.

Ques. 78 What tree provides us with the tincture of benzoin?

Ans. The benjamin tree, of Java.

Ques. 79 What tree provides us with the base used for suppositories?

Ans. The cacao tree of Mexico and South America.

Ques. 80 Where is the largest known collection of woods?

Ans. At Yale University in New Haven, Conn. There are over 52,-000 scientifically labeled specimens of wood and shrubs.

Ques. 81 How many products have been listed in which wood enters into in some degree?

Ans. More than 10,000 products, and wood enters to some degree into the manufacturing processes or delivery of practically all other products.

Ques. 82 What tropical tree starts to deteriorate after seven years of age if it is not cut?

Ans. Balsa wood.

Ques. 83 What wood was probably named because its appearance resembles raw beef?

Ans. Beefwood, from British and Dutch Guianas.

Ques. 84 What is the whitest known wood and what is the blackest?

Ans. American holly and Gaboon ebony.

Ques. 85 What has long been the favorite wood for making the top-grade pipes?

Ans. Briar root. Over 10,000 tons a year are consumed.

Ques. 86 What is the wood from which practically all lead pencils are made?

Ans. Red cedar.

Ques. 87 What wood has long been considered one of the best for the planking of boats?

Ans. The Atlantic white cedar, because of its light weight and firmness of texture.

Ques. 88   What American trees are becoming extinct because of the blight that is killing them?
Ans. American elm, which is attacked by the Dutch elm disease.

Ques. 89   What trees are called "the oldest and biggest of living things"?
Ans. The giant sequoias, of California.

Ques. 90   From what wood is English harewood produced?
Ans. The English sycamore.

Ques. 91   What wood provides us with decorations at Christmastime?
Ans. The American holly, with its berries and leaves.

Ques. 92   What tree provided the early American settlers with a substitute for coffee?
Ans. The Kentucky coffeetree.

Ques. 93   How many woods are referred to in the Bible?
Ans. About twenty-one.

Ques. 94   What wood from Cuba and other places is noted for its large use in the making of bows for archers?
Ans. Lemonwood.

Ques. 95   What wood is known as African walnut?
Ans. Lovoa.

Ques. 96   How many species of oaks are growing in the U.S.?
Ans. Over fifty different species.

Ques. 97   What American wood is used for dyewood and the making of bows?
Ans. Osage orange.

Ques. 98   How many different species of trees are there classified under the name of palm throughout the world?
Ans. Nearly 1,200.

Ques. 99   What tree was originally believed capable of renewing the youth of the human race?
Ans. Sassafras.

Ques. 100   How was Brazilian rosewood named?
Ans. Because of the odor of roses from the freshly cut trees.

Ques. 101   What wood when burning will produce restful slumber and also kill canaries?
Ans. Ceylon satinwood.

Ques. 102   What tree, while not producing the berry, has the name of one of our most tasteful berries?
Ans. The strawberry tree.

Ques. 103   What African wood is often used as an alternative for the European beech?
Ans. Abura, from Nigeria.

Ques. 104   What South American wood resembles greenheart and can also be used as a substitute for teak?
Ans. Acapu.

Ques. 105   What west African wood resembles Burma teak and has been used as a substitute for teak?
Ans. Afrormosia, from west Africa.

Ques. 106   What tree has been called the "bark cloth tree"?
Ans. Antiaris from west Africa because the natives used the inner bark for making a white cloth.

Ques. 107   What wood is called Nigerian satinwood?
Ans. Ayous, from the west coast of Africa.

Ques. 108   Which tree provides us with cacao butter?
Ans. The cacao tree.

Ques. 109   Which tree supplies us with cascara?
Ans. The cascara tree.

Ques. 110   What tree supplies us with quinine, used for malaria?
Ans. The chinchona tree from Peru.

Ques. 111   From what tree is cocaine obtained?
Ans. The coca trees of Colombia and Bolivia.

Ques. 112   What tree is responsible for Coca-Cola and other cola drinks?
Ans. The kola tree, of western Africa.

Ques. 113   What tree provides us with strychnine?
Ans. The nux vomica of India.

Ques. 114   What tree provides us with many of our tranquilizers?
Ans. The rauwolfia, from India.

Ques. 115   What tree provides the oil that permits the successful treatment of leprosy?
Ans. The chalmoogra.

Ques. 116   How long has coffee been used as a beverage?
Ans. Only about 250 years.

Ques. 117   What tree provides us with our chocolate?
Ans. The cacao.

Ques. 118   How long has the apple tree been cultivated and how many species are there?
Ans. For over 3,000 years and with 6,500 horticultural varieties.

Ques. 119   What European wood in figure resembles bird's-eye maple?
Ans. Alpine burl or European white birch.

Ques. 120   For what purpose is apple wood particularly utilized?
Ans. For the heads of golf clubs.

Ques. 121   When is a tree not a tree?
Ans. When it is a papaya tree.

Ques. 122   What wood has been favored many times in the construction of church altars?
Ans. American butternut.

Ques. 123   What wood, when cut on the quarter, very much resembles sapele?
Ans. Danta, from the Gold Coast.

Ques. 124   What tree does the wood come from which has the most offensive odor—one that can best be described as similar to rotten cabbage?
Ans. Essia, from the west coast of Africa.

Ques. 125   How many seeds are there to the pound, from the fruit of the holly tree?
Ans. Over 30,000.

Ques. 126   What wood from Borneo has the same figure as our native bird's-eye maple?
Ans. Jongkong.

Ques. 127   How did the American smoketree receive its name?
Ans. Probably because the small yellow and purplish flowers that appear in clusters, when they turn to a rosy haze, have the look of a puff of smoke or a thin film spreading over the foliage.

Ques. 128   How did snakewood receive its name?
Ans. The markings in the wood are similar to those seen on the backs of many snakes.

Ques. 129   What commercial value has American sourwood?

Ans. Outside of landscaping, only for certain extracts from the sap of the tree. These are used in medicine for the treatment of fevers.

Ques. 130 How was the strawberry tree named?

Ans. Because of the fruits produced, which are orange-red to a bright scarlet color, round in shape and rough on the outside, with small, tiny grains.

Ques. 131 What wood has a peculiar scent similar to that of old shoe leather?

Ans. Teak.

Ques. 132 Which tree has the largest leaf of any tree?

Ans. Indian teak, which has a leaf 10 to 20 in. in length and 7 to 14 in. in width, of oblong shape.

Ques. 133 How is the weight of teak logs reduced so that they will not sink in water?

Ans. Before felling, the trees are first girdled completely round into the heartwood, in which condition the trees die, and in about three years become lighter than water. Then they are cut down.

Ques. 134 What tree has its cortical tissue ground up to form a filler for certain floor coverings?

Ans. Cork oak tree.

Ques. 135 What tree is stripped of its bark every ten years and continues to grow and thrive for 150 years or more?

Ans. Cork tree.

Ques. 136 How many pounds of rubber does each rubber tree yield in a year?

Ans. An average of 4 to 5 lbs.

Ques. 137 Who was the first one to report the existence of rubber in South America?

Ans. Christopher Columbus, on his second visit.

PART TWO

Woods from Abura to Zebrano

Description of
Individual Woods

For uniformity and convenience of reference, information on the different woods is given as indicated in the following list. Except for a few woods, the derivation or origin of the scientific name is also included:

1. Preferred common name
2. Scientific name—in italics
3. Derivation
4. Other common names
5. Brief description of tree, size, peculiarities, etc.
6. Range of species—native range and, in some instances, areas of cultivation outside of native habitat
7. Color of wood
8. Physical properties of wood, as specific gravity
9. Seasoning behavior

[137

10. Strength properties
11. Dimensional stability (shrinkage)
12. Workability
13. Utilization
14. Other information

As you will note, not only the preferred and scientific names have been given, but whatever other common names are in sufficient usage in various parts of the world to warrant their being mentioned. The preferred common, scientific and other common names have all been listed alphabetically in the "Index of Woods" at the back of this book—1,200 or more names in all. When referring to any particular wood, you can quickly locate its description by turning to the page number given in this index.

ABURA *Mitragyna ciliata* (Mitra— headdress; gyna—pertaining to the female organ of the flower; ciliata—bearing hairs)

This tree is known also as BA-HIA and SUBAHA.

It is a relatively small tree, growing in Nigeria. The wood is of a pinkish brown or light yellow color and is without figure. In Europe, where it is particularly used in furniture, it is often substituted for European beech.

This wood shows a tendency to split, but in seasoning it dries very rapidly without any difficulty. It is a very stable wood when seasoned, but will buckle if bent. Since it is a popular wood, a good deal of the timber is exported from Africa in the form of boards and planks. The width in lumber averages about 8 in., and the length, 8 ft.

ACAPU *Vouacapoua americana* (Vouacapoua—probably derived from a native name "wacapou," "wakapo" or "acapu"; americana —of America)

The weight per cubic foot is 63 lbs. and the tree is native to South America.

This valuable timber strongly resembles the dark-colored greenheart. It has light and dark lines similar to partridge wood and also could be used as a substitute for teak, although it is harder and more difficult to work than teak.

Acapu stands up well and a fine finish can be obtained on the surface.

AFRORMOSIA *Afrormosia elata* (Afr—pertaining to Africa; ormosia—pertaining to the legume genus *Ormosia;* elata—elevated)

This tree is known also as KO-KRODUA, RED-BARK, DEVIL'S TREE, BONSAMDUA and by other names.

It is a medium-sized tree, growing in west Africa, and the weight is 45 lbs. per cubic foot. It is sometimes found in the forest along the banks of rivers, but generally it grows on stony and rocky ground. The tree at times has a crooked stem. The bark is blotched with red and orange, which is why it has acquired the common name of red-bark. The figure runs from a straight grain to some mottle.

After it has been cut for some time, it resembles Burma teak, changing from a yellow color to a warm brown with exposure to air and light.

Afrormosia is considered an attractive wood and it works satisfactorily with all tools. It is sometimes used as a substitute for teak, the main difference being that this wood, after repeated scrubbings, remains a dark color. It is useful for decking.

AFZELIA *Afzelia africana* (Afzelia —after Adam Afzelius, 1750–1837, a Swedish botanist; africana —of Africa)

This wood is known also as ALIGNA, APA, BILINGA, COUNTERWOOD, MAHOGANY-BEAN TREE and UVALA.

The trees grow in Nigeria. Logs may be obtained as large as 4 to 5 ft. in diameter with lengths of 30 ft. or more, usually straight and cylindrical. The wood weighs 50 lbs. per cubic foot.

The color varies considerably from a golden-brown to a reddish brown shade, the color darkening appreciably upon exposure. The grain is irregular and often interlocked; the texture is coarse but even. Afzelia is an exceptionally stable wood, being comparable to teak in this respect, and is often used as a substitute for teak. It also has a distinct resemblance to iroko. No particular trouble has been experienced in seasoning, and the timber can be kiln-dried satisfactorily from the green condition. The wood is very durable and is reported to be proof against termites and the teredo. The hardness of this wood is comparable to oak.

The wood works well and is used in general paneling and for doors and high-grade cabinetwork. During World War II, afzelia was accepted as a substitute for teak in the United Kingdom for use in shipbuilding and for switchboards, laboratory benches, etc.

AGALAI or AGLAY *Chukrasia velutina* (Chukrasia—origin of name unknown; velutina—velvety)

This wood is known also as HULANHIK. It is a large tree, growing in Burma and the Cochin China province of Vietnam, and is hard and heavy, weighing around 45 lbs. per cubic foot. The sapwood is light brown in color and the heartwood is of different shades of reddish brown and brown, sometimes with a striped effect.

Agalai works well with tools and takes a high polish. It produces fine-quality timber, suitable for the better classes of furniture, cabinetwork, interior paneling of rooms, etc.

AGBA *Gossweilerodendron balsamiferum* (Gossweiler—after

John Gossweiler; dendron—tree; balsam—a gummy substance; ferum—to bear)

This wood is known by the names MODORON, TOLABRANCA; and, although somewhat misleading, it is known also, because of its appearance, as NIGERIAN CEDAR or PINK MAHOGANY.

The wood comes from Nigeria. It is a huge tree with a height of as much as 125 ft. and diameters up to 5 and 6 ft. This tall tree is often clear of branches up to over 100 ft. The girth is often very large, one known specimen measuring 21 ft. It is found in the rain forests, where it frequently forms local pockets. The trunk has the appearance of a round log set on end with no root swelling at all at the base. If the trunk is wounded or notched, thick gum or oleoresin exudes and hardens into large lumps. This is often sold in Africa and used as an illuminant and for other purposes.

The wood is unusual because of its light weight, only 32 lbs. per cubic foot when dried. It is of a pale cedar-brown appearance, resembling pale mahogany, with similar ribbon-grain characteristics when sawed on the quarter. There is little difference in color between the sapwood and heartwood. The latter is slightly darker, but the line of demarcation is somewhat indefinite.

This timber is easily dried and has little tendency to warp or split. However, while being kiln-dried, some gum exudation may be noted; therefore in the selection of the wood, it is advisable to obtain timber free of gum. Agba is resistant to decay and is about as strong as our Honduras mahogany.

It is an easy wood to work with most hand and machine tools, but sometimes there is a slight tendency for the saws to stick because of the gumminess of the wood. It is somewhat similar in working quality to Honduras mahogany but a bit milder to work with. It takes stain and polish well and an excellent finish can be obtained.

Agba is an excellent wood and undoubtedly one of the most useful timbers from west Africa.

AILANTHUS *Ailanthus altissima* (Ailanthus—native Mollucan name; alt—high; issima—a superlative)

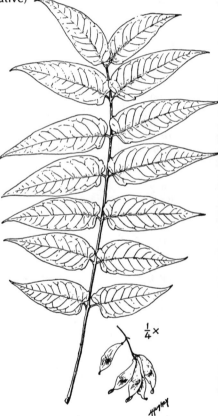

$\frac{1}{4}$×

This wood is known also as PARADISE TREE and STINKING CHUN, because of the very disagreeable, obnoxious odor, which is said to aggravate catarrhal infections. In China it is known as CHINESE SUMACH and also TREE OF HEAVEN, which is a translation of the local name Amboyna, though it has no relation to the wood known as Amboyna.

Ailanthus is native to China, but now may be found throughout most eastern parts of the United States. It weighs approximately 38 lbs. per cubic foot. It is not very well known or used. Because its color and graining resembles ash so closely, it could easily be mistaken for it. The great width of its annual rings is the main distinguishing mark in comparison to ash. It is a very rapidly growing tree and if permitted, would soon crowd out the more desirable trees.

This is the wood referred to in the book and the motion picture entitled *A Tree Grows in Brooklyn.*

ALBIZZIA *Albizzia ferruginea* (Albizzia—after Filippo del Albizzia, eighteenth-century naturalist; ferruginea—rusty-colored like iron)

This wood is found in east Africa and weighs about 45 to 50 lbs. per cubic foot. It has a reddish brown, warm color and generally shows a stripe when sawed on the quarter.

Although the wood is hard and heavy, it is not durable when used for outside construction, but for general purposes it is an all-around hardwood. In east Africa, and also on the west coast of Africa, it is used to a certain extent for canoes.

ALDER, EUROPEAN *Alnus glutinosa* (Alnus—a Roman plant name; glutinosa—like glue)

This tree originated in Europe and weighs between 26 and 41 lbs. per cubic foot. The wood is a light brown, tinged with red, and is soft, light and brittle. It is used in the manufacture of soles of shoes and in cheaper cabinetwork. It also has long been used in the manufacture of gun powder.

ALLACEDE *Wallaceodendron celebicum* (Wallace—after Alfred Russel Wallace; dendron—tree; celebicum—of the Celebes Island)

This Philippine wood is of the same botanical classification as banuyo. It is a coarse-grained wood of light reddish brown cast with a dark brown broken stripe and sometimes a mottled figure. A fair amount has been used in the veneer form for the manufacture of furniture and for general fixture work.

ALMIQUE *Manilkara jaimiqui* (Manilkara—derivation unknown; jaimiqui—from the native name)

This wood is known also as ACANA and GONSELLA.

The wood comes from Cuba and has a deep, rich red color, with an oily appearance. It is principally used for inlay work and various types of turning, and takes a lovely polish.

ALPINE BURL or EUROPEAN WHITE BIRCH *Betula alba* (Betula—ancient Latin name for birch; alba—white)

This wood is obtained from the forests of Finland, Sweden and

Norway and sold in this country under the name ALPINE BURL. However, in Europe it is commonly known as KARELIAN BURL and NORWAY BURL BIRCH, and sometimes the veneers are advertised and sold as FLAMY BIRCH.

In figure, this wood resembles bird's-eye maple, with swirls in a light tan surface covered with tiny V-shaped figures. At times this species contains a fiddleback figure.

ALSTONIA *Alstonia   congensis* (Alstonia—after   Charles   Alston, 1683–1760, English botanist; congensis—of the Congo)

This is a rapidly growing tree, widely   distributed   throughout tropical Africa. It has such rapid growth that it is often found replacing trees from clearings in the forests. The growth rings are readily seen by a change in the color of the late wood. However, there is very little difference in the color of the heartwood and sapwood. When the tree or lumber is freshly cut, a faint odor resembling that of Fuller's earth may be detected.

It can best be described as having   a   pale   oatmeal,   off-white color, and it darkens very little upon exposure. What seems to

widely   separated,   will   be   found upon   examination   to   be   latex ducts. This latex in the bark and wood   remains   in   liquid   form   for a   long   time   and   may   be   seen oozing   from   the   ends   of   boards when   they   are   resawed,   despite the   fact   that   they   were   originally sawed many years before.

Alstonia is an easy wood to dry and does not present any problem   when   being   worked   with tools. In Africa this timber is subject to attacks by termites. It is generally used for household implements such as spoons, ladles and stools, and also for drums.

AMBOYNA *Pterocarpus   indicus* (Ptero—winged;   carpus—fruit;   indicus—of India or Indies)

The native Malayan name for this wood is ANGSANA. In some dictionaries it is KIABOOCA; this means twisted wood, and is applied to burls imported from Amboyna   and   Borneo.   Amboyna wood   was   so   named   because   it was originally shipped from the island of Amboyna.

Coming from Borneo, this tree has   a   wide   range   of   growth throughout   the   East   Indies   and   a large variation in size, from small trees to 90 ft. high, with diameters of   2   to   3   ft.   The   wood   has   a weight of 39 lbs. per cubic foot.

The wood is brown, tinged with yellow   or   red,   but   changes   with age to a dull brown leather color. It   is   marked   with   little   twisted curls and knots in a manner more varied than bird's-eye maple. To the naked eye, it is difficult to distinguish   between   the   burls   of   amboyna wood and thuya. The wood has   a   fairly   coarse   grain   and   is difficult   to   work   with   power   or hand   tools   because   of   the   ex-

Quarter-sliced striped amboyna or narra with mottle figure.

treme hardness and the quantities of gum in the pores. These characteristics tend to dull the edges of the tools.

Amboyna wood was used to a large extent in the manufacture of furniture during the Empire period, from 1804 to 1814. It has, however, become very scarce—almost a rarity—particularly in this country, and is available only in the veneer form.

Wood of the same botanical classification as amboyna, when received in this country in log form, is known as narra. It is of a rose to deep red color, some of a golden-yellow, having a distinct stripe when manufactured on the quarter. Some of the logs contain a ripple figure. It is a hard and heavy wood, not very strong or durable, but suitable for manufacture into veneers for furniture and high-grade interior work.

ANDAMAN MARBLEWOOD *Diospyros marmorata* (Dios/pyros—fruit of the gods; marmorata—like marble or marbleized)

This is a medium-sized tree, averaging over 50 lbs. per cubic foot and its growth is restricted to the Andaman Islands, Ceylon and part of India.

The bark is yellow in color and the sapwood is pinkish brown and clearly defined from the heartwood, which is dark gray with streaks of dark brown and black. A hard, heavy wood, it resembles in many ways Macassar ebony, being used for the same purposes. When the seasoning process is not too hurried, the wood seasons well.

It is a difficult wood to work with hand tools because of its extreme hardness, and power saws require special spacing and shape of teeth for easy cutting. However, it is a fine wood for all turning purposes and useful for decorative furniture.

ANDIRA *Andira inermis*

This wood is known also as BITTERWOOD, BOIS PALMISTE, CABBAGE-BARK, MACAYA, MOCA, PARTRIDGE WOOD and PHEASANT WOOD.

This evergreen tree is considered one of Mexico's valuable woods. Occasionally it grows to 100 ft. in height. It has a ragged bark with a very disagreeable odor. The color of the wood is similar to old mahogany and the grain is like old English oak, being of coarse texture, fairly straight. It is heavy, hard, strong and durable and has a beautiful figure.

Andira is difficult to work with, but it can be finished smoothly. In the solid form, it is used for umbrella handles, billiard-cue butts, and canes; in the veneer form, it is particularly adaptable for the paneling of large rooms, churches and interiors.

ANDIROBA *Carapa guianensis* (Carapa—native name; guianensis —of Guiana)

This wood is known also as CARAPA, CEDRO or MACHO, CRABWOOD and DENERARA.

It originates in northern South America, is reddish brown in color and when quartered has a nice stripe and parallel, irregular rays.

Andiroba is generally scarce but available at times in the veneer form. It is used in furniture and cabinetmaking.

ANTIARIS *Antiaris africana* (Antiaris—Javanese name of the gum resin from the upas tree; africana —from Africa)

This large tree, 100 ft. or more in height, with a diameter of 3 ft. or more, emanates from the west coast of Africa and in Ghana is called the BARK CLOTH TREE. In Nigeria it is sometimes called FALSE IROKO. It is closely related to the upas tree, the botanical name of which is *Antiaris toxicaria*.

The wood is soft, 25 lbs. per cubic foot, and has been called the bark-cloth tree because the inner bark was formerly used to make a white bark cloth in certain parts of west Africa. The tree is easily distinguished since its smooth bark is at times a pale, dirty white and at other times yellowish or almost pure white in color, with many numerous wart-like growths.

Antiaris will season without difficulty but requires extreme care after the tree is cut, otherwise a blue stain will develop. It is a good, all-round, lightweight utility wood and works well with both hand and power tools. In west Africa this wood has been used principally in the manufacture of canoes, but some logs are now being exported for the manufacture of veneers.

Unreliable rubber collectors in the past have used the pale-colored latex which the wood contains as an adulterant to rubber.

Antiaris, known as chen chen, comes from the west coast of Africa. Color of wood is white to yellowish with pronounced ribbon figure.

APPLE *Malus pumila* (Malus—classical Latin name for apple; pumila—small)

The apple tree from Europe has a weight of 48 lbs. per cubic foot. The heartwood is hard and reddish brown while the sapwood is light red. If not handled carefully, this wood is apt to warp and split when drying. Apple wood is used for a variety of purposes, but is particularly utilized for the heads of golf clubs. It is the state tree of Michigan.

ARARIBA *Centrolobium* spp. (Centro/lobium—center lobe, a reference to the winged fruit)

In Brazil, where this wood originates, it is known also as AMARILLO, BRANCA, ROSA and VERMELHA. In the United States it is generally marketed under the name BALAUSTRE and occasionally as CANARYWOOD.

It is a fairly small tree with an average length of 8 ft. Diameters of the log run from 6 to 8 in. It is shipped from the port of Rio de Janeiro. The background color of the wood is usually yellow with red and black streaks. The lumber is sometimes used in naval architecture, and in the veneer form it is employed for decorative purposes in cabinetwork.

ASH, BLACK *Fraxinus nigra* (Fraxinus—classical Latin name for ash; nigra—black)

Black ash is marketed also under the name BROWN ASH, HOOP ASH, SWAMP ASH and WATER ASH. Much of the northern black ash is converted into veneers of very attractive figure and marketed under the name NORTHERN BROWN ASH.

The general growth of these trees runs along the Atlantic coast, from Canada down as far south as Virginia, and westward to Mississippi and Minnesota. In earlier times, in Indiana, this was the favorite wood used in weaving all types of baskets. The tree gen-

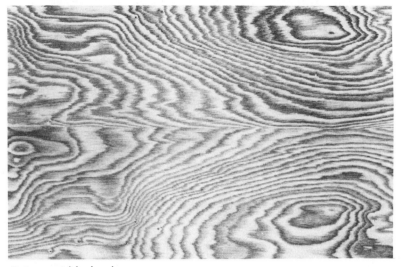

Rotary-cut black ash.

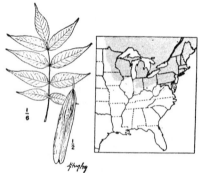

key, France and Hungary. The color of this wood is grayish white, except that which grows in Hungary, and this tends to be brownish white to white.

The logs are usually rotary cut into veneers and produce very wavy, distinct, sometimes black, streaks and dark graining. This ash, while available in the veneer form, in burls and half-round, is scarce and is fairly costly.

erally grows in lowlands and swamps, which explains how it receives its different names. This wood is grayish brown to light brown in color and often produces burls of high quality. Among items made from this ash are chair bottoms and barrel hoops.

ASH, GREEN *Fraxinus pennsylvanica* (pennsylvanica—of Pennsylvania)

This tree is known also as BLUE ASH and WATER ASH.

It is found throughout eastern Canada and most parts of the United States east of the Rocky Mountains. It is a good-looking tree and one of the ashes that is often planted for shade and ornamental purposes in landscaping. Green ash lumber is often marketed with the white ash and is

ASH, EUROPEAN *Fraxinus excelsior* (excelsior—elevated, high)

This is also known as ITALIAN OLIVE ASH.

The tree grows in England, Tur-

White ash tree yields an important American cabinet wood.

European ash logs being marked for mill and export, Bolu Province, Turkey.

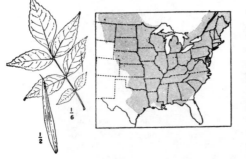

used for the same purposes, as handles of all kinds, baseball bats and novelties.

ASH, OREGON *Fraxinus velutina* (velutina—velvety)

This is a fairly small tree with a height of from 50 to 70 ft. and diameters from 14 to 30 in. This ash is particularly interesting, as it is the only species of ash found on the Pacific coast, where it extends all the way from British Columbia, in a narrow belt through the mountains, to southern California. It grows best in rich, lowland soil and when found in higher elevations, the tree is greatly dwarfed and frequently crooked.

Oregon ash is one of the most valuable hardwoods throughout the West Coast area. While lighter in weight than the eastern ashes, other characteristics are quite similar and it is used for about the same purposes.

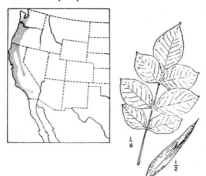

ASH, WHITE *Fraxinus americana* (americana—of America)

This is a heavy wood with an average weight of 42 lbs. per cubic foot. The heartwood is brown to dark brown, sometimes with a reddish tint. White ash is often confused with hickory but the zone of large pores is much more distinguishable in ash than in hickory.

This wood is strong and stiff, has good shock resistance and is noted for its excellent bending qualities. It is used almost exclusively for all types of sports and athletic equipment such as baseball bats and long oars. Almost universally it is also used for handles of shovels and spades, and

the long handles of forks, hoes and rakes. In the lumber form it is particularly valuable for the bent parts of chairs. Occasionally, high-grade logs are cut into veneers which are very attractive in decorative work.

ASH, WHITE MOUNTAIN *Eucalyptus regnans* (Eu/calyptus—true cover; regnans—to rule, probably referring to the lordly size of this species—to 350 ft.)

This tree, from Tasmania, is known also as TASMANIAN OAK.

Flat-sliced American white ash, light brown, open figure.

Eucalyptus, an impressive family of large Australian trees, has many species being utilized for lumber and veneer under a variety of names, including white mountain ash. The veneer sample here is striking. It has an overall golden hue with brown and pink accents. The figure is said to be blistered.

Mountain ash forest in Australia. This species is the tallest of more than 500 species of eucalyptus, reaching up to 250 feet in height.

It is probably the largest hardwood in the world and one of the tallest—some trees have been reported in excess of 326 ft.

The *Eucalyptus* species, largely of Australian origin, produces a great variety of woods with wide range of texture, color and behavior, and the principal wood in this species is the White Mountain ash. It has a tan to golden-brown color, sometimes pinkish, and a blistered figure, fiddleback and with straight grain. It is very strong and durable and works well. Locally it is used for bridges, wood paving and other structural uses, but it is also suitable for use by cabinetmakers.

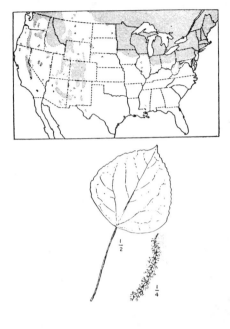

ASPEN, QUAKING *Populus tremuloides* (Populus—the classical Latin name; tremul/oides—resembling the European aspen, *P. tremula*; tremul—trembling)

Aspen crotch.

This tree grows throughout the northeastern, northern and western parts of the United States as far north as Alaska. It is a short-lived tree, decaying early in life when approaching full growth. The bark is thin and whitish or gray-green in color. Quaking aspen is one of the lightweight hardwoods, averaging around 26 lbs. per cubic foot.

This aspen shrinks very little and in bending properties it ranks with the best of hardwoods. It has a tendency, though, to split under the action of nails or screws. The wood seasons very easily by air-drying or kiln-drying. It is fairly easy to finish to a smooth surface with hand or power tools, takes stain very poorly, but can be painted.

Producers of cheese have always preferred this wood for use

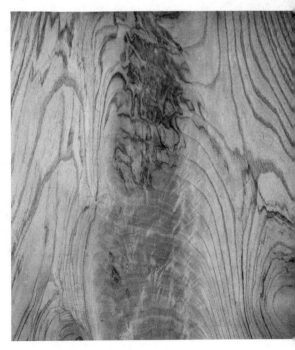

Quaking aspen, known for its white bark and its leaves that tremble in the wind. Where forked trunks or forked branches are large enough this aspen yields highly valued crotch veneer.

Avodiré, mottle, from Africa, pale gold with changing highlights.

as containers because it is light in weight, of light color and free from any odor or taste.

Highly figured logs of aspen and also some crotches are occasionally cut into veneers, which are generally available to craftsmen. It has long been one of the perfect woods for the manufacture of high-grade excelsior. When sawed into lumber it is also used for paper pulp and matches.

AVODIRÉ *Turraeanthus africana* (Turrae—after Anton Turra, eighteenth-century Italian botanist; anthus—flower; africana—from Africa)

This wood is known also as APAYA, APPAYIA, OLON and by other names.

It comes from the Ivory Coast, the Gold Coast and Liberia, in west Africa. It originally came into the United States with African mahogany logs, shipped from the west coast of Africa. Avodiré is a fairly lightweight wood weighing

around 20 lbs. per cubic foot. In the past it has been offered for sale as African satinwood, African furniture wood and African white mahogany.

The wood has a golden-yellow color with a firm, clean grain that can become a smooth, highly polished surface. It is very strong in relation to its light weight.

Avodiré is available both in lumber and veneer form. Large quantities of this wood have been used in the manufacture of store fixtures and furniture and in decorating the interior of fine offices and homes, and it is used quite extensively for various effects in marquetry.

AYAN *Distemonanthus benthamianus* (Di—two; stemon—stamen; anthus—flower; benthamianus—after Bentham, a nineteenth-century English botanist)

This wood is also known as BARRE, EYEN and MOVINGUI. Because of the color, the grain and

Striped ayous.

the general beauty of the wood, it is also called NIGERIAN SATIN-WOOD.

This is a tall tree, often 90 ft. or more in height, moderately hard and heavy, about 45 lbs. per cubic foot, and grows in the forests of west Africa, through Ghana, the Ivory Coast, Nigeria and the French Camerouns.

Ayan has a bright yellow and orange color. It is said to be durable and termite-proof. It is a wood that is easy to season, providing the lumber is not exposed to the full force of the wind or direct sunlight until it has dried. This timber cuts smoothly, exhibiting a fine, lustrous appearance, and works easily with both hand and power tools. It has been used for flooring, and the veneer is used in cabinetwork. The wood, however, has to be filled well when finishing in order to obtain a high polish.

AYOUS *Triplochiton scleroxylon* (Triplo—pertaining to threes; chiton—an outer covering; scler—hard; xylon—wood)

This wood is known also as AFRICAN WHITEWOOD, OBECHE, SAMBA, OKPO, WAWA and ABACHI.

It is a fairly large tree with an average diameter of 30 to 36 in. and a weight of 25 lbs. per cubic foot, emanating from the Gold and Ivory Coasts and the French Camerouns. It is creamy white to light yellow in color, has a fine stripe when cut on the quarter, is fairly soft but firm, with a medium grain and even texture. In strength it is about equal to our American whitewood and it will not withstand heavy wear.

The logs deteriorate so quickly when cut that prompt transportation facilities are essential. Though light in weight, it is remarkably strong in relation to its weight.

At first glance one would get the impression of wooliness, but it works easily, and a smooth surface is quickly produced which takes a fine polish. A large amount of this wood is manufactured into veneers.

BALDCYPRESS *Taxodium distichum* (Taxodium—having the appearance of *Taxus*, the yew; distichum—two-ranked, the leaves being in two rows)

This cypress has various names in different states. A few of them are BLACK CYPRESS, BUCK CYPRESS, COW CYPRESS, RED CYPRESS, SOUTHERN CYPRESS, SWAMP CYPRESS, WHITE CYPRESS and YELLOW CYPRESS.

The natural growth of cypress covers a large area along the Atlantic coast from Delaware to Florida and westward through all the Gulf states to Texas and through most of the mid-Atlantic states, northward to Indiana and Illinois. The appearance of the wood varies somewhat according to where the tree grows, but it is usually found in wet, low bottomlands and swamps.

The wood in the southern swamps is darker in color than that which grows farther north on drier land. Some of the baldcypress has light streaks through a dark background and this makes an attractive figure. The heartwood varies in color from a light yellowish brown to a dark brown. The foliage is light green in color, something like celery in appearance, and in the far south the trees are usually found covered with drooping Spanish moss.

Baldcypress is a very durable wood and quite resistant to decay. It is medium hard, strong, with close, straight grain, and is fairly heavy. When rubbed, the wood has a greasy feeling. Cypress fingers are considered more valuable than all other American woods for durability in greenhouse construction, coffins and wooden drainboards.

Crotches cut from baldcypress trees are offered in the market, when available, under the name faux satine.

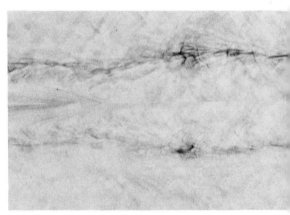

Top: Faux satine (baldcypress) crotch.

Bottom: Flat-cut.

BALSA *Ochroma lagopus* (Ochroma—paleness; lago/pus—rabbit foot)

This tree, from Central and South America, obtains a height up to 70 ft. and is one of the lightest woods. Balsa wood was used by the natives of Central and South America for making boats and canoes, which is probably the original source of its name, the word balsa being the Spanish name for raft.

The wood is a whitish, pale yellow color, exceedingly porous and relatively very elastic and strong for its light weight. Under favorable circumstances, balsa trees are ready for cutting when they are seven years old. Older trees often develop rot at the base and become worthless. The lighter-colored wood is by far the best, weighing 5 to 10 lbs. per cubic foot, while the darker wood of old trees may weigh up to 25 lbs. per cubic foot.

Its lightness and good working properties favor its use as a packing material for highly finished surfaces. Because of its extreme lightness and relative strength, it is used extensively in the manufacture of model airplanes.

During World War I this wood came into great prominence, as it was in demand for many purposes, including the packing of armor plates for battleships. Impregnated with a hot paraffin solution, the wood was used extensively for life rafts because of its great buoyancy.

Today, in the United States, it is used as insulation for refrigerator cars and lifesaving appliances.

BAMBOO *Bambusa gramineae* (Bambusa—typifies a tribe, Bambuseae, of the Poaceae; gramineae—grasslike)

Bamboo is often treelike, with woody stems growing from underground root stock, often crowded to dense clumps. It occasionally reaches 120 ft. in height. The slender stem is hollow and, as generally in grasses, has well-marked joints or nodes, at each of which the cavity is closed by a strong diaphragm. It grows throughout the tropical zone, extending into the subtropical and even into the temperate zone. Tropical Asia is richest in this species, the plant extending into Japan and to an elevation of 10,000 ft. or more in the Himalayas. There are very few bamboo plants in Africa. In South America they reach the snow line. Three species are natural to the United States, thriving best in the cotton states and the valleys of southern California.

Bamboo is considered one of the fastest-growing plants. In Ceylon, species have been observed to grow 16 in. a day. Importation of living bamboo and bamboo seeds has been forbidden in the United States since 1919 because of danger from pests.

In the United States, the use of bamboo includes furniture, landscape ornaments, fences, etc.

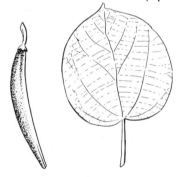

Left: With room to spread, the baldcypress becomes a beautiful, pyramidal tree. Right: Grove of beech dominated by large, marketable specimen, easily identified by its blue-gray smooth bark.

Clump bamboo stands up against hurricanes much better than most other plants and trees. In Oriental countries, the bamboo has been called "one of nature's most valuable gifts to uncivilized man," for its use is almost endless. The soft shoots, just beginning to grow, are cut off and served like table asparagus. They are also salted and eaten with rice, prepared in the form of pickles. Joints of sufficient size form water buckets; smaller ones, bottles. In places in Borneo, bamboo is used for cooking utensils. It is used extensively as a timber wood, and houses are made entirely of the products. Complete sections of the stem form posts or columns; split up, it serves for floors or rafters; and interwoven in latticework, it is used for the sides of rooms, admitting light and air, and in shipping of all kinds. Some of the strongest plants are selected for masts of boats of moderate size, and the masts of larger vessels are sometimes formed by several joined bamboo stems. Bamboo is used in the construction of all kinds of agricultural and domestic implements and in the materials and implements required in fishery.

Bows are made by the union of two pieces bound with many bands. With the septa bored out and the lengths joined together, bamboo is employed to carry water to reservoirs or gardens. The outer cuticle of the Oriental species is so hard that it forms a sharp and durable cutting edge, and it is so siliceous that it can be used as a whetstone. When cut into thin strips, it is one of the most durable and beautiful materials for basket making. In China the interior portions of the stem are beaten into a pulp and used in the manufacture of the finer varieties of paper. Bamboo is exported, to a considerable extent, to Europe for the use of basket makers and for umbrellas and walking sticks.

BANAK *Virola koschnyi* (Virola —possibly referring to greenness; koschnyi—after Koschny)

This tree grows beside swamps and in forests along river valleys, from Panama to British Honduras and Guatemala, often reaching a height of 85 ft. and a diameter of from 6 to 40 in. The bark is unusual, as it is red and contains red sap which flows like blood from a wound. The wood resembles somewhat the paler-colored mahoganies, being pinkish brown when cut but darkening upon exposure. In British Honduras this is considered one of the more important woods.

Care is required in seasoning to prevent warping and splitting. It is a wood of medium hardness

and from 35 to 40 lbs. per cubic foot in weight, with generally a straight grain.

In strength it is comparable to the American whitewood. This wood is easy to work if tools are kept in sharp condition. The principal difficulty in marketing the wood is that a large quantity of the logs are damaged from stain and pin worms. The clean logs, however, are suitable for manufacture into veneers and the cheaper type of furniture.

BASSWOOD, AMERICAN *Tilia americana* (Tilia—the classical Latin name; americana—of America)

This wood is known also by other names in various states, such as AMERICAN LINDEN, BEETREE, BLACK LIMETREE, LIME TREE, LINN, LINDEN, WHITEWOOD, WICKUP and YELLOW BASSWOOD.

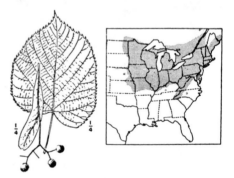

It grows throughout the eastern half of the United States and more than half the total quantity is found in the Great Lakes states. This is a lovely-shaped tree and grows well in sandy soil near streams. The heartwood is creamy white to creamy brown and sometimes reddish.

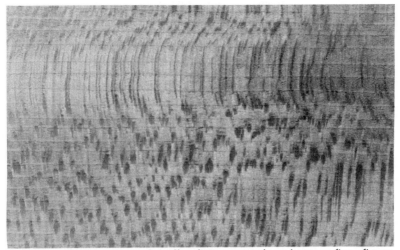

American beech. Exceptionally fine example of cross-fire figure. Flecked areas are similar to lacewood.

Basswood is a lightweight hardwood, averaging 26 lbs. per cubic foot, and it is fairly easy to air-dry or kiln-dry, staying in place well after seasoning.

The wood is weak, however, and there is a large shrinkage involved. The tree grows fast and has a heavy foliage, and therefore is good for landscaping and a fine tree for shade.

The largest percentage of the basswood in this country is cut into lumber, the greatest portion of which is used for crates and boxes, the manufacturing of sash, doors and general millwork. Also, a considerable amount is manufactured into veneers for various specialized purposes and particularly as core material for the manufacture of panels.

BEECH, AMERICAN *Fagus grandifolia* (Fagus—the classical Latin name, from the Greek word meaning to eat, in reference to the edible nuts; grandi/folia—large-leaved)

American beech grows in the United States from Maine to northern Florida and westward into Wisconsin and Texas. It is one of the heavier woods, having an average weight of 45 lbs. per cubic foot, and is readily distinguishable from other native species by its heavy weight and the conspicuous rays and tiny pores.

It is rated high in strength and shock resistance and, when steamed, is readily bent. However, considerable care must be taken during seasoning because

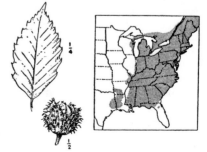

the wood is subject to a very large shrinkage. If careful attention is not given during this period, checks and discolorations, in addition to warping, will be encountered.

Beech is used not only in the lumber form but also in veneering. It is particularly suitable for food containers, since it does not impart taste or odor.

BEEFWOOD *Mimusops* sp. (Mimusops—monkey face)

This wood, growing in British and Dutch Guiana, is known locally under many different names, including BULLY TREE, BULLET WOOD, RED LANCEWOOD, HORSEFLESH.

The wood from Dutch Guiana —Surinam—is of far better quality than that from British Guiana, which often contains considerable knots. This wood is generally exported in the form of square-hewn logs, from 8 to 18 in. square and in lengths from 12 to 30 ft.

The color of this wood is a dull plum red and somewhat resembles raw beef—which is probably the reason it was so named. Beefwood is very durable and stands exposure, but on the other hand is subject to attacks from worms and the teredo.

When planed, the wood has a very smooth surface which glistens with minute shining specks of substance contained in the pores. A very fine polish can be obtained. This wood has long been in demand for the best umbrella sticks because of its great strength. It is also used in making the cheaper quality of violin bows and in archery for the footings of arrows.

BILLIAN *Eusideroxylon zwageri* (Eu/sider/oxylon—true ironwood; zwageri—after Zwager)

In Borneo and the Malaya Peninsula, this plentiful, hard wood is commonly known as IRONWOOD. It is one of the hardest woods from those countries, weighing 70 lbs. per cubic foot. The color varies from light brown when first cut to almost black upon exposure to light and air. Most of this timber is used in the construction of wooden buildings, as it seems to be entirely impervious to white ants and teredos. Locally it is used for all types of heavy construction and is one of the best woods for telegraph and telephone poles, railway ties and piling.

BIRCH, PAPER *Betula papyrifera* (Betula—classical Latin name for birch; papyr/ifera—paper bearing, in reference to papery bark)

This species is known also as CANOE BIRCH and MOTHER TREE.

Paper birch grows in a greater number of localities than any other birch. It grows practically across the entire country of Canada from Alaska to Labrador and across the northern part of the United States from coast to coast, and is the state tree of New Hampshire.

When growing in the forest, it is the easiest birch to distinguish because of its smooth white bark. It reaches heights of from 55 to 75 ft. with diameters from 2 to 3 ft. The wood is white in color and there is little difference between the sapwood and heartwood. This birch is very easily worked and finishes smoothly.

One of its principal uses is in

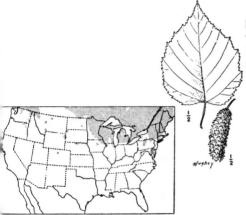

This is the tree that we remember from our school days from the "Song of Hiawatha," written by Longfellow: "Give me your bark oh birch tree, I a light canoe will build me."

BIRCH, RIVER *Betula nigra* (nigra —black)

This is another species of birch, which is known also as WATER BIRCH, RED BIRCH and BLACK BIRCH. It is named river birch because it is always found along streams, brooks and swamp areas, growing across the southern part of our country from Florida to Texas and as far northward as New England.

This wood is more or less of similar texture and is used for the same purposes as other birches. The principal difference is that the bark on the branches of the younger trees is very smooth and has a lustrous reddish brown color as the tree grows older.

Birch logs can be stored with perfect safety for many years if they are kept immersed in fresh water. One large veneer firm recently learned of a large number of logs that had been buried in Lake Superior for sixty-three years on the site of an old sawmill. They had their men inspect the logs beneath water and then pur-

the form of candleholders for table decorations. It is the birch that you see in many forms in souvenir shops as baskets, toy canoes or postal cards. A large amount of this wood is also manufactured into dowels and toothpicks.

Because the bark of this tree has inner layers of orange-and-tan color, it permits easy peeling from the tree to obtain these bark layers. The peeling does not injure the tree unless the entire bark is removed. This is the tree which furnished the Indians with wigwams and various utensils and canoes, and today in some states it is still known as canoe birch for this reason.

The tree is very ornamental, often growing in clusters of three. The reason it is also called mother tree is that it is frequently planted in memory of mothers. For example, around the Capitol grounds in Washington it was planted to honor the mothers of the nation, and on the grounds of the White House to honor the mothers of U.S. Presidents. It is also planted in Arlington Cemetery and known as National Mother's Tree. While ornamental, it is not as long-lived or as large as the other birches.

Top: The Kemijoki River, Finland, brings logs to mills and ships. Finland is one of principal sources of Alpine burl, also known as European white birch. Bottom left: Yellow birch in Wisconsin, early spring. A superior specimen. Bottom right: Yellow birch in scenic summer view, New York state.

chased the entire lot. They were fine, large logs of birch timber, and when they were taken into the mill produced some very fine veneers. The only loss involved was a small length from each end of the log, which had to be cut off because of the effect of the water.

BIRCH, SWEET *Betula lenta* (lenta —flexible or tough, referring to the twigs)

This birch is known also as BLACK BIRCH and CHERRY BIRCH.

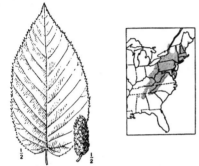

It grows mainly in the Adirondacks, in the eastern Appalachian area, although it can be found as far south as the northern Gulf states. The wood is brown in color, tinged with red, and the sapwood is thin and light brown or yellow. It has a heavy, very strong, hard, close grain, distinct but not prominent. Birch veneer is generally rotary cut and sliced and is used in all types of cabinetwork.

BIRCH, YELLOW *Betula alleghaniensis* (alleghaniensis—of the Allegheny Mountains)

This wood is also known as GRAY BIRCH, SILVER BIRCH and SWAMP BIRCH.

It grows in Canada, through the Great Lakes and in the New England states, and as far south as North Carolina. Yellow birch is creamy or light brown in color, tinged with red, with thin, nearly white sapwood. The curly or wavy figure is often prominent, both in the rotary and sliced veneer. It is a heavy, very strong, hard, close-grained wood of even texture.

The wood works easily, takes a finish nicely and is available in both the lumber and veneer form. It is used in the manufacture of furniture and interior woodworking for doors and door fixtures, and is especially valuable for cupboards, school seating, etc., because of its durability and strength.

Rotary-cut yellow birch, highly figured.

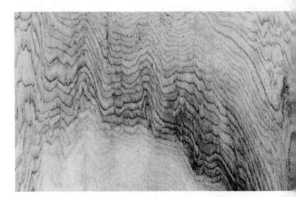

BITTERWOOD *Vatairea lundellii*

Locally this wood is known also as BITTER ANGELIM and MOUNTAIN COW-WOOD, the latter name because the purplish brown bark, about ½ in. thick, is often chewed on by mountain cows.

Bitterwood grows from southern Mexico to Brazil and is so named because of the extreme bitterness to the taste. The bitterness obtained from chewing a small splinter of the wood will remain for a long time.

At times these trees grow as high as 125 ft. with diameters of 3 ft. The heartwood, which is yellow when first manufactured, darkens to a warm golden-brown color. The wood is coarse, about 45 lbs. per cubic foot in weight, and has large pores. Its strength is somewhat superior to Honduras mahogany, but it is a much more difficult wood to work with. Its principal use in Brazil is for general building and as an all-around utility wood.

BLACKBUTT *Eucalyptus pilularis* (Eu/calyptus—true cover; pilularis—globular, pertaining to the spherical fruit)

This tree is found only in the forests of New South Wales, Victoria and Queensland, along the coast and in the tablelands directly behind the coast. It is a large tree, one of the tallest in the eucalyptus family and is at times referred to as one of the best-growing in Australia. The wood is very heavy, generally over 60 lbs. per cubic foot, and unusually hard. The bark is stringy and often black on the lower part of the trunk, which is the reason why it is commonly called blackbutt. However, this condition changes and it is not a reliable identification for the wood. The heartwood is a pleasing pale light red color to pinkish brown, with small difference between the sapwood and heartwood. This wood is quite similar to tallow-wood.

In the countries in which it grows, because of its durability to the elements, it is often used on outside construction. It is particularly desirable in the shipbuilding industry for planking. However, the silica generally found in the wood quickly dulls the edges of all cutting tools. Smaller sections of the tree are of special value for fence posts, because of their long life.

Blackbutt tree. Enormous size, straight trunk, and black bark characterize this Australian eucalyptus.

BLACKGUM *Nyssa sylvatica* (Nyssa —the name of a water nymph, so-called because the first described species, *N. aquatica,* grows in water; sylvatica—of the woods)

Although this wood is known principally as BLACK TUPELO, it also is called BOWL GUM, PEPPERIDGE, STINKWOOD, WILD PEARTREE and YELLOW GUM-TREE.

These trees are found in practically all states east of the Mississippi and, like the water tupelo, grow wherever there is swampland and abundant water supplies as ponds or streams.

All four woods of the tupelo family are similar in appearance and texture and very difficult to distinguish from one another. They all have a tendency to warp, owing to the interlocking grain of the wood, which also makes it difficult to split and nail.

Blackgum and water tupelo both take a good finish, but blackgum glues well, which the water tupelo does not. A better grade of lumber and a large quantity of veneers are obtained from the blackgum tree, and the logs, when manufactured into veneers, have an attractive figure.

The wood is used for paper pulp and general miscellaneous items of manufacture such as baskets, crates, cigar boxes, etc.

Blackgum tree, also called tupelo in veneer form.

BLACKWOOD, AUSTRALIAN

Acacia melanoxylon (Acacia— sharpen, probably a reference to the spines borne by many species; melan/oxylon—black wood)

This wood grows in Tasmania and throughout Australia. The color varies from a rich reddish brown to almost black, with bands of golden-brown. Blackwood has a close grain, very often curly, and an attractive mottled figure. Care has to be taken to see that it is properly seasoned.

This wood is easily worked and will produce a fine polish. A limited quantity is converted into veneer and used for furniture work, marquetry and the paneling of interior rooms.

Blue paloverde tree, distinguished as the state tree of Arizona. Seldom harvested for wood.

BLUE PALOVERDE *Cercidium floridum* (Cercidium—a weaver's comb; floridum—full of flowers)

This is a small tree, no more than 12 to 30 ft. tall and 15 in. or more in diameter. It is the state tree of Arizona, one of the three species of blue paloverde native to the United States and the loveliest in appearance.

The wood has little value. It can be detected when burning because of its very unpleasant odor. However, in contrast, it offers a food value from its pealike pods.

BOARWOOD *Symphonia globulifera* (Symphonia—grown together; globulifera—bearing globules or spheres)

In British Honduras it is called WAIKA CHEWSTICK and is known in the West Indies as HOG GUM.

This is a large tree, growing in height from 60 to 120 ft. and as much as 3 ft. in diameter. It is widely distributed throughout Central America and the northern part of South America, extending from Guatemala and British Honduras down through Peru and Brazil, and in Trinidad and the British West Indies.

Usually boarwood is found in the lowland forests and occasionally grows alongside palms. It is a hard, medium-heavy wood, about 40 to 45 lbs. per cubic foot. The bark contains a yellowish brown gum which darkens with exposure and sometimes has the resemblance of pitch.

The sapwood is almost pure white, while the heartwood is yellow to a grayish brown or a pale olive brown, and several of these shades in the form of stripes may appear on a single piece of lumber. Considerable difficulty is experienced in seasoning, during which time it must not be exposed to the direct sun. Protection is necessary to the ends of the boards to prevent their drying out too rapidly.

This wood is comparable in strength to the American oak, and while it is not as well known, except in the country it grows in, some of it is used as plywood on a small scale in Europe. Throughout Central America and the West Indies it is generally used in the ordinary forms of carpentry and for boxes.

BOSSE *Guarea cedrata* (Guarea—from guara, a native name from Cuba; cedrata—pertaining to cedar)

This wood is known also as PIQUA, AFRICAN CEDAR, CEDAR MAHOGANY, CEDRON, OBOBO, OBOBONE, KWI and SCENTED GUAREA.

The tree grows on the Gold and Ivory Coasts, is medium large in size, and at times logs up to diameters of 5 ft. are exported. The wood has a pleasing pink to light mahogany color, has a fine grain and comes in stripes and mottles. The amount of sapwood is small and whitish in color; the heartwood is pinkish brown, darkening upon exposure, but not to the same extent as true mahoganies. The main characteristic of this tree is that it is generally superior to the American mahogany. The grain is either straight or wavy and the mottle figure is fairly common, but the stripe is far less frequent than that found in sapele. The plain-cut stock shows a small zigzag figure. When freshly cut, a strong cedarlike scent results; occasionally the boards and veneers will be gummy, which has a dulling effect on saws. However, these gum spots may be easily sanded off.

The logs are a good size for widths and lengths, and the wood is stiff, tough and strong, comparing favorably with Honduras mahogany, but being considerably harder.

BOXWOOD, WEST INDIAN *Gossypiospermum praecox* (Gossypiospermum—having seeds like cotton, *Gossypium*; praecox—before or earlier to develop, precocious)

This tree, found in Venezuela, Colombia and the West Indies, reaches a height of 65 to 70 ft., generally without a single knot through its entire length. At the very top the tree branches out into a turf of foliage.

The color is yellowish white, and this wood is of the same family as elm, with a leaf similar to the elm, two sides of which are unequal at the base. As a rule it is a straight-grained wood, close, firm and smooth, and of uniform, fine texture. Occasionally logs will be found with irregularities. Chalky deposits will be found both in the heartwood and sapwood.

It is an extremely heavy and hard wood, easy to work, and is very satisfactory for turnery as well as carving. In this country it is used extensively for inlay work, in inlaid borders and many types of marquetry designs, and occasionally for handles of tools, brush backs, and various mathematical instruments and backs of scientific and weather instruments. In some countries a great deal of it is used in the manufacture of small combs.

BRIAR *Erica arborea* (Erica—the heath; arborea—treelike)

Briar grows on small trees or shrubs and is a wood much sought for the manufacture of the finest grades of pipes. It grows principally in countries around the Adriatic Sea, Turkey, Algeria and the island of Corsica. One hundred years ago the French town of St. Claude was the original manufacturing center for all briar pipes, but this industry has now spread to practically all countries.

The wood for the pipes is obtained from the roots of the tree

Bubinga with stripe-and-mottle figure.

Striped bubinga.

when it is generally twenty-five years or more of age and usually from 9 to 14 ft. high. The roots lie from 6 to 12 in. beneath the surface of the ground, and any roots 4 in. or more in diameter are considered acceptable. Occasionally some roots are obtained as large as 8 in. After being procured, they are roughly trimmed, piled in large heaps and watered frequently to prevent the roots from drying. They are constantly kept damp until they are ready to be cut into the blanks for the pipes. After this, they are boiled to improve the color and reduce

danger of splitting. It is reported that over ten thousand tons a year are used.

From time to time the popularity of the wood has changed; sometimes the straight-grained wood is the most desired; at other times the burl or bird's-eye figure is preferred.

BUBINGA *Didelotia africana* (Didelotia—probably after Didelot; africana—of Africa)

This tree grows principally in Gabon and the Camerouns and when rotary-cut is known as

KEVAZINGO. It is known also as ESSINGANG. While the botanical classification of bubinga has been given by some, it should not be accepted definitely until it has been further verified. It is a wood which has obtained its name from the vernacular name of bubingo. The French have referred to it in the trade as BOIS DE ROE D'AFRIQUE.

The average weight per cubic foot is 57 lbs. and the logs, when received in this country, are tremendous in size. Logs have been received which weigh as much as 10 tons. The color varies in different logs from a pale to deep red, though the color is uniform in individual trees. It also comes in striped and mottled figures. Bubinga is valuable as a veneer for cabinetwork.

BUCKEYE *Aesculus glabra* (Aesculus—ancient Latin name of a European oak; glabra—smooth, hairless)

The twigs and flowers of this tree have a most disagreeable odor when they are crushed or broken, which is why it also has been given the names STINKING BUCKEYE and FETID BUCKEYE.

This tree grows in the central states from Alabama to Pennsylvania. While originally it was brought from Germany, from the earliest days it has been associated with Ohio and is the official tree of that state.

Buckeye is a rather small to medium-sized tree and in many ways resembles in appearance the horse chestnut. It is called buckeye because of the large seeds, which resemble the eye of a buck deer. Incidentally, these seeds are poisonous.

Buckeye is light in weight, soft in texture and nearly white in color except for streaks that sometimes occur from staining. It is a good-looking tree and generally bears leaves in the spring earlier than almost any other species.

Early settlers used an extract from the bark for medicine.

In lumber form the wood is easily distinguished by the appearance of ripple figures. It is used in the manufacture of paper pulp, various types of woodenware and splints and artificial limbs. Some of the logs are also converted into veneers.

BULLET WOOD *Mimusops globosa* (Mimusops—monkey face; globosa—spherical, probably referring to the fruit)

This wood, which comes from Brazil, the Guianas and Venezuela, is also known as BALATA, BEEFWOOD, RED LANCEWOOD and WILD BILLY.

It is reddish brown with a purple cast, hard and heavy, and one of the strongest woods known. It is produced only in the lumber form and in limited quantities.

BUTTERNUT *Juglans cinerea* (Juglans—the classical Latin name of the walnut, meaning the nut of Jupiter; cinerea—ash-colored, pertaining to the bark)

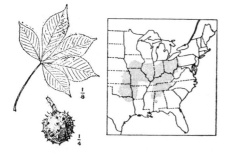

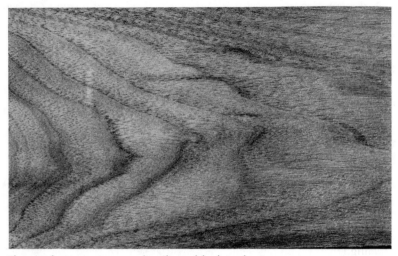

Flat-cut butternut, same family as black walnut.

The kernel of the nut is delicious and so rich and oily that the name OIL-NUT has sometimes been given to this tree.

It grows from Quebec down through the northeastern sections of the United States, westward to South Dakota and as far south as Arkansas, Mississippi and Alabama.

This wood is in many ways very similar in characteristics to American black walnut and has at times been called white walnut. Like walnut, the nuts are edible and highly prized. The sap obtained is sweet, and a syrup may be produced that is similar to syrup from the maple tree. Butternut wood is lighter in weight and not as strong and durable as black walnut. It is soft in texture but coarse-grained. The wood is easily worked with all types of tools, very sharp tools being desirable because of the softness of the wood. Lovely interior paneling has been done with butternut, and a small amount used in the manufacture of furniture. Also, many church altars have been made of this wood. It is also used by wood carvers.

CAMPECHE *Sickingia tinctoria* (Sickingia—probably after Franz von Sickingen; tinctoria—dyed)

This wood is known by a number of different names, among them CARRETA, CORALITO, NADARA ROSITA, PALO ROSATO, PAU BRAZIL, QUINA ROJA and RED INDIA INK. It has long been associated with the red dye made from the bark, and small quantities have been brought into New

York for use as a dyewood under the name ARARIBA ROSA.

Campeche grows up to 60 ft. in height and with diameters from 15 to 18 in. The wood has a fine texture and straight grain, but little commercial value. It works well, and locally in Brazil is used for making fancy articles, bowls and spoons, and also for interior construction and general carpentry.

CAMPHORWOOD *Cinnamomum camphora* (Cinnamon—from the ancient Greek, *kinnamomon;* camphor—from the Arabic *kafur,* meaning resin)

This tree grows in Japan, China and Formosa and is a difficult wood to obtain. In China and Formosa, capital punishment has been the penalty for cutting down camphor trees. This is known as

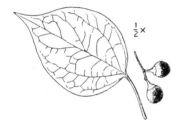

the true camphorwood and the strong scent of camphor will last hundreds of years. The wood weighs about 41 lbs. per cubic foot and is light yellow to brown in color. There is little demand for it.

Oftentimes wood of the cinnamon tree (*Cinnamomum zeylanicum*) is sold in place of the true camphor. However, this wood shrinks, warps and swells. As long as it is in existence it has the strong scent of paregoric or balm of aniseed. The well-known seamen's trunks made in China and sold today in eastern markets as camphorwood are generally made of this inferior cinnamon tree, only a small portion being made of camphorwood, to produce the scent of camphor.

There is another type of camphorwood from Borneo which does not have an odor like camphor. This wood also shrinks and can only be used after at least two years of air seasoning followed by kiln drying.

From Madagascar there is also a camphorwood (*Hernandia voyroni*), which has a strong and consistent odor of camphor but is greenish brown in color, has a rough grain and is difficult to work with tools.

CAMPHORWOOD, EAST AFRICAN *Ocotea usambarensis* (Ocotea—a South American Indian plant name; usambarensis—of Usumbura, capital of Ruanda-Urundi, Belgian trust territory in Africa)

This large tree emanates from Kenya, in east Africa, at altitudes anywhere from 7,000 to 8,000 ft. and higher. It is one of the largest trees growing in Kenya.

When freshly cut, the wood is a pale, greenish color, but darkens to a deep brown with exposure to air and light. It is light in weight, weighing around 35 lbs. per cubic foot, and has a distinct aromatic scent which probably is the reason for the name of camphor, though it differs entirely from the Asiatic camphorwood and no camphor is present in the tree. The leaves also contain an aromatic oil. This wood is closely related to the African stick wood and British Guiana greenheart.

This camphorwood needs to be dried fairly slowly to avoid any warping. With hand or machine tools the wood is easily worked, and locally it has been used in the manufacture of railway coaches and furniture, and small quantities have been exported to other markets. A fine example of the use of this wood can be seen in the Post Office at West Kensington, London, where all of the trim and cabinetwork has been done in this wood.

CANALETE *Cordia alliodora* (Cordia—after Valerius Cordus, 1515–1544; alliodora—smelling like an onion, *Allium*)

This tree, growing in Venezuela, is reddish brown in color, works easily, is strong and is used locally for furniture, house construction and joinery. Occasional logs have been brought into this country and manufactured into veneers.

CANARIUM *Canarium schweinfurthii* (Canarium—in reference to the Canary Islands; schweinfurthii —after Schweinfurth, a German botanist)

This is a large tree, often obtaining a height of 100 ft., which grows throughout the west coast of Africa. In France it is known as AIELE, and sometimes it has been called WHITE MAHOGANY.

The wood is almost white in color, occasionally slightly pink, which later may turn to a pale brownish tint upon exposure and drying. When first cut, the bark is strongly aromatic, with a resinous odor, and contains a gum, nearly white in color, which, after solidifying, resembles wax used for candles and burns freely.

Canarium is of medium texture and weight and when cut on the quarter shows a prominent stripe. It has often been used in place of African mahogany, for after being stained the appearance is so similar that it is deceiving to almost anyone who does not have a thorough knowledge of these timbers. It also resembles obeche in appearance, texture and color, except that it is somewhat harder and a little finer in texture.

It is a wood one does not care to work with, as a rule, because the edges of the tools are quickly dulled, because of the amount of gum the wood contains. It should always be cut on the quarter because of its tendency to warp.

Canarium is used for shelving, interior fittings and general purposes.

CAPOMO *Brosimum alicastrum* (Brosimum—edible; alicastrum— wild wheat)

This wood, from Central America, is also known as BREADNUT, LAREDO, LERADO and OJOCHE.

It has a yellowish sapwood and a reddish heartwood. Capomo, which is hard, is generally manufactured into veneer on the quartered form, and shows a cross-ripple figure with considerable luster.

CARACOLI *Bucida spinosa* (Bucida—from ox, referring to the hornlike galls on the fruit caused by a mite; spinosa—spined, with spines)

This is a small tree, found in abundance along the coast of the West Indies and known by the names BLACK OLIVE TREE, BULLET TREE, GREGORY WOOD, OLIVE-BARK TREE and PRIETO.

The heartwood is of an olive-brown color. Caracoli has very little export value and it is fairly difficult to work with tools. Locally it is used for general carpentry and furniture work, and because of its high durability, for pole posts and railroad ties. The bark of this tree is used in tanning.

CASCARILLA *Coutarea hexandra* (Coutarea—derivation unknown; hex/andra—ten stamens)

It also is called AMARGO, CAPARCHE, PAKERI and QUINA.

This tree, often with a height of over 100 ft. and a straight trunk, 18 to 36 in. in diameter, grows from Mexico to Argentina and throughout all of southern Brazil. The heartwood is a pinkish brown color; it is hard, strong and heavy and has a uniform fine texture. This wood is easy to work with, takes a high polish and is highly esteemed locally for use in furniture.

CATALPA, SOUTHERN *Catalpa bignonioides* (Catalpa—the American Indian name; bignonioides —appearing like *Bignonia,* a vine of the same family)

This tree grows in the eastern half of the United States from Maine to the Gulf of Mexico and is recognized by the long seed pods, which look like string beans

and remain on the tree throughout the winter. These pods are from 9 to 12 in. in length, and in some states, this tree is known as the bean tree. There is also a northern catalpa tree very similar in characteristics to the southern species.

Catalpa wood is soft and weak and has a slightly aromatic odor. The supply of the lumber is limited. Locally it is used for fence posts, and it is also suitable for handles and picture frames, because of its lasting qualities.

CATIVO *Prioria copaifera* (Prioria —probably meaning earlier or first; copaifera—after the genus *Copaifera*; copai—the Tupi Indian "copaiba," the copaiba tree yielding a medicinal resin; fera—to bear or yield)

In the trade this wood is known also as SPANISH WALNUT, TABASARA and TAITO.

It is the only broad-leaved tree in South America occurring in large groves. The tree grows to a height of 100 ft. with average diameters of 24 to 36 in., and larger specimens are not uncommon. The rather thick bark is smooth or with fine warts, and is a mottled gray-green on the surface but reddish brown beneath.

In its unfinished condition, the

wood is not very attractive in appearance, showing a number of narrow oily streaks and veins. With only a wax finish, however, a surface luster develops, with a rich striping of brown and many nicely variegated tones and shades such as one sees in English oak. When dry, the wood is odorless and without taste.

Its principal use in this country is for making veneers in limited quantity and it is recommended for making fine furniture. Cativo is worthy of attention from interior decorators for use in paneling rooms.

CEDAR, ATLANTIC WHITE *Chamaecyparis thyoides* (Chamaecyparis—from the Greek name for ground cypress, a dwarf shrubby Old World composite which resembles a dwarf cypress; thyoides—like *Thuja*, a related genus)

It is known also as FALSE-CYPRESS, JUNIPER, SOUTHERN WHITE CEDAR, SWAMP CEDAR and WHITE CEDAR.

This tree, native to the Atlantic seaboard from Maine to northern Florida, reaches a height of 60 to 80 ft., with diameters up to 3 ft. It grows along small streams and

the edge of freshwater swamps and has a gray to light reddish brown bark, smooth but in loose platelike scales which peel off easily into long strips.

Because of its durability, it serves well for fences, poles, shingles, etc. It is a wood in great demand for boat work and canoe construction because of its light weight, uniform texture and close grain. Also, it is a good wood for craftsmen to use and is excellent for making many novelties.

CEDAR, EASTERN RED *Juniperus virginiana* (Juniperus—ancient Latin name; virginiana—of Virginia)

Middle Tennessee has produced more red cedar than any other part of the United States, but the bulk of production has been confined to a few counties which produce a higher class and more aromatic variety of wood than found elsewhere.

This widely distributed tree is called red cedar in most states. It grows slowly and thrives in almost any soil and situation, except deep swamps, and the trees often stand wide apart or solitary, yet in some states they grow in

Top: Sawing Spanish cedar at a sawmill in Santarem, Brazil. Lower
left: Eastern red cedar. Lower right: Catalpa tree.

Aromatic eastern red cedar.

almost impenetrable thickets, particularly in Texas and the southern states. This cedar is red in color and the thin sapwood is nearly white. The grain is very fine and even except for occasional knots.

There is little trouble experienced with warping or shrinkage, and the heartwood is considered as durable as any other American wood. It has a delicate, agreeable fragrance. This odor is disagreeable to insects and for this reason chests and closets of cedar are highly appreciated as storage places for garments which are subject to the ravages of the moth and buffalo bugs.

Tests have proven that red cedar is 80 percent as strong as white oak. The wood is easily worked. Although the most general use at the present time is for lead pencils, few people who sharpen one and smell the fragrant wood stop to wonder where it comes from.

Cedar was long used as one of the best woods for skiffs and other light boats and it was occasionally employed in shipbuilding for the upper parts of vessels. A little of it is still used for trim and finish, particularly for canoes, motorboats and yachts. Early chest makers selected clear lumber because it could be had and was considered to be better, but modern chest manufacturers cannot obtain sufficient clear stock and make do with boards filled with knots. The wood is finished with oils, the natural color remains, and the knots give chests a pleasing rustic effect.

An extract from the fruit and leaves is used in medicine, and oil of red cedar, distilled from the wood, in making perfume. To the taste, this cedar is sweet.

CEDAR-OF-LEBANON *Cedrus libani*

This is the tree made famous by numerous biblical references. It is a large cone-bearing evergreen tree with irregular spreading crown of horizontal branches. The bark is dark gray, becoming fissured and scaly. A native of Asia Minor and Syria, it is being seeded in warm climates in Atlantic, Gulf and Pacific regions of the United States. Harvesting is prohibited in its native lands.

CEDAR, PORT-ORFORD *Chamaecyparis lawsoniana* (Chamaecyparis—from the Greek name for ground-cypress, a dwarf shrubby member of the sunflower family which resembles a dwarf cypress; lawsoniana—after Peter Lawson and Sons, nurserymen of Edinburgh, who introduced this species into cultivation)

Locally this wood is called LAWSON'S CYPRESS and is known also as OREGON CEDAR and GINGER PINE, as the wood has a pungent gingerlike odor, and when freshly cut a spicy, bitter taste.

This beautiful evergreen tree is found on the western slopes of the Pacific coast from Coos Bay in Oregon southward to Humboldt County, in elevations up to 5,000 ft. The tree has a long, clear trunk 80 to 100 ft. high before any branches appear, and it runs in diameter from 22 in. to 12 ft. and in height up to 200 ft.

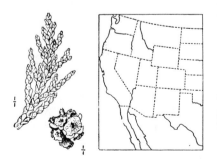

Port-Orford cedar is a pale yellowish white to yellowish brown color. The wood is of fine, even grain and light in weight. It is particularly durable.

This wood is one of the favorites for archers, being used for arrows, and it is also used in Venetian blinds and boat construction, and for furniture. It has long been the best wood for storage-battery separators.

CEDAR, SPANISH *Cedrela mexicana* (Cedrela—a cedar; mexicana—from Mexico)

This wood is known also as BRAZILIAN CEDAR, CEDRO and HONDURAS CEDAR.

It grows in every country south of the United States except Chile. The wood is light red in color, straight-grained and soft in texture; occasionally it is wavy and mottled. One of the principal uses of Spanish cedar is in the manufacture of cigar boxes. It is also used in boat building and pattern making, and for lead pencils and furniture.

CEDAR, WESTERN RED *Thuja plicata* (Thuja—from the Greek *thuia*, an aromatic wood highly prized in ancient times for choice, durable furniture and probably a juniper; plicata—folded, probably a reference to the scalelike leaves)

This tree is known also as CANOE CEDAR, GIANT ARBOR VITAE, IDAHO CEDAR, PACIFIC RED CEDAR, SHINGLEWOOD and STINKING CEDAR.

It grows all the way from southern Alaska to northern California and eastward to Montana and Idaho. It flourishes in moist soil and grows from sea level up to high altitudes in the Rocky Mountains. It is a slow-growing tree, large and long-limbed, reaching up to 200 ft. and diameters of 14 to 16 ft.

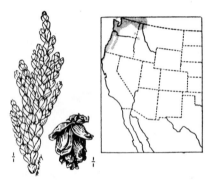

Western red cedar is a dull red in color but loses most of its reddishness upon exposure to the air. It has a distinctive odor although different in nature and degree from the characteristic pleasant odor of eastern red cedar. The wood is straight-grained, fairly coarse in texture, without any pitch, but it is easily worked with tools and takes a good finish.

The greater part of this species of cedar is used for shingles and miscellaneous millwork, boat building, etc.

CEIBA *Ceiba pentandra* (Ceiba— a native name; pent/andra—five stamens)

This tree, originating in west Africa and Mexico, is known also as KOPAK, ODOUM and SILK COTTON TREE.

The wood is a reddish gray color, sometimes with yellowish or grayish streaks, and is very absorbent, coarse-textured and soft when green but brittle when dry. In the lumber form it is used for tables, plates, trays and simple furniture.

CHERRY, BLACK *Prunus serotina* (Prunus—Persian, or an old name for peach; serotina—late, probably referring to the late-maturing fruit)

Flat-cut cherry, cross figure.

This cherry is known also as CHOKE CHERRY, RUM CHERRY, WHISKEY CHERRY, and WILD CHERRY.

It grows generally through the eastern part of the United States, the largest supplies located in the Appalachian Mountains in New York, Pennsylvania and West Virginia. Black cherry is usually easily distinguished from other native species because of its distinctive color, the bark being dark with irregular scales which peel off easily, and with light to dark reddish brown heartwood.

This wood is comparatively free from checking and warping; it stays in place well after seasoning, but has a moderately large amount of shrinkage during seasoning. It is a fairly heavy wood, averaging around 35 lbs. per cubic foot, moderately hard, stiff and strong.

The fruit of this tree is about the size of a pea and the purple, juicy, colored pulp surrounding the seed has a bitter taste but is edible and used principally to flavor jelly and beverages, especially in the making of rum cherry, cherry cider and a drink called cherry bounce. This is the reason why some of the common names mentioned above were given to this wood.

The wood is used for carving and works fairly well with all types of hand tools. Large amounts are used for backing blocks on which engravings and electrotype plates, used in printing, are mounted. In the cabinetmaking trade this wood has also been called New England mahogany. Choice logs are cut into veneers for furniture, cabinetmaking and musical instrument work.

Flat-cut American cherry. This example of typical figuration is especially useful in identifying one of the leading furniture and architectural woods. Color is light reddish brown.

Black cherry growing in Gainesville, Florida.

CHESTNUT, AMERICAN *Castanea dentata* (Castanea—the classical Greek and Latin name; dentata —toothed, referring to the leaf margin)

This tree grows throughout the eastern part of our country and westward into Michigan and Illinois. It is generally a broad tree with a short trunk and large, overhanging branches. (Longfellow referred to this when he wrote, "Under the spreading Chestnut tree the village smithy stands.")

American chestnut is well known for the delicious nuts it produces. They have long been a delicacy, but are becoming harder to obtain each year. In addition to the nuts, the bark from this tree has been a valuable product, being the principal supply of the tannin used in the leather industry. However, a fungus disease, known as chestnut blight, has almost entirely exterminated these trees, and no control for this disease has yet been found. Small insects eat the tree after it has been killed by the blight and the lumber has been sold as "wormy chestnut." Furniture, picture-frame moldings and other articles have been made from wormy chestnut.

CHINABERRY *Melia azedarach* (Melia—a classical Greek name for the ash tree; azedarach—from the Persian, meaning noble tree)

This tree, emanating from China and India, is known also as CHINATREE, CHINESE UMBRELLA TREE, INDIANA SOAP PLANT, SOAP BERRY and the TEXAS UMBRELLA TREE.

The chinaberry, so named because it originates in China, has long been used in that country as an ornamental tree. The wood, which is light reddish tan with tints of yellow, while attractive in appearance, has little value as lumber, but it may be worked easily with tools and takes a good finish, making it suitable for use where obtainable.

COCOBOLO *Dalbergia* spp. (Dalbergia—after N. Dalberg, 1735–1820, a Swedish physician)

This wood comes from Nicaragua and western Costa Rica and has an average weight of 62 to 76

lbs. per cubic foot. The color of the heartwood varies greatly from light to deep red and the hues of the rainbow, and the grain runs fairly straight to interwoven.

Cocobolo is of high durability, but the wood is unsuited for gluing. If the smooth surface is rubbed with a cloth it will acquire a waxy finish without the use of any oil, wax, shellac or filler. Lengthy immersions in soapy water has little effect on the wood except for a slight darkening in color.

When working with cocobolo, care must be taken to protect oneself from the fine dust, as it produces a poisoning similar to ivy poisoning. It can become very painful. When affected, a person usually has to remain away from work for a week and then may never again be able to be in a room where there is any cocobolo dust.

This wood is used principally in the cutlery trade for knife and tool handles of all kinds. It is also used for scientific instruments, brush backs, steering wheels for boats, canes, chessmen, buttons, forks and spoons. Occasionally, highly figured logs have been cut into veneers, but the supply is limited.

CORDIA *Cordia fragrantissima* (Cordia—after Valerius Cordus, 1515–1544; fragrantissima—very aromatic)

This wood, native to Burma but growing occasionally in other parts of the East Indies, is known also as KALAMET.

Cordia has a reddish brown color, sometimes intermixed with darker streaks and beautiful mottled markings. When cut on the quarter, it produces a silver grain like that of our American sycamore. The wood seasons without difficulty and is of moderate weight and hardness.

Principally, this wood is of value because of its unusual fragrance. Like all odors in woods, however, it is strongest when first cut and as it dries out and becomes older the scent gradually disappears.

Only small quantities of cordia have been used so far in the lumber form. It can be worked with both hand and power tools.

CORK OAK TREE *Quercus suber*

This evergreen oak, growing in southern Europe and along the North African coast but principally cultivated in Spain and Portugal, provides the world with its supply of cork for forming bungs and bottle stoppers. Its lightness, combined with strength, is particularly suitable for life buoys, belts and jackets. Because of its lightness, softness and nonconducting properties, it is also used for hat linings and soles of shoes. Chips and cuttings are ground up and combined with linseed oil, gums, rubber and other materials to form floor coverings. Cork is also used in making artificial limbs.

The tree reaches a height of 30 ft. and the outer layer of bark, by annual additions from within, gradually becomes a thick, soft homogeneous mass having the compressible and elastic properties upon which the economic value of cork depends. The first stripping of the cork takes place when the trees are from 15 to 20 years old. Subsequently, the bark is removed every 8 or 10 years during the months of July and August. The tree continues to live and thrive under the operation for 150 years and upward, the quality of the cork improving with each period. The quality of the first stripping is very poor and is suitable only for a tanning substance or for forming rustic work in ferneries, conservatories, etc. The second stripping, still coarse, is suitable for making floats for nets and similar work.

There are other trees growing in different parts of the world which are known as cork wood but do not produce cork like *Quercus suber*. *Anona glabra*, a tree with a buttressed base which grows in southern Florida and the West Indies, is sometimes used locally, particularly the roots, as a substitute for cork in floats for fishing nets, stoppers of bottles and the like. It is known also as ALLI-GATOR APPLE, MONKEY APPLE, POND APPLE and BOBWOOD. *Ochroma lagopus*, the source of balsa wood, is sometimes called cork wood. *Pterocarpus officinalis*, growing in Jamaica, southern Mexico, throughout Central America and northern South America, is known in Venezuela as cork wood.

The wood *Leitneria floridana*— a small tree growing in the swamps of Florida, Georgia and Texas—has cork wood as its only common name. The wood is very light and brittle but has no commercial value because of its size and scarcity.

COTTONWOOD, EASTERN *Populus deltoides* (Populus—ancient Latin name; deltoides—triangular in reference to the leaf shape)

This tree is known also by several other names, including ASPEN COTTONWOOD, CAROLINA POPLAR, RIVER POPLAR, WATER POPLAR, YELLOW COTTONWOOD.

The tree grows to a height of 100 ft. or more, with a diameter from 5 to 8 ft. It is at its best in moist soil, along the banks of rivers or edges of swamps. It has a wide distribution in this country and to the early pioneers in the Midwestern plains the trees proved invaluable for shade and timber, and the leaves helped to feed the livestock. The bright green, broad leaves have a feathery appearance and flutter in the breeze like the quaking aspen. This is the state tree of Kansas.

The wood of this tree is very similar in texture and appearance to that of the other eight or ten species of this family. The tree was named from the cottony fluff that is attached to the seeds.

The color of the wood is creamy white, and the heartwood is white to light brown. It has a smooth, even texture and is slightly lustrous in appearance. Difficulty is experienced in seasoning cottonwood, owing to the large amount of warpage, but it is easily worked with tools and is a favorite wood for manufacturing boxes and packing crates because it takes the stencil ink so well. It is also used for rough carpentry work, excelsior, firewood, pulpwood and low-priced commercial veneers.

COURBARIL *Hymenaea courbaril*
(Hymenaea—membrane; courbaril—the native name)

In the West Indies it is often referred to as STINKING TOE, in British Guiana it is known as LOCUST, and in South America under such names as ALGARROBO, GUAPINOL and JATOBA.

This tree grows in the West Indies and in South America, up to 100 ft. in height and 3 to 4 ft. in diameter. It is strong and hard, averaging around 60 lbs. per cubic foot. While the sapwood is often white in color, the heartwood is a reddish brown to brown with pronounced darker stripes. The bark is fairly heavy and contains an orange or yellowish gum which in fossilized forms is sometimes dug up on sites which probably contained trees of this species. This gum is used in the manufacture of special types of varnishes and cements. Like our paper-bark birch, this bark may be stripped off in large sheets; it likewise is used in the construction of canoes.

Courbaril has a characteristic of woods in the family of Leguminosae; when the wood is planed it seems to glow from within. It turns well in the lathe but is difficult to work with tools. Generally, it is used for large construction work as in shipbuilding and general types of carpentry.

CRAB APPLE *Malus pumila*

It is known as CRAB, CRAB TREE and GARLAND TREE.

This tree is native to southeastern Europe and central Asia, usually growing wild individually, and it has become naturalized in the northeastern part of North America. It is a small tree, 20 to 30 ft. in height and 10 to 12 in. in diameter. The wood is hard, heavy, pinkish to grayish brown in color, somewhat like the appearance of pearwood but with more color variation, and heavier and harder.

It is a fairly difficult wood to work with, has a dulling effect on tools, but is unusually fine for turning and for carving because of the even texture. It holds its place well when manufactured. Formerly it was one of the most popular woods for handles of handsaws and it is also used for the heads of wooden mallets.

The tart red fruit, called crab apples, are used for making preserves and jellies.

CRAMANTEE *Guarea excelsa*
(Guarea—from guara, a native West Indian name; excelsa—tall or elevated)

Growing in British Honduras, this wood is very similar to the scented Guarea of west Africa and the alligator wood of Jamaica, even though separated by several thousand miles. It grows to a height of 100 ft. or more, with good-sized diameters, and weighs about 35 lbs. per cubic foot.

The heartwood is very similar in appearance to a pale-colored mahogany, but the grain is coarser in texture. The tree also bears white, scented flowers.

If seasoning is slow, no difficulties are encountered. The wood has good strength and other properties, comparable to its weight. Satisfactory logs are produced for sawing or for manufacturing into veneers. If the wood is turned, considerable sanding is necessary to ensure a good surface, but it may be worked with tools as desired.

CUMBARÚ *Amburana cearensis* (Amburana—a native name; cearensis—after a state, Ceara, in Brazil)

This wood, growing in Brazil, is known also as AMBURANA, ROBLE and TREBOL.

The wood is light in weight, around 35 lbs. per cubic foot, light brown or a yellowish tinge in color, and of coarse texture. Great value is placed on the seeds of this tree; they have a lovely scent and are used in perfuming toilet soaps and snuff. The resin of the bark contains a fragrant oil used in medicine, and the wood contains the same pleasant scent, which is more noticeable when the wood is freshly cut.

This wood takes a very smooth finish and stays in place. Generally, it is used in northeastern Brazil for construction like crating and carpentry and it is often used in the manufacture of furniture in Argentina.

DAHOMA *Piptadenia africana* (Pipt—to fall; adenia—a gland or the genus *adenia* (?); africana—of Africa)

It is known also as ATUI, BANZU, DAB'EMA, EKHIMI, MUSESE, MPEWERE, SINGA, TOM and TOUM.

This is a large tree of 110 ft. or more in height and grows through-

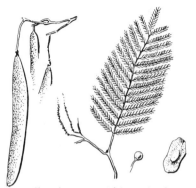

out all of west Africa. It is a straight-grained wood, of fairly coarse and woolly texture. The heartwood ranges in color from grayish brown to a warm golden-brown color. The texture is uniform, however, and the wood weighs around 38 lbs. per cubic foot.

Dahoma is a very difficult wood to kiln-dry because it tends to collapse and distort, and there is a large shrinkage. Until the wood has been dried, it has a very disagreeable odor; when freshly cut, it has the unpleasant smell of ammonia and the sawdust is irritating to the eyes. Also, when the wood is dry, it may cause irritation and sneezing spells while one is working with it.

The strength value of this wood is good, resembling that of iroko; it has somewhat the appearance of iroko and has been used as a substitute when iroko was scarce. It is reported to be taking the place of that timber on the Gold Coast. The wood is very durable and resistant to termites.

Dahoma works well but has a dulling effect on tools. While small quantities have been exported, it has not met with too much favor, owing to the irritation caused when working with it and to the offensive odor.

DANTA *Cistanthera papaverifera* (Cist—a box; anthera—anthers; papaver/ifera—poppy bearing)

This small tree from the Gold Coast and Nigeria is known also as APRU, EPRO, KOTIBÉ, OLBORBORA, OTUTU, OVOUÉ and TSANYA.

The average diameter of the exported logs is from 18 to 30 in. and the weight per cubic foot is 46 lbs. The wood is reddish brown in color, even textured and generally has a narrow stripe when cut on the quarter, when it very much resembles sapele. The grain is typically interlocked and this produces the ribbon figure. Danta seasons fairly well but has a tendency to warp, and care must be taken to avoid overrapid drying.

It is a wood that is used generally where extreme strength is required. In Europe it has a large use, similar to American birch, for handles of tools. When the surface is planed, it has somewhat of a greasy feel. This wood works well with most tools but has a tendency to pick up on quarter-sawed material. However, it turns excellently, takes a good finish and polishes well.

DINUANG *Octomelis sumatranus* (Octo/melis—light apple trees; sumatranus—of Sumatra)

This tree is known also by other names, such as BILUAN, DANUANG and DINONANG.

Dinuang grows in the moist lands and banks of rivers in the Philippines, Borneo and Sumatra, where there are forests composed entirely of this species of tree. It is a large tree with a height, at times, of over 70 ft. and diameters of 30 in. or more. However, it is a very lightweight wood, averaging 25 lbs. per cubic foot. While there is a large amount of sapwood, it is hardly different in appearance from the heartwood. The wood has little figure or grain, is reddish brown in color, and the nearer the center of the tree, the darker the wood is.

There is no problem in seasoning this wood and it works easily with power or hand tools. At times it has been included in shipments of white lauan from the Philippines, but is inferior in strength and texture.

The wood has no special uses. In a general utility way it is suitable for the same purposes as other light hardwoods.

DOGWOOD, FLOWERING *Cornus florida* (Cornus—the Latin name of the cornelian cherry dogwood of Europe, *Cornus mas*, from the word horn, referring to the hardness of the wood; florida —flowering)

This tree is known also as ARROW WOOD, CORNEL, CORNELIAN and FALSE BOXWOOD.

The tree is small, between 30 and 40 ft. high, and 12 to 18 in. in diameter and is generally found at its best in the rich soils along the banks of streams in the eastern part of the United States from

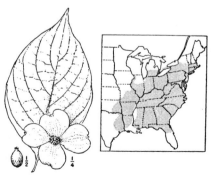

Flowering dogwood.

New York to Florida and westward to Michigan. Dogwood is the state tree of Missouri and Virginia and is also native to Texas.

Of the twenty or more species of dogwood in the United States, nine of which are trees and the rest flowering shrubs, the *Cornus florida* is the most beautiful of them all. It has a yellowish brown color, a cubic weight per foot of 50 lbs., and when the tree flowers bloom, it is perhaps the most beautiful sight in the botanical world.

Early colonists prepared a medicine from the bark of this tree for the treatment of malaria. While this is not done today, some of the essence of dogwood is still used in parts of the south, in whiskey taken as a home remedy.

Dogwood is used for making shuttle blocks, golf-club heads, wood engravings and charcoal for gunpowder.

DURIAN, WILD *Cullenia excelsa* (Cullenia—probably after Cullen; excelsa—high)

This wood, native to the island of Ceylon, is occasionally found also in southern India, where it is known as KATUBODA.

It is a medium-weight wood, averaging around 40 lbs. per cubic foot, mostly straight-grained, and an attractive pinkish gray and reddish brown in color. An interesting feature about this tree is that it bears annually large prickly fruits up to 6 in. in diameter, but these are not edible.

Macassar ebony, flat-cut.

After logging, this timber has to be removed from the forest and converted quickly, otherwise it stains and then decay sets in. However, it dries without trouble and is an easy wood to work with.

Little of this wood has been used outside the country it grows in. Small quantities of veneers have been manufactured, but it is generally used for all-around purposes in carpentry, partitions in buildings, furniture backings, etc.

EBONY *Diospyros* spp. (Diospyros —fruit of the gods)

The woods of this genus, belonging to the family of Ebenaceae, are widely distributed throughout the tropical and mild temperate regions of the world and consist of about three hundred species of shrubs and trees.

Ebony was among the articles of merchandise brought to Tyre as described in Ezekiel 27:15, and Herodotus stated that the Ethiopians every three years sent a tribute of two hundred logs of this wood to Persia. It was used by the kings of India for scepters and images, and also in drinking cups as a supposed antidote for poison.

The best kinds are very heavy, deep black, and consist of heartwood only. Because of its color, durability, hardness and susceptibility of polish, ebony is much used in cabinetwork, inlaying, turned articles and piano keys of top-grade instruments.

The most important varieties of ebony originate in the East Indies and in Ceylon, the best of the species being the *Diospyros ebenum*, which grows in abundance in the flat country west of Trincomalee, in Ceylon. This tree is easily distinguished by the smallness of its trunk, its jet-black charred-looking bark, beneath which the sapwood is perfectly white until the heartwood is reached. This wood is believed to excel all other varieties for the fineness and intensity of its dark color. However, a large percentage of the East Indian ebony is produced by the species *Dio-*

Quarter-sliced Macassar ebony, four-piece match.

spyros melanoxylon, a large tree growing to a height of 60 to 80 ft. and 8 to 10 ft. in circumference. These logs are streaked with yellow or yellowish brown and are sometimes known as golden ebony or Macassar ebony. They are manufactured into veneers and sliced across the heart and on the quarter to produce fine, pronounced stripes.

The ebonies in Africa are available in the form of short logs or billets, with diameters of from 2 to 12 in. and lengths of 2 ft. and longer. The weight of ebony varies from 45 to 70 lbs. per cubic foot.

Of the American species of *Diospyros,* the largest and only one of commercial importance is the common persimmon, which is described under that name later on in this book.

Because of its extreme hardness and the dulling effect on tools, ebony is difficult to work, though it finishes smoothly and produces a high polish.

Locally, some of the light-colored sapwood is used in the manufacture of tool handles. In the solid form ebony is used for turning and carving and in the veneer form for inlay work.

EKKI *Lophira alata* (Lophira—helmet tufted; alata—winged)

This wood is known also as AKOURA, AZOBE, BONGOSSI, HENDUI, KAKU and RED IRONWOOD.

It grows along the west coast of Africa and is a very heavy wood, weighing 65 lbs. per cubic foot. The tree is large and produces logs up to 55 in. in diameter.

Ekki has a deep, chocolate-brown color, sometimes turning to a dark red, and has a prominence of white defects in the pores. The wood is used when great strength is required, as in flooring, where the wood is subject to a good deal of wear. It is extremely difficult to season, however, because of the tendency to warp and split. Ekki is very resistant to decay and, as far as is known, is the most durable wood in west Africa, exceeding oak and teak as far as strength is concerned.

This timber is hard to work with hand tools, but can be worked by machine with less trouble. It holds its shape well when manufactured and a good finish can be obtained.

ELM, AMERICAN *Ulmus americana* (Ulmus—the classical Latin name; americana—from America)

This elm grows throughout the eastern United States, except in the Appalachian highlands and southern Florida.

It is a moderately hard and heavy wood, averaging 35 lbs. to the cubic foot and reaching a height of 100 ft. or more and a diameter of from 3 to 6 ft. It is the state tree of Massachusetts, Nebraska and North Dakota.

There are approximately eighteen elm species known throughout the world, six of them native to the United States. Out of the six, the American elm is the handsomest and largest. It is not unusual for this tree to reach an age of two hundred years. It grows in rich, moist lands along streams and is one of the favorite trees supplying shade to lawns and streets. Unfortunately, the Dutch elm disease has wrought tremendous loss to our elm-shaded parkways and avenues.

The heartwood of this elm is brown to dark brown in color, sometimes containing shades of red. American elm, like the rock elm, has to be seasoned carefully to prevent warping.

Quarter-sliced American elm.

American elm, widely regarded as the most beautiful and graceful of broadleaf trees.

Flat-sliced American brown elm.

Like all of the commercial elms, this wood has excellent bending qualities. However, there is a large shrinkage. A good part of the lumber is used principally for containers for furniture and dairy and poultry supplies. Because of its excellent bending qualities it is also used for barrels and kegs, and for the bent parts of chairs. A smaller percentage of it is manufactured into veneers for plywood used in the panel and cabinet trade, which sometimes is sold under the name prinz wood or apatalae. When quarter-sliced, it is especially nice for decorative inlay work in furniture.

ELM, CARPATHIAN BURL *Ulmus procera* (procera—leader, chief or noble)

This tree is known also as ENGLISH ELM.

It grows in France, England and the Carpathian Mountains, varies from an almost brick-red to a light tan and has a beautiful medium-to-fine burl. However, defects of all kinds are found in almost every burl and a great deal of repair work is necessary before the burl can be used. This wood is used in fine cabinetry and decorative areas.

Importation of the logs has been banned in this country be-

Carpathian elm burl.

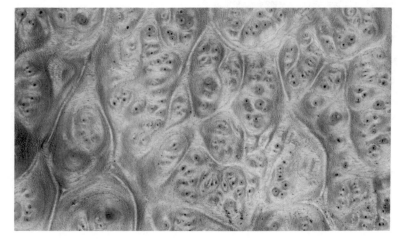

cause of the elm disease. Only manufactured veneers are allowed to enter and these are quite rare and expensive.

ESSIA *Combretodendron africanum* (Combreto—from the genus *Combretum;* dendron—a tree; africanum—from Africa)

It is known also by various other names, such as ABALE, BOSAKI, MINZU and WULO. This tree grows along the west coast of Africa from Sierra Leone to Ghana. In Ghana it is known as ESIA and OSA.

The tree is large, often reaching 130 ft. in height and about 30 in. in diameter. The wood is moderately heavy and hard, averaging around 35 lbs. per cubic foot, fairly straight-grained and coarse-textured. However, it is very attractive in appearance, the heartwood being pinkish brown and mottled with reddish brown shades. One can easily distinguish this wood as it is being logged in the forests or sawed in the mill, for it has an offensive odor which can best be described as similar to that of rotten cabbage.

Care has to be taken in drying the wood, and it is reported not to be very resistant to decay. The wood has a feeling of harshness to the touch. With careful attention, a good finish may be obtained.

Its principal use in Africa is in the manufacture of canoes, but in recent years small quantities have been exported to foreign markets.

FAUX ROSE *Dalbergia greveana* (Dalbergia—after N. Dalberg, 1735–1820, a Swedish physician; greveana—probably after a person)

This wood, from the island of Madagascar, is known also as FRENCH ROSEWOOD and MADAGASCAR ROSEWOOD.

Faux rose is pinkish brown in color and has a striped figure when manufactured on the quarter. It is used in the manufacture of furniture and for decoration on musical instruments.

FIR, BALSAM *Abies balsamea* (Abies—the classical Latin name of the silver fir, *Abies alba,* of Europe; balsamea—ancient word for balsam tree, referring to the resinous pockets or blisters in the bark)

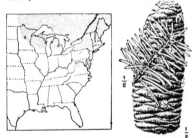

This tree is known also as CANADA BALSAM, EASTERN FIR and FIR-TREE. It grows throughout eastern Canada as far west as Alberta and through New England along the Appalachian Mountains as far south as Virginia. This could really be called the Christmas tree, as it is one of the choicest —and the one most used—for Christmas trees throughout the country. The deep blue-green needles are shiny on the surface and light underneath, with blunt ends. They have a strong, lasting aromatic odor and large quantities are used for balsam pillows because of this pleasing scent and their softness. It is considered the best-shaped evergreen.

Left: Douglas fir. Above: Balsam fir.

The resin obtained from this tree is important in optical work, being used as a cement for the glass. Botanists also use it for mounting microscopic specimens.

Balsam fir is soft in texture, straight-grained, light in weight and cuts easily with tools. It is very useful in the manufacture of food containers, since the wood is odorless and does not impart taste to the contents.

FIR, DOUGLAS *Pseudotsuga menziesii* (Pseudo/tsuga—false hemlock; menziesii—after Archibald Menzies, 1754–1842, Scottish physician and naturalist, who discovered it in 1791 at Nootka Sound on Vancouver Island)

This fir is known also as DOUGLAS SPRUCE, FIR, YELLOW FIR, RED PINE, RED SPRUCE, RED FIR, OREGON PINE and by other names.

It grows in the northwest, from British Columbia and western Alberta throughout our northwestern states, to as far south as Arizona, New Mexico and a small portion of Texas. The tree grows to tremendous girth and height, one of the tallest being 415 ft., and a single record tree has produced over 70,000 board feet of

high-grade lumber. This fir is one of the most important of our domestic commercial woods. It is estimated that over 490 billion feet remain growing, 75 percent of this in the states of Oregon and Washington. Douglas fir has been made the official state tree of Oregon.

While the wood varies considerably, according to the particular part of the country it comes from, it is strong, medium hard and heavy. The wood is a yellowish and very light tan color. The bark is very thick, often 12 in., rich, reddish brown and deeply fissured. This is a rapidly growing tree and its grain is attractive to many because of the large prominent growth rings seen when it is manufactured into rotary-cut veneers.

The wood is difficult to work with hand tools, but machines easily and glues well. It is a poor wood for painting and does not absorb preservatives. Its principal use is as the main wood for the manufacture of veneers for plywood construction.

FIR, GRAND *Abies grandis* (Abies —the classical Latin name of the European silver fir, *Abies alba*; grandis—large)

It is known also as GIANT FIR, YELLOW FIR, ROUGH-BARKED FIR and OREGON WHITE FIR.

This tree is found exclusively along the Pacific coast, from Vancouver well down into California, and eastward into the Rockies through Montana and Idaho. It has been called a stately tree because of its fine, straight trunk, tapering to a narrow crown. The tree needles are shiny, deep yellow-green on the top surface and

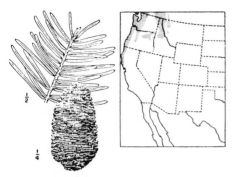

prominently white on the underside. The bark is of a brown color with splashes of gray-white and is deeply and closely furrowed.

As the wood is light in weight, soft but firm and almost white in color, with the absence of odor and stain, the wood is highly desirable for containers of all kinds, particularly food containers. The main use, however, is for paper pulp.

FUSTIC *Chlorophora tinctoria* (Chloro/phora—greenish yellow yielding; tinctoria—useful as a dye)

The wood is called MORA in Mexico and AMARILLO in Bolivia.

This tree grows in Central America and the West Indies, is a hard and heavy wood weighing around 50 lbs. per cubic foot, and is bright golden or greenish yellow in color.

Fustic is a durable wood and does not warp. It saws and planes well and is used for mill rollers and occasionally in cabinetwork. One of the chief values of this wood is the yellow dye it produces.

GABOON *Aucomea klaineana* (Aucomea—possibly after the na-

tive "okoumé"; klaineana—after Klaine, a collector in west Africa)

This tree is known also as ANGOUMA, GABOON WOOD, OKOUMÉ and ONGOUMI.

It is found only in the French Congo, Gabon and Spanish Guiana. Gaboon grows to a large size and at times the diameter at the ground may run from 4 to 8 ft., but its growth is limited. It is light in weight, averaging 25 lbs. to the cubic foot, and closely resembles African mahogany, at times being given the name of mahogany.

This wood seasons easily, with no tendency to damage, and in the solid form works well with both hand and machine tools. It takes a good finish and glues easily, and this is why it is particularly desired for the manufacture of plywood.

GEDU NOHOR *Entandrophragma angolense* (Ent/andro/phragma— within the male membrane; angolense—from Angola)

This tree also has the names ABENBEGNE, BUDONGO MAHOGANY, EDINAM, KALUNGI, TIAMA, TIMBI.

Botanically, it is a close relation to sapele, with the exception that the color is darker in appearance and with a less-pronounced stripe. Like sapele, it is also a large tree and the average weight is 35 lbs. per cubic foot.

This wood seasons easily but should never be used unless fully seasoned, or it is liable to warp. It has good strength value for its weight but is slightly inferior to African mahogany and sapele in this respect. It is easy to work with hand or machine tools and in all directions of the grain, taking an excellent polish if the grain is well filled.

It is used in veneering, general furniture manufacture and cabinetmaking, and a considerable quantity is used in shipbuilding.

GONÇALO ALVES *Astronium fraxinifolium* (Astronium—star; fraxinifolium—with leaves like ash, *Fraxinus*)

This wood has been sold in this country under the name BOSSONA, which was given to it by the late Albert Constantine, Sr.

Gonçalo alves is a wood with distinctive markings and belongs to the large group of over four hundred species of trees and shrubs scattered throughout the world belonging to the sumach family.

This is a hard, heavy, close-grained wood which takes a glass-like finish, and craftsmen may obtain striking effects in combining it for decorative purposes with other woods. Another use of this is for dampers in grand pianos.

GREENHEART *Ocotea rodiei* (Ocotea—a South American Indian plant name; rodiei—after Rodie, a French physician)

Greenheart comes from British Guiana and the West Indies and is a heavy, strong and hard wood, weighing approximately 65 lbs. per cubic foot. Its color varies from light olive-green to nearly black. As a rule, the logs have a straight grain and are unusually free of knots and defects. The sapwood is quite thick, but it cannot be distinguished from the heartwood. The grain is fine, and smooth, and has a feel of coldness to the touch.

Greenheart is very strong and is a close second to teak in resisting the white ant. Occasionally worms may attack the sapwood, but they do not penetrate into the heartwood.

An interesting fact about this wood is that unusual care has to be taken when it is being sawed. Immediately after the saw has entered the log and air is admitted, the entire log may split apart with considerable noise. In one known instance, part of the log flew upward, penetrating the roof of the sawmill. To prevent such accidents, it is customary to put a strong chain around the log immediately over the part that has passed the saw. These logs are usually long, from 20 to 60 ft., and are hewn square from 10 to 24 in.

Many people are susceptible to this wood. Those working with it must be very careful not to get any splinters, which will have a poisonous effect.

Most of this wood is used locally in the construction of docks, ships, flooring and piling, and for fishing rods. A fine sample of greenheart can be made into an exceedingly small top joint of a fishing rod which will bend to an unusual extent before breaking.

GUAMBO *Phoebe ambigens* (Phoebe—the Greek goddess of the moon, hence bright or radiant; ambi/gens—variable race)

This tree from Central America is very similar to the Brazilian imbuya. It is dark yellow-brown in color, lustrous, moderately heavy and so similar it may actually be the same wood. Also, the coarse texture and cross grain are very like those of imbuya.

Guanacaste, more generally known as kelobra.

GUANACASTE *Enterolobium cyclocarpum* (Entero/lobium—intestine lobe; cyclo/carpum—circle fruit, a reference to the twisted beanlike fruit)

This wood, emanating in Guatemala, British Honduras and Mexico, is known also as JENISERO, KELOBRA and PAROTA.

The color of the wood is brown with a greenish cast and sometimes streaked. It is of coarse texture and has a large figure with wavy lines. It is fairly scarce. Lumber is available, but generally it is manufactured into veneers on the quarter, producing some crotches and swirls. Guanacaste is used in furniture and cabinetmaking.

GUM, MURRAY RED *Eucalyptus camaldulensis* (Eu/calyptus—true cover; camaldulensis—probably after a place name, i.e. Camaldula)

This wood, from eastern Australia, is known also as LONG BEAK.

It is a heavy wood, about 52 lbs. per cubic foot, and renowned for its strength and resistance to fungus diseases. A great deal of it is used for wood paving.

GUM, SOUTHERN BLUE *Eucalyptus globulus* (globulus—globules)

Blue gum, growing in New South Wales, Tasmania and Victoria, has a life span of three hundred years and at full maturity reaches a height of up to 250 ft., with large diameters. It has been transplanted to other countries and is an ornamental tree in England, but it is very sensitive to cold weather and many die in severe temperatures. The tree is named after the pale blue color of the bark, which in no way is reflected in the color of the wood. The heartwood is a lovely light pinkish color. It is a heavy wood, averaging 48 to 52 lbs. per cubic foot.

Considerable care has to be taken in seasoning, otherwise

much distortion and splitting will result in great waste. It is strong and unusually resistant to fire.

The usual run of these trees is not particularly attractive, but an occasional tree has a high fiddle-back figure which is prized for furniture and cabinetwork. The leaves of this tree, and also those of other species of eucalyptus, contain a volatile oil which, after distillation, produces the oil of eucalyptus.

GUM, SPOTTED *Eucalyptus maculata* (maculata—spotted)

Spotted gum is one of the better-known trees growing along the coast of New South Wales and Queensland. The wood is a brown shade with tendencies to gray; the bark is whitish, smooth and mottled with various colored spots —perhaps the reason the tree is so named. It is coarse, somewhat like oak, and some of the lines have a particularly wavy figure, which is sought after for use in paneling.

Though care is required in seasoning the wood properly, it works easily but has a tendency occasionally to dull the teeth of the saw. As it is figured and light in color, it is sometimes used as a substitute for satinwood, though it is not as good.

In Australia, spotted gum is probably used in more varied types of work than any of the other eucalypt timbers. It is used in heavy construction and paneling of rooms and flooring, and is a favorite wood in the ship-building industry for framing, stem and sternposts and for planking beneath the water line. It is also often used for cabinetmaking and the manufacture of furniture.

HACKBERRY *Celtis occidentalis* (Celtis—the classical Latin name of a species of lotus; occidentalis —western)

This tree is known by several names, one of the most prominent being SUGARBERRY. It is known also as BASTARD ELM,

Hackberry is related to sugarberry and has similar uses.

HACK TREE, HOOP ASH and NET-
TLETREE.

It grows from southern Canada
throughout the eastern part of the
United States and is found in large
quantities in the lower Mississippi
Valley. For proper growth the tree
requires much moisture and a rich
soil. The tree is somewhat similar
to that of elm in appearance. It
reaches a height of 30 to 50 ft.
and the best specimens reach 130
ft.

The heartwood is light yellow;
it is a fairly soft, coarse-grained
wood and works well with any
type of tool. The lumber is generally sold along with ash and
elm, and it is much used in the
manufacture of farm implements.
Hackberry takes a very fine finish
and has an attractive appearance
when finished in the natural color.
Some of it is used in furniture and
cabinetwork and for other general
purposes similar to elm and ash.

HALDU *Adina cordifolia* (Adina
—crowded; cordi/folia—heart-
shaped leaves)

Emanating in Siam, this wood is
similar to wood of the same name
from the Himalayan regions of
India. It is a heavy wood, averaging around 45 lbs. per cubic
foot. In some sections of India the
tree is girdled, some time previous to felling, to decrease its
weight in handling.

The wood is bright yellow when
first cut and darkens with time to
an attractive reddish brown color.
It is straight-grained and in drying
no difficulties are encountered,
nor is there any trouble in working it with any type of tool.

Occasionally figured logs are
found and these are used for cabinetwork and interior paneling.

HAREWOOD, ENGLISH *Acer
pseudoplatanus* (Acer—the classical Latin name for maple; pseudo/
platanus—false *Platanus*, the sycamore in United States)

This tree, sometimes referred to
as SCOTCH PLANE, ENGLISH
SYCAMORE, or WEATHERED SYC-
AMORE, probably received the
latter name because the lumber
turns to a light brown color when
it seasons in the open instead of
remaining white.

This wood is not to be confused
with the original harewood tree
that grows in Santo Domingo and
is known as Pino Matcho, which
is yellowish and has a luster. The
Santo Domingo wood is not used
commercially and is practically extinct.

English harewood, or gray harewood, as we now know it, is one
of the products of the sycamores
of Western Europe and the British
Isles. It is white in color, similar
to the American maple. When
sold in this country in this form,
it is known as English sycamore.
In its natural form it is highly desired for its lovely white color,
and is particularly adaptable for
staining to any color desired. Outside of holly, this wood is the
nearest to white that can be obtained.

When this wood is dyed a silver-
gray color, it is sold under the
common name English gray harewood. It is interesting to note that
while many people in this and
other countries have attempted to
secure the silver-gray color, only
one firm located in London has
been successful in obtaining the
finest color and most permanent
results. The logs are first cut into
lumber or veneer and then placed
in large vats where the dye is
forced through the wood by hy-

English gray harewood with fiddleback figure.

draulic pressure. Generally it is used in the veneer form because of the high cost in lumber form.

The wood weighs approximately 37 to 42 lbs. per cubic foot and is a straight-grained timber which is easy to work, but difficulty is encountered when planing the highly figured logs. Particular care has to be given in the seasoning of the wood, not because of splitting or warping, but to prevent any staining or discoloration.

The wood is very much in demand for fine interiors and modernistic furniture, and the type of figure most desired is a strong fiddleback figure with straight grain.

HEMLOCK, EASTERN *Tsuga canadensis* (Tsuga—Japanese name for native hemlock; canadensis—of Canada)

Eastern hemlock ranges in size from 80 to 100 ft., though trees as high as 160 ft. have been recorded, with diameters of 4 to 6 ft.

The largest percentage of growth is in the northeastern states, but in the production of pulp, timber

and tannin, Michigan now leads. It is also the state tree of Pennsylvania.

In Canada, eastern hemlock is the chief supply of material for their tanning industries. It supplies pulp for various types of paper and it is estimated that over 13 billion feet of eastern hemlock are still standing.

HEMLOCK, WESTERN *Tsuga heterophylla* (hetero/phylla—various leaved)

It is known also as ALASKA PINE, HEMLOCK SPRUCE and PACIFIC HEMLOCK.

This is one of the important

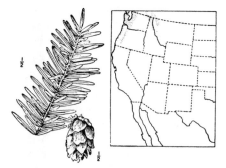

HICKORY *Carya ovata* (Carya—classical Greek for nut; ovata—egg-shaped, referring to the nut)

There are some sixteen species and twenty varieties of hickory in North America, and the largest stands of true hickories are located in the lower Mississippi Valley region. True hickories include such trees as shagbark hickory, shellbark hickory, pignut hickory and mockernut hickory. Of these,

trees in the Northwest. It grows along the coastline from Alaska to central California and eastward through Idaho and Montana at fairly low mountainous altitudes. Of the ten species of hemlock, this is the largest and reaches its greatest growth in the extreme northwestern portions of Oregon and Washington. It is the state tree of Washington. The most extensive growth is in Alaska, estimated as much as 63 billion board feet, and somewhere around twice this quantity in the United States.

Western hemlock differs from eastern hemlock in that the wood is of very fine texture, light in weight and straight in grain, and has about the same workability as pine. It has a thick bark, 1½ in., is dark reddish brown and deeply marked. The needles are under an inch in length, flat, narrow, grooved and rounded on the end, like the eastern species. The small cones are twice the size of the eastern species.

Western hemlock is used for the making of quality paper, the largest output of the wood going into newsprint, and in the lumber form for all types of general manufacture. Practically all the commercial lumbering is confined to the ⌐states of Washington and Oregon.

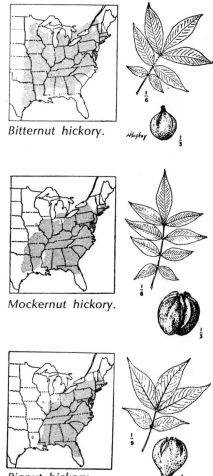

Bitternut hickory.

Mockernut hickory.

Pignut hickory.

Top left: Western hemlock. Top right: Eastern hemlock. Bottom left: Shagbark hickory. Bottom right: Bluegum, member of the eucalyptus family, 110 years old, stands 105 feet tall, measures 8 feet in diameter.

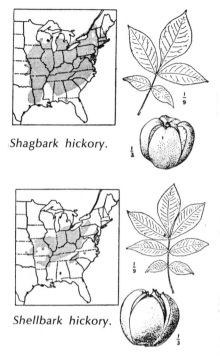

Shagbark hickory.

Shellbark hickory.

avoid checking, warping and other seasoning defects. Under magnification, the end grain shows numerous white lines paralleling the growth ring. Nearly 80 percent of the true hickory goes into tool handles, for which its qualities make it especially suitable. Other uses include agricultural implements, athletic goods and lawn furniture.

HINOKI *Chamaecyparis obtusa* (Chamaecyparis—from the Greek name for ground-cypress, a dwarf shrubby member of the sunflower family which resembles a dwarf cypress; obtusa—blunt)

This is one of the most highly prized woods in Japan and is one of the five royal trees which were reserved for imperial and religious uses in ancient times. The palaces of the Mikado and the temples were built of hinoki.

This wood is of a pale yellow straw color with wavy marks caused by intermittent darker streaks. It weighs approximately 22 to 25 lbs. per cubic foot, has a fragrant, agreeable scent and a lustrous sheen. Hinoki is used for the finest interior work and for buildings.

Hinoki also comes from Formosa, but this timber differs from the Japanese species, being of a bright yellow-brown, resembling somewhat the baldcypress of the United States, and is harder and heavier, and has a more marked grain than Japanese hinoki. Its strong, aromatic scent is not as pleasant as that of the Japanese wood.

HOLLY, AMERICAN *Ilex opaca* (Ilex—the classical Latin name of *Quercus ilex*, holly oak of Europe,

the most important commercially is the shagbark (*Carya ovata*). This species grows in the northeastern United States to southwest Mexico. It is light cream in color, extremely tough and resilient, though quite hard and unusually heavy. It is used in veneers, skis, molding and bent plywood, which requires extreme strength.

The heartwood of the true hickory is brown to reddish brown and the wood is very hard and heavy, averaging from 42 to 52 lbs. per cubic foot. Some woods are stronger than hickory and others are harder, but the combination of strength, toughness, hardness and stiffness possessed by hickory has not been found to the same degree in any commercial wood.

Hickory has a very large shrinkage and must be carefully dried to

which has hollylike leaves; opaca —dark, in reference to the dull green foliage)

About 175 species of holly are dispersed in various parts of the world, the largest number occurring in Guiana and Brazil. The largest trees are found in southern Arkansas and eastern Texas, while the holly growing in the New England states is always very small. Holly varies in size from small, straggly bushes to well-formed trees 50 or 60 ft. high and 2 to 3 ft. in diameter. It is the state tree of Delaware.

The wood of holly is white, light in weight and has almost a total absence of any figure, no matter which way the wood is

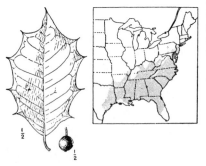

worked. There is only a small quantity of holly cut into veneers and lumber each year. It must be cut in the winter and manufactured before the hot weather, or else it discolors and then the pure white color is not obtained. It approaches ivory color more closely than any other American wood.

The principal value of holly is not in its wood but in the leaves and berries. The gathering of holly leaves and berries is an industry of much importance, and along the eastern coast of Maryland there are annually over ten thousand persons engaged in securing branches for manufacture into sprays and wreaths.

The American holly, which is always thought of for decoration during the holidays, can be described as one that wears its decorations the year round. Its broad leaves, unlike other native American evergreens, with their needlelike leaves, always make an outstanding appearance.

The fruit of this tree is food for the wild turkey and other birds, as well as deer. The seeds are small, over thirty thousand to a pound, and widely distributed through the forest by the birds. The seeds of holly are a long time in germinating and lie buried in the soil until the second year. Anyone who plants them without knowing this may despair too soon. The trees are widely scattered and never found growing together.

The wood is used for inlay work, on small musical instruments and as keys for pianos and organs, and brush-back manufacturers use it for their choicest brushes. Engravers also find it suitable for various classes of work. It is occasionally worked into small articles of furniture, but probably never is used on large pieces.

HOPHORNBEAM, EASTERN *Ostrya virginiana* (Ostrya—Latinized form of the Greek *ostrua*, a tree with very hard wood)

Growing in Indiana, this species originally came from Great Britain and continental Europe. It is known also as IRONWOOD in several states of this country and in Ontario.

It is yellowish white in color, close-grained, hard, tough and strong, weighing about 51 lbs. per

American holly. This is a fine specimen of the tree that yields wood nearly as white as ivory; in scarce supply.

cubic foot. Engineers make use of this wood for cogs in machinery and agricultural implements.

HORNBEAM, EUROPEAN *Carpinus betulus* (Carpinus—classical Latin name; betulus—similar to birch, betula, in reference to the leaves)

It is known also as IRONWOOD.

This medium sized tree, from 40 to 65 ft. in height and with diameters averaging from 20 to 24 in., grows in Europe and Canada. The heartwood is white with an occasional yellow or greenish tinge. It is of fine, uniform texture, about the weight of oak, and is considered one of the hardest woods growing in England. Because of the texture and hardness, it is considered superior to beech. At times in Europe it is stained black and used as a substitute for ebony in fancy articles and the backs of brushes.

Hornbeam is a very difficult wood to work, except when turned on the lathe, but when thoroughly dried it will take a fine finish. It is a favorite wood with manufacturers of wooden bench screws, tool handles and mallets, where great strength is required. Occasionally it is manufactured into veneers.

IDIGBO *Terminalia ivorensis* (Terminalia—border or terminus; ivorensis—from the Ivory Coast)

This is a large tree of 100 ft. or more in height and from 3 to 5 ft. in diameter, growing on the west coast of Africa—the Ivory Coast, Gold Coast and Nigeria. The heartwood is pale yellow with darker colored pores. It is of average weight, around 35 lbs. per cubic foot, and has a tendency to split badly in seasoning unless proper care is given. However, after seasoning it is a stable wood and easy to work with.

Logs have been cut into rotary veneer for the manufacture of plywood, and figured logs are sliced on the quarter to develop wood suitable for interior paneling.

IMBUYA *Phoebe porosa* (Phoebe —the Greek goddess of the moon, hence, bright; porosa—porous)

This wood is known also as BRAZILIAN WALNUT, CANELLA and IMBUIA.

This is a fairly fine-textured wood, growing in Brazil, and it weighs from 42 to 46 lbs. per cubic foot. The heartwood is yellowish or olive to chocolate-brown, either plain or beautifully corrugated and figured.

When properly seasoned, the wood stays in place and is considered durable. Imbuya has a spicy, resinous scent and taste, most of which is lost in drying. In sawing this timber, the fine dust which arises is particularly irritating to some and can cause sneezing.

In Sao Paulo in Brazil, imbuya is considered one of the most important woods and is used for high-grade flooring, furniture, interior trim and fixtures. It has a medium luster, is easy to work with and will take a high polish. However, exports have not been too large, as the local demand for the lumber has been about equal to the supply.

INDIAN SILVER GREY-WOOD *Terminalia bialata* (Terminalia— border or terminus; bi/alata—

East Indian laurel, figured. Known also as India walnut.

two-winged, probably in reference to the fruit)

Originating in the Andaman Islands, this timber is sold in various wood markets of the world as DERDA, INDIA WALNUT, INDIAWOOD and IXORA.

An unusual feature of this tree is that it produces two different kinds of wood in color. One is of yellow straw color with variegated dark-colored streaks, which is generally marketed as white chuglam; and the other is considerably darker in color and is sold as Indian silver greywood. It is one of the largest trees growing in that area, 140 ft. or more in height, with a diameter of 3 ft.

The wood is medium heavy, averaging a little over 40 lbs. per cubic foot, has a medium texture, and is strong, although in working it there is a tendency to split. A large majority of the wood is manufactured into veneers, in which form this difficulty is not of importance. The wood takes a very high and lovely finish. It is used in high-class cabinetmaking and decorative work.

IPÉ *Tabebuia avellanedae* (Tabebuia—after a native Brazilian plant name; avellanedae—drab); often called PAU D'ARCO.

Growing in the forests of Brazil, the tree presents a beautiful appearance. It is one of the tallest trees of the Amazon region, reaching a height of 170 to 200 ft. The wood is plentiful throughout Brazil. Logs are available as long as 100 ft. and the weight per cubic foot is 70 lbs.

Ipé has a lustrous brown color, occasionally with a greenish tinge, resembling a dark greenheart but with a much closer and finer grain. Occasionally logs are highly figured with a small mottle and broken roe, and the veneers obtained from these logs are similar to a dark golden-brown Ceylon satinwood. High-grade veneers are produced from these logs both in America and Europe.

IPIL *Intsia bijuga* (Intsia—a native name in Madagascar; bi/juga—two pairs, probably in reference to the leaflets)

Striped iroko with mottle figure.

In England it is known as BOR-
NEO TEAK, though it has none of
the qualities of teak.

Ipil grows in the Philippines. It
is a heavy wood, averaging 61
lbs. per cubic foot, and hard—
sometimes being considered one
of the ironwoods. The color is a
warm brown. With the passage of
time and exposure, this color
darkens to black.

IROKO *Chlorophora excelsa*
(Chloro / phora—yellow-green
bearing or yielding; excelsa—high
or distinguished)

Iroko, originating on the west
coast of Africa, is also known as
AFRICAN or NIGERIAN TEAK (although in no way related to the
teak family), MVULE, ODOUM,
OROKO, IREME and FRAMERE.

The tree is large in size and it
is not unusual to have logs up to
5 ft., but the average size is generally around 30 in. The color
varies from a light brown to a
rich golden brown. The wood is
heavy, 40 lbs. to the cubic foot,
not as strong as teak but often
used as an alternative. The heartwood has unusual natural durability.

The wood is not difficult to
work with and does not have the
effect of dulling tools as quickly
as when working with genuine
teak, except when the logs have
a defect known as "stone." When
quartered, the wood looks somewhat like teak and is used for
furniture and architectural panels.

IRONWOODS

OVER A PERIOD of many years,
seldom a week or a month has
passed in which some visitor to
my office has not brought up, as
one of the topics of conversation, the ironwood that grows in
his particular state or country; also
in letters there is often the mention of ironwood. This interest is
confined not only to the United
States but also is displayed by overseas visitors and correspondence.

From this personal experience we are led to believe that the common name "ironwood" is not given by individuals to any single species of wood but is generally applied to whatever wood in any particular section of the country is considered the densest and the hardest—in the absence of any knowledge of what the wood actually is.

There are, in fact, over eighty distinct botanical species of wood which are listed in various parts of the world and referred to as ironwoods. In the alphabetic description of woods in this book, the following woods are referred to as ironwoods:

Billian
Hophornbeam, Eastern
Hornbeam, European
Ipil
Mesua
Pau d'Arco
Pau Ferro
Pyinkado
Quebracho

Other woods referred to as ironwoods have not been described in this text because of the lack of general interest. A few of them are: American hornbeam or blue beech, referred to as ironwood in a few New England states; honey mesquite, known as ironwood in Texas; red ironwood in Queensland, also known as Cooktown ironwood; leguminous iron bark; and gangaw (*Mesuaferrea*), which is native to India, Burma, Ceylon and the Andaman Islands, and also called locally Indian rosechestnut and ironwood.

IVORY, PINK *Rhamnus zeyheri* (Rhamnus—the old Greek name; zeyheri—after Zeyheri)

This wood is often said to be rarer than diamonds and it is almost impossible to obtain. It is the royal wood of the Zulus and may be cut only by the chief of the tribe and his sons. When a chief's son is able to fell a tree and fashion a spear from the wood, he is considered to have reached manhood. Any other member of the tribe who cuts or possesses the wood is subject to death.

It is a medium-sized tree, from 20 to 40 ft. high, with diameters from 7 to 12 in., growing very occasionally on rocky soils in Rhodesia, Transvaal and Natal.

The tree produces small black berries, in appearance resembling those on the buckthorn tree. The wood is extremely heavy and of very fine texture and rich color, though with little figure.

Pink ivory works very easily, takes a fine polish, and is an excellent wood for special turnings. Very attractive pieces of jewelry can be fashioned by those few who have been fortunate enough to obtain a piece of this wood. Since it is so scarce, it is more a museum piece than an article of commerce.

IVORYWOOD *Balfourodendron riedelianum* (Balfouro/dendron—Balfour's tree; riedelianum—after Riedel)

Ivorywood grows in Brazil and has a close, compact grain, displaying a smooth surface resembling ivory, which no doubt is the reason for its name. It weighs from 47 to 52 lbs. per cubic foot and is of a light yellow color with a greenish tinge. It is a rare wood, highly esteemed in Argentina, but not generally commercially used.

JARRAH, CURLY *Eucalyptus marginata* (Eu/calyptus—true cover; marginata—enclosed with a border)

Curly jarrah grows in western Australia and is considered one of the most valuable native woods. It is found in greater profusion than practically any of the other important commercial trees. Diameters as large as 6 ft. are encountered, and heights of 120 ft. or more.

Fairly heavy—averaging around 50 lbs. per cubic foot—the wood is hard and often has a wavy grain. It is of a rich red color, which darkens with exposure, resembling old American mahogany. A great deal of care is required in seasoning, since the wood is subject to a large amount of shrinkage and will if not handled carefully. Where a large amount of curly figure is prominent, it produces some difficulties in working. It is used for carving, furniture and interior work. Quantities of the curly logs are cut into veneers.

JĔLUTONG *Dyera costulata* (Dyera—after W. T. Thistleton Dyer, English botanist; costulata—with small ribs, probably in reference to the ribbed leaves)

Coming from Malaya, this tree often grows higher than 200 ft. and has a diameter of 5 and 6 ft. It is a fairly light wood, averaging about 30 lbs. per cubic foot, and of soft but firm texture. The wood has a very plain appearance, is off-white in color when first manufactured, with no difference between the sapwood and heartwood, but after exposure to the air it has a yellowish tint.

The main value of this wood is in the latex, the greatest portion of which is used in the manufacture of chewing gum. Also, jĕlutong is used in the making of plywood boxes and cores for plywood. Little if any of the timber is exported.

JONGKONG *Dactylocladus stenostachys* (Dactylo/cladus—finger twig; steno/stachys—narrow spike, e.g., of grain)

Jongkong grows in Borneo, has a cubic weight per foot of about 33 lbs. and is pink in color. It is a particularly interesting wood, as it has the same figure as our bird's-eye maple.

THE JUNIPERS

THE FOUR leading species of juniper trees are similar in that none of them produce any large quantities of usable lumber. The lumber is used for lead-pencil stocks, the making of novelties and, locally, for fence posts and fuel. The four junipers and their leading characteristics follow.

JUNIPER, ALLIGATOR *Juniperus deppeana* (Juniperus—the classical Latin name; deppeana—in

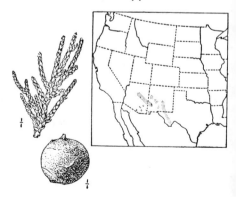

honor of Ferdinand Deppe, d. 1861, German botanist)

This tree also is called CHECK-ERED-BARKED JUNIPER, MOUNTAIN CEDAR and OAK-BARKED CEDAR.

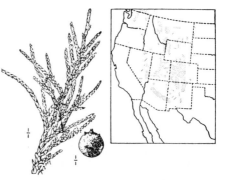

It is native to the deserts in southern New Mexico and Arizona and to southwestern Texas, growing in the higher mountainous elevations from 4,000 to 10,000 ft.

Alligator juniper has a short, large trunk from 2 to 4 ft. in diameter and is different from the other junipers. It has a dark, red-brown bark that varies from 1 to 3 in. thick and is marked in a checkered pattern, resembling alligator hide.

Local Indians use the dry berries to grind into a flour which is used in the preparation of cakes.

JUNIPER, CALIFORNIA *Juniperus californica* (californica—of California)

This wood is known also as CEDAR, BERRIED-CEDAR, JUNIPER and WHITE CEDAR.

California juniper is close to the western juniper and at times it is almost impossible to distinguish it. However, this species is more of a broad, round-top shrub with heavy, odd-shaped branches.

JUNIPER, ROCKY MOUNTAIN *Juniperus scopulorum* (scopulorum —of rocky cliffs or crags)

This juniper is known also as COLORADO JUNIPER, RED CEDAR, ROCKY MT. RED CEDAR and WESTERN JUNIPER.

It is found in the higher mountain regions of western Canada, southward to Oregon and Ari-

zona. It is not quite as tall as the alligator juniper, ranging in height from 20 to 35 ft. It is one of the most desirable woods for use in the manufacture of novelties, because of its beautiful color and the closeness of the grain.

JUNIPER, WESTERN *Juniperus occidentalis* (occidentalis—western)

This juniper often is called SIERRA JUNIPER, WESTERN RED CEDAR and YELLOW CEDAR.

It is native to the Pacific coast through the states of Washington and Oregon. It grows on rocky soil and canyon sides, in elevations up to 10,000 ft. The berries of this tree mature in two years, are blue-black in color, small in size, about ¼ in. in diameter and have a tough skin. They have a strong, aromatic odor, sweet to the taste, and are appreciated by both the Indians and the birds.

KABUKALLI *Goupia glabra* (Goupia—after one of the native Guiana names, goupi; glabra—hairless, smooth)

In Brazil and British Guiana, where this wood grows, it is known as CUPIUBA and KABU-KALLI, respectively.

It is a large tree, reaching a height of from 100 to 130 ft., with a comparatively slender trunk (up to 3 ft. in diameter) and branches up to 60 ft. The wood is of a light reddish color which, when aged, loses some of its reddishness and turns more to brown. When freshly cut, it has a very strong, penetrating odor, which is noticeable for quite a distance. Both the odor and the disagreeable taste of the wood diminish with age, though the odor is never entirely absent from the dried wood.

A heavy wood, averaging around 50 lbs. per cubic foot, it is used in Brazil and British Guiana for naval construction and wooden buildings. Native tribes use it in the manufacture of canoes. Until recently, this wood was not exported in any large quantities for commercial use.

KATON *Sandoricum indicum* (Sandoricum—after a Malayan plant name; indicum—of India)

This tree grows in Thailand, where it is known as KAPON, and in Burma, where it is known as THITTO.

It is an evergreen, found in the forests, generally 60 ft. in height. The wood varies considerably in color, the sapwood ranging from a yellowish to a pink color and the heartwood from a grayish brown to a red resembling mahogany. It is a fairly light wood, 30 to 40 lbs. per cubic foot, of medium texture and generally showing a well-defined stripe.

Katon seasons easily and works with little difficulty. It finishes smoothly and takes a high polish. In the East, where it grows, its main use is for boat building, but it is also a most suitable wood for cabinetwork and furniture making.

KAURI, FIJI *Agathis vitiensis* (Agathis—a ball of thread; vitiensis—from Fiji)

This wood grows in the Fiji Islands, where its native name is NDAKUA NAKANDRE.

It is found in the heavy rain forests on the islands of Vanua Levu and Vanikoro, usually on hillsides from 1,500 to 3,000 ft. above sea level, but it does grow in lower and higher altitudes than these. The wood can be classified as one of the more valuable softwoods. It has a pale yellowish sapwood with a heartwood slightly darker, and it is difficult to tell where one merges into the other. It is a close, even-textured wood of average hardness.

Kauri contains a valuable resin. When it is collected, a great many trees of this species are ruined. A large rectangular piece of the bark is removed, 2 to 3 ft. in size, and this area is warmed by a fire close to the trunk, below the scar, so as to hasten the flow of the resin. Because of this injury the tree frequently dies.

The wood is easy to work with and is used in the manufacture of furniture, high-class joinery work and boat building. It also makes good veneers.

KAURI, NEW ZEALAND *Agathis australis* (australis—southern)

This wood, found only in New Zealand, weighs from 30 to 39 lbs. per cubic foot and has lightness and elasticity. It has a pleasant and agreeable odor when worked and has been found to be more durable than pine, one of its uses being for the masts of boats.

Forest of giant kauri trees, New Zealand's best native softwood.

Coffeebean wood has porous texture, conspicuous annual ring markings which show as brownish red striping, and light yellowish brown sapwood. Comes from Kentucky coffeetree.

KENTUCKY COFFEETREE *Gymnocladus dioicus* (Gymno/cladus— naked branch; dioicus—male and female flowers on separate trees)

This tree also is known as AMERICAN COFFEEBEAN, CHICOT or "DEAD TREE," COFFEE NUT, KENTUCKY MAHOGANY, MAHOGANY BEAN and STUMP-TREE.

Kentucky coffeetree grows in western New York, as far west as South Dakota and Oklahoma, and southward to Tennessee. The roasted seeds of this tree were long used by early settlers of the country as a substitute for coffee, which explains its name.

The tree is not very attractive. The wood is rather heavy and coarse-grained, with the color varying from a light brown to a reddish brown. It blooms late in spring and the leaves are the first to drop off in fall, which is the reason for the name chicot. It is a durable wood and used a great deal for railroad ties and fence posts.

Western juniper.   *Kentucky coffeetree.*

Kingwood.

KINGWOOD *Dalbergia cearensis* (Dalbergia—after N. Dalberg, 1735–1820, Swedish physician; cearensis—of Ceara, a state of Brazil)

Emanating from South America, this small tree is known also as VIOLETE.

It weighs about 75 lbs. per cubic foot and is exported in the form of logs from 3 to 6 ft. long, in diameters from 4 to 8 in., with the sapwood removed.

Kingwood is of a rich, violet-brown color, shading at times almost to black, and streaked with varying lighter and darker lines of golden yellow. It has a bright luster, fine, uniform texture, and very smooth surface, and stays in place with little expansion. An unusually high polish can be obtained. While this is a beautiful cabinet wood when first used, it becomes more so as it is toned with age, the wood seeming to have a transparent surface and metallic sheen. Examples of this fine wood can be seen in furniture of French

manufacture. It is well named, for it is truly the wood of kings.

It is generally manufactured into veneers by cutting it across the heart and used in the manufacture of fine marquetry work and occasionally in lumber form for articles of turnery. However, its exportation is very limited, and it is quite scarce in the general market. When available, it is generally in the veneer form.

KOA *Acacia koa* (Acacia—the classical Greek name of a thorny Egyptian tree; koa—the native name)

Emanating only from the Hawaiian Islands, koa grows from sea level and moist soil to the top of volcanic mountains. It is from these high, exposed places that the best figured wood is obtained.

Some of the early history of this wood in its native country can be seen in the naming of this tree, which in Hawaiian is koa-ka—koa meaning soldier, bold and valiant;

Old koa trees on the Island of Hawaii.

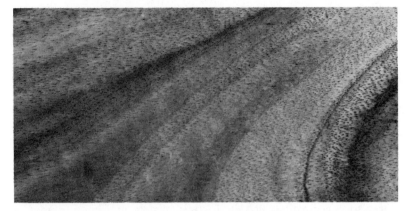

Koa wood, native of Hawaii, is used for ukelele cases. Portion of koa crotch, top specimen, is a lustrous rainbow in shades of brown. Bottom specimen shows fiddleback figure.

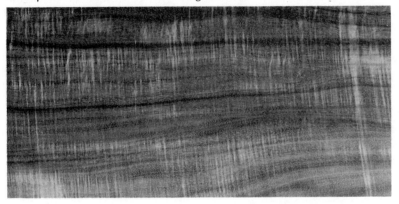

ka meaning irregular in habit. The first part of the name probably originated from the fact that in early times the Hawaiians, renowned for their seafaring abilities, used these large trees for making dugout canoes in which they made sea trips of great distances. Ka doubtless comes from the fact that this tree can adapt itself to a wide variety of climates and soil conditions.

Koa wood is excellent for musical instruments, as it has high resonant qualities. The world-famous Hawaiian ukeleles are always made of koa wood. Also, because of the fiddleback figure and the fine finish it takes, it is an ideal wood, particularly in the veneer form, for making fine furniture.

KOKKO *Albizzia lebbeck* (Albizzia, after Filippo del Albizzia, eighteenth-century Italian naturalist; lebbeck—the Arabic common name)

Kokko is common throughout Ceylon and in the Andaman Islands, and in the latter country is the principal wood used in the workshops of the convicts. The wood is a deep brown with a stripe effect and unusually large pores. Kokko, or coco, as it is also known, has not been used in this country in any large quantities, in comparison with other fancy woods.

KUROKAI *Protium decandrum* (Protium—after the sea god Proteus; dec/andrum—ten stamens)

It also is known as INCENSE TREE.

This species of wood is found throughout the dense forests of British Guiana and in forests along the Amazon River, and grows with a long, slender trunk often as high as 50 ft., the total height of the tree at times being 90 ft., with an average diameter of 20 in. The heartwood is pinkish brown in color with variegated darker lines at irregular intervals. It is a mod-

erately hard wood, though fairly light, weighing about 35 lbs. per cubic foot.

The wood requires care during the drying period in order to avoid defects, but it works well after being dried.

Considerable quantities of odorous, pale-colored resin or balsam is found in the bark, and this the natives use in medicines and in producing incense, hence the name incense tree.

The wood from British Guiana is similar to the lighter grades of crabwood with the exception that the surface is brighter in color. Locally it is used for the manufacture of furniture, taking a good polish after a careful filling of the pores.

LACEWOOD *Cardwellia sublimis* (Cardwellia—after Cardwell; sublimis—uplifted, exalted)

Lacewood, growing throughout

Lacewood, quartered. Also known as silky oak. Light pink to light reddish brown with silvery sheen. Flaky, speckled figure. Dark flecks in illustrated sample measure from 1/16 to 1/4 inch. Some sycamore and planetree veneers have similar flecking.

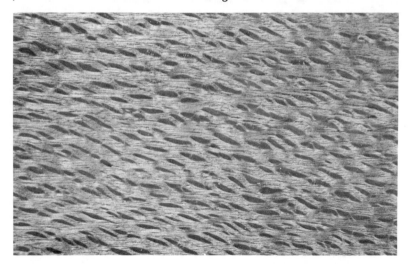

Australia and Europe, is marketed in this country also as SILKY OAK and SELENA.

The logs vary in color from what might be called a shell pink to a light reddish brown and they have a striking figure, varying from a small lacelike pattern to a large splashlike figure.

Locally it has been used for years in panels and trim work of fine residences and banks, for railings, doors and the like. It is a good wood for many types of cabinetwork where a striking and unusual appearance is desired.

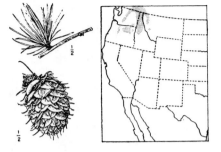

LARCH, EUROPEAN *Larix decidua* (Larix—the classical name of this species; decidua—deciduous, pertaining to the leaves which fall in the autumn)

This species is obtained principally from the Alps and Carpathian Mountains, growing in high altitudes, up as far as the tree line. It is a tall, graceful evergreen, at times reaching a height of 140 ft. and more, though generally averaging 80 to 90 ft., with diameters up to 3 ft.

The heartwood is reddish or brownish, averaging around 35 lbs. per cubic foot. In drying, it requires care so as to prevent the resin content from proving troublesome in working. It is one of the most valuable softwoods used in the United Kingdom and has been used for the planking of boats below the water line, for posts and other outdoor work.

LARCH, WESTERN *Larix occidentalis* (occidentalis—western)

The western larch grows from Montana through northern Idaho, Washington, Oregon, and south-eastern British Columbia. This species is similar to the eastern larch, in that it sheds its needles every fall, but generally it grows on slopes and elevations from 2,000 to 7,000 ft., whereas the eastern larch grows in swamps and lowlands.

The bark is a dull reddish brown and of conspicuous appearance, and a galactan gum is extracted from the wood, some of which is used commercially. The wood closely resembles the Douglas fir, but it is not used for veneers, as it is far inferior in quality. It is rather difficult to work this wood with tools and it does not hold paint, but it can have a natural or stained finish.

Western larch is mostly used for the cheaper grades of furniture, boxes, various kinds of poles, railroad ties and posts, and in the manufacture of fiberboard and craft wrapping paper.

LAUREL, CALIFORNIA *Umbellularia californica* (Umbellularia—refers to the umbrella-shaped flower clusters; californica—of California)

Other names of this tree are ACACIA BURL, CALIFORNIA OLIVE, MYRTLE, MOUNTAIN LAUREL, PEPPERWOOD and SPICE TREE.

California laurel produces highly-prized veneer burl known as myrtle burl.

This tree grows on the West Coast of the United States, especially in southern Oregon and northern California. The most beautiful for varied types of figure and coloring is found in Oregon. A rich golden brown and yellowish green in color, the wood has a wide range from light to dark shades and there is a mixture of plain wood, mottle and cluster burls. It produces a stump and burl figure also, with a scattering of dark purple blotches.

Great care is necessary in the seasoning of the green wood, as it will check and warp if not properly handled. However, it is a hard and strong wood, and the burls from Oregon are favored, in the veneer form, by cabinetmakers.

California laurel is an evergreen and is distinguished from others by a strong, aromatic odor when the leaves are crushed. The leaves have been used as a substitute for bay leaves in flavoring meats and soups.

Magnificent, highly figured veneers may be obtained from this wood, and they will take an excellent polish for use in decorative panels and fine furniture. Wood turners also prize this wood for turning bowls, candlesticks and other items.

LEADTREE, GREAT *Leucaena pulverulenta* (Leucaena—to whiten, as the flowers; pulverulenta—powdered, referring to the dusty-appearing foliage)

This tree is found generally in the southern part of Texas and in northern Mexico and has many of the characteristics of black locust, with the exception that it is considerably softer in texture.

Great leadtree is noted for its flowers, which bloom from early spring until summer. They have delicate colors—shades of red and purple—and a fragrant odor. This, combined with the lacylike pale, light-green foliage, makes it valuable for ornamental purposes. Locally some lumber is produced, but it is not generally offered in the market.

LEMONWOOD *Calycophyllum candidissimum* (Calyco/phyllum —cup/leaf; candidissimum—very bright white)

It also is known as DEGAME SPARS and LANCEWOOD, but is in no way related to the American lemon tree.

This is a small to medium-sized tree, from 40 to 65 ft. high and 8 to 20 in. in diameter, growing in Cuba and from southern Mexico through Central America to Colombia and Venezuela. In bloom it is beautiful and conspicuous because of the large white calyx lobes. The heartwood is brownish, not sharply demarcated from the thick and nearly colorless sapwood; it has a low luster and is of fine, uniform texture.

Lemonwood is similar in strength, toughness and resilience to hickory. It is without any distinctive odor or taste and is difficult to work. It does not split easily and is not resistant to decay, but holds its place well when manufactured and takes a high, glossy polish.

Locally the wood is used in making agricultural implements, tool handles, various articles of turnery and frames of buildings. Practically all of the timber exported comes from Cuba and in this country its principal use is in the manufacture of bows by the archery trade.

LIGNUM VITAE *Guaiacum officinale* (Guaiacum—from the Carib Indian name; officinale—pertaining to drugs; gum guaiac, derived from this species is a drug)

Lignum vitae is native to the West Indies, the northern coast of South America and the western coast of Central America. The average size of the logs produced ranges from 4 to 6 ft. in length and from 4 to 24 in. in diameter. The heartwood is of a greenish black color, and upon being exposed to light and air, grows darker. It is the hardest, heaviest and closest-grained wood known and has a density almost equal to iron. The weight is about 83 lbs. per cubic foot with a specific gravity of 1.3. The high resin content of lignum vitae, which runs about 30 percent of its weight, consists of a natural gum, which combined with its pressure-resisting quality, renders this wood admirably suited for an increasing number of mechanical purposes where the introduction of lubrication is not practical or reliable. Originally it was supposed to contain marvelous medicinal qualities, but little is now used in medicine.

As lignum vitae has the ability to withstand the great working

pressure of 2,000 lbs. per square inch and has resistance to the action of many mild chemicals and acids, it has a limitless variety of uses. Lignum vitae bearings are used in various applications and equipment such as clocks, dishwashing machines, exhaust fans, air-conditioning units and underwater in marine equipment. It is used as rollers for awnings, elevator gates, dryer equipment, and moving heavy boxes weighing two to four tons. A few of the miscellaneous uses of lignum vitae are die-cutting blocks, lemon-squeezer cups, drainboards for

chemicals, thrust blocks for propeller shafts, guides for cables and band saws, the construction of acid tanks, mallets of all kinds, thrust bearings for outboard motors, and washers for rotating sprinklers, wheels and casters. The wood turns very well. For drilling, ordinary high-speed twist drills should be used, as carpenters' auger bits are not suitable. Holes may be tapped successfully by hand, but external threads are difficult to cut and should be avoided if possible.

Applications of lignum vitae can be found in almost every industry and range from tiny rollers for Venetian blinds to propeller-shaft bearings in the largest liners.

LIMBA *Terminalia superba* (Terminalia—border or terminus; superba—highest, superb)

Limba, emanating from west Africa, also is known as AFARA, FRAKE, KORINA and OFFRAM.

It is a large tree, with wood of a pale yellow to light brown color and of medium texture and hardness. There may be some tend-

Straight-stripe limba.

A valuable stand of handsome black locust with feathery crowns, graceful pinnate leaves and deep-furrowed orange-brown bark.

ency to split if the lumber is nailed, but the wood stains and takes a good polish. Limba produces good, clean timber which is suitable for architectural paneling and general woodworking.

LOCUST, BLACK *Robinia pseudo-acacia* (Robinia—in honor of Jean Robin, 1550–1629, herbalist to kings of France; pseudo/acacia—false *Acacia*)

It is known by a number of names in various states, such as ACACIA, FALSE ACACIA, HONEY LOCUST, PEA FLOWER and WHITE LOCUST. In Great Britain it is often known as ROBINIA and acacia, though it does not belong to the true family of acacias.

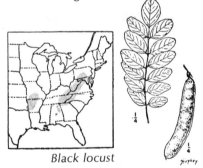

Black locust

Black locust, the most prevalent and valuable of the five species of locust found in this country, also grows in the eastern and southeastern part of Canada. It is a small tree with very rough and furrowed bark of an orange-brown color. Black locust is desired for conservation purposes, as it is an excellent tree for providing a

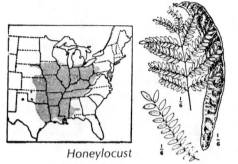

Honeylocust

windbreak and preventing soil erosion.

The wood is very hard, heavy, stiff and strong, and because of its durability when exposed to the ground, locust posts are most highly prized. However, it is a very rapid-growing, short-lived tree which succumbs to the locust-borer insect. While it is easily worked by machine tools, it is difficult to work with hand tools, but will take a good finish.

LOLAGBOLA *Pterygopodium oxy-phyllum* (Pterygo/podium—winged-foot; oxy/phyllum—sour leaf)

This large, well-shaped tree is found in the equatorial forests of Africa, which includes the Belgian, Portuguese, French and British territories. It varies in height from 45 to 55 ft., with an average diameter of 30 in., and has a straight trunk. One of the unusual characteristics of the wood is that old trees often shed their bark in long strips. The heartwood is an attractive brown color, striped with reddish lines when cut on the quarter. Sometimes a cross figure is found. After the trees are cut, very rapid removal from the forest and early manufacture into lumber or veneers are necessary,

as the logs are subject to attack by pinhole borers and other defects.

Lolagbola weighs about 35 lbs. per cubic foot when dried and is fairly soft in texture, and the large amount of resin the wood contains does not cause serious dulling of cutting edges during manufacture. The lumber works well, and logs are regularly sent to South Africa, where they are manufactured into veneers for plywood.

LOVOA *Lovoa klaineana* (Lovoa —after the Lovo River; klaineana —after Klaine, a collector in west Africa)

In the United States this wood is known as TIGERWOOD; outside the United States it is known generally as AFRICAN WALNUT, and in Africa it is often called ALONAWOOD, BENIN WALNUT, CONGOWOOD, LOVOAWOOD and NIGERIAN GOLDEN WALNUT.

Lovoa is a large tree growing in Africa, and produces logs up to 48 in. in diameter and 24 ft. long. It has a very attractive bronze yellowish brown color, occasionally showing dark streaks. When the wood is quarter-sawed or cut, it shows a very pleasing ribbon-stripe figure. With the exception of the name, it does not have much resemblance to the European or American walnut, in most respects being nearer to a mahogany.

The wood seasons well and glues easily. An excellent finish can be obtained by scraping and sanding. After the pores are filled, a fine polish can be produced. It can be rip-sawed easily and cleanly, though it is somewhat

Lovoa, which is known also as tigerwood.

weaker than our American walnut. Hand-turning needs care and sharp tools to avoid tearing, and for the same reason drills need to be kept sharp or the fibers will tear out at the bottom of the drill hole.

Under normal conditions, plentiful supplies are available in the form of logs, boards and planks. It is a decorative timber, widely used in the making of furniture, in paneling and in veneers. Selected material is occasionally stained and used as a substitute for mahogany, especially fake antique furniture. It is used also for gunstocks and inlaying.

Lovoa, stripe shown here, comes in crotch figuration too. This yellowish brown wood with mild cross flecks has a pronounced, silky lustre. Known also as benin.

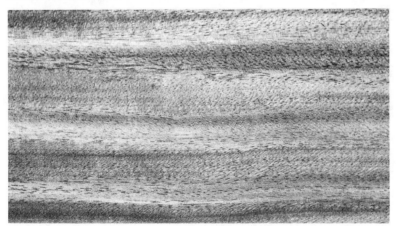

MACA WOOD *Platymiscium,* sp. (Platy/miscium—broad stem, probably in reference to the wide trunk diameter)

This tree grows in northern South America and Central America and is known also as BLEEDING HEART, BRAZILIAN PADAUK, FALSE ROSEWOOD, GRANDADILLO, MACACAHUBA and MEXICAN TULIPWOOD.

It is a rich reddish brown in

Texas madrone Arbutus texana. *This stand of tall, straight evergreens in Hays County, Texas, is honored as National Champion Texas Madrone. It grows taller than the often shrub-like Pacific madrone, has smaller leaves, and yields similar wood that is easier to process.*

color with irregular grain and sometimes shows a stripe. It is a fine wood for borders and decorative work and is used in furniture and musical instruments and for knife handles.

MADRONE, PACIFIC *Arbutus menziesii* (Arbutus—the classical Latin name of *Arbutus unedo*, the strawberry madrone of southern Europe; menziesii—after its discoverer, Archibald Menzies, 1754–1842, Scottish physician and naturalist)

It has several local names, generally LAUREL, MANZANITA and MADRONE.

Madrone or madroño (the Spanish name) grows along the Pacific coast from British Columbia southward to central California and reaches its greatest development in the redwood forests of northern California, where the trees are sometimes 100 ft. high and 5 to 7 ft. in diameter. It varies greatly in size, depending upon the quality of the ground, from a small shrub to a tree that spreads its branches wide enough to shade a gathering of around 2,000 men. The branches of a large tree will cover an area from 8,000 to 10,000 square ft. When madrone grows in the open, it has wide

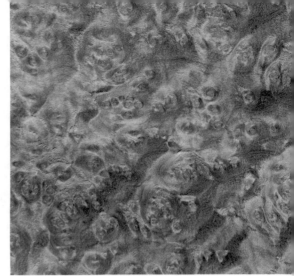

Madrone burl, pale reddish brown.

limbs like a southern live oak, but in a forest the trunk rises tall and straight, bringing the crown into the sunlight and fresh air. It usually grows mixed with other forest trees, but sometimes large stands are encountered by themselves.

The wood is pale, reddish brown, resembling apple wood in tone but not quite as dark. Its weight is 44 lbs. per cubic foot and the wood is porous with very small pores.

It presents extreme difficulty in seasoning, as the wood warps and checks easily. However, it is a beautiful wood and presents a fine appearance when worked into furniture. It is particularly suitable for turned work, bowls, novelties and souvenirs, as the wood polishes almost to the smoothness of holly. Large burls grow on the tree and these are much sought after by furniture manufacturers and inlayers.

Madrone wood is in great demand by the manufacturers of gun powder, as they find this one of the best sources of charcoal suitable for making gunpowder.

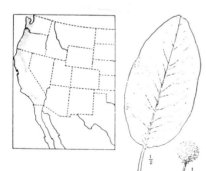

Southern magnolia, older than recorded history of man. This family of trees yields large quantities of lumber and veneer.

MAGNOLIA, SOUTHERN *Magnolia grandiflora* (Magnolia—in honor of Pierre Magnol, 1638–1715, director of the botanical garden at Montpellier, France; grandi/flora—large-flowered)

It is known also as BAT TREE, BIG LAUREL, BULLBAY, LAUREL and the SWEET MAGNOLIA, and is the official state tree of Mississippi and Louisiana.

Southern magnolia grows along the Atlantic coastline, from central Florida northward to North Carolina, and along the Gulf of Mexico, from Florida throughout Louisiana and eastern Texas. It is a shapely tree, growing up to 90 ft. in height, and has a large trunk up to 4 ft. in diameter.

There are eight species of magnolia native to the eastern part of the United States, of which this is one, and a part of the thirty-five species known throughout the world. Magnolias have been traced back long before the coming of man. In the early centuries the Chinese cultivated magnolias in order to preserve the buds, which they used in seasoning rice and also in medicine.

Southern magnolia has thick leaves which are dark green above and silvery color underneath. A fine example of this species grows close to the south portico of the White House, in Washington, where it was planted by Andrew Jackson in memory of his wife, Rachel.

The southern magnolia tree produces well over half of all the magnolia timber used commercially—for all types of cabinetwork, interior finishes and turnery; a good deal is cut into veneers and is also used for boxes and crates.

MAHOGANY, AFRICAN *Khaya ivorensis* (Khaya—from the native name for this tree, Khaye; ivorensis—Latin name for the Ivory Coast)

Several species of mahogany come from the west coast of Africa, the most important being

Khaya ivorensis. The mahogany that is exported to Europe is often sold under different trade names, according to the ports through which the logs are exported. Various types commonly known to the trade are LAGOS and BENIN MAHOGANY, from Nigerian ports; HALF-ASSINE and SEKONDI MAHOGANY, from the Gold Coast, also GRAND BASSAM, from the Ivory Coast.

The tree is large, sometimes very large, and excellent cuttings both for width and length can be obtained for use as lumber or veneers. In most cases the trees range from 100 to 150 ft. in

African mahogany, highly figured crotch.

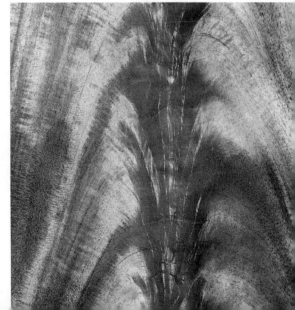

Mahogany, quartered, mottled.

Mahogany, quartered, broken stripe.

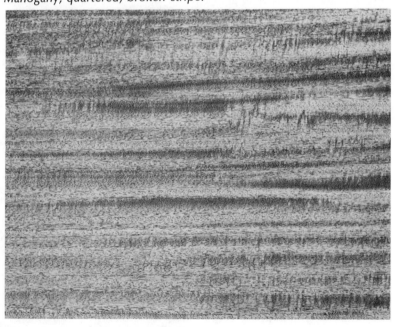

height, with a trunk clear of branches up to 90 ft. The diameter varies from 3 to 6 ft. and considerably more at the base, which is usually buttressed. After felling, the logs are frequently squared by natives, using adzes, in order to avoid transporting unnecessary amounts of useless timber for long distances and to remove the sapwood to prevent the attacks of ambrosia beetles, which cause pinholes.

Freshly sawed or cut African mahogany varies from a light to deep pink color, which gradually darkens to various shades from a light brown to a dark reddish brown when exposed to air and light. African mahogany is probably the most widely used of the true mahoganies at present, as it is the cheapest and can readily be obtained in all sizes. It is of coarser texture than the New World mahogany and has the disadvantage that it is more likely to warp.

The wood seasons rapidly without any particular attention and is very stable when dry, having less tendency to split than the American or New World mahogany, though it is not quite as strong.

Owing to its interlocked grain, African mahogany is rather more difficult to work than the Honduras variety; nevertheless it is fairly easy to work both with hand and machine tools, though there is a tendency for the grain to pick up when planing. It veneers very well.

African mahogany produces more figured logs than the New World mahogany, and the various types of figures are much more pronounced. It has long had an important established place in the construction of furniture of all classes, in boat building, and in the manufacture of high-grade plywood.

MAHOGANY, NEW WORLD

THE MAHOGANIES of this hemisphere belong to the genus *Swietenia* (after von Swieten, a Dutch physician), the source of the original or true mahogany. This is the premier cabinet wood of the world. It grows in southern Florida, the West Indies, Mexico, Central America, Colombia, Venezuela, and the upper Amazonian region. The genus was described by Jacquin in 1760 with a single species, *Swietenia mahagoni* from the Bahamas.

Three South American species of *Swietenia* have been proposed, but each has been based on specimens from a single tree and, for all practical purposes, may be considered mere forms of *S. macrophylla*.

Mahogany is the most valuable timber tree in tropical America. Its use by European colonists and explorers dates back at least to the sixteenth century. According to George N. Lamb (*The Mahogany Book*, 2nd ed., pp. 8–10), "the earliest surviving use of Mahogany is that of a rough-hewn cross preserved in the Cathedral of St. Domingo and bearing the legend: 'This is the first sign planted in the center of this field to mark the beginning of this magnificent temple in the year year 1514.' The cathedral, completed in 1550, has much carved mahogany woodwork, some of it considered the finest in the world, still in splendid condition after nearly four centuries in the tropics. Mahogany was early estab-

This is a valuable stand of Honduras mahogany being cultivated in Honduras, Central America. The trees are 6 years, 9 months old. The average height is 29.1 feet, and the diameter at breast height (DBH as officially designated) is 4.4 inches. Harvesting of this stand will start when the trees are about 60 years old. At that time the average diameter will be 30 inches or more.

lished as a ship-building wood and Cortez used it for the construction of ships for further voyages of discovery. . . . The first known European use of mahogany was in the Escorial begun by Philip II of Spain in 1563 and completed in 1584. . . . The earliest use of mahogany known in England was in Nottingham castle built in 1680."

No one knows when mahogany was first introduced into England, but it was probably used in shipbuilding long before it became fashionable for furniture, its identity concealed under the nondistinctive name of cedar. In an account of the trees of Bermuda about 1619 (*The World Displayed*, London, 1760, vol. 4, chap. 12), the native cedar is described as "firmer and more durable than any of its kind we are acquainted with and answers in every respect to oak timber. It is therefore used in shipbuilding." Certain rooms in Nottingham castle were wainscoted and floored in 1680 with "Cedar wood," as shown by the original bill for the timber, but contemporary evidence of the hardness and beauty of the woodwork leaves no room for doubt that the wood was mahogany. It was probably to avoid the confusion with other kinds of cedar

(*Cedrela* and *Juniperus*) that the English settlers began to use the name mahogany, presumably a term of native origin. Its first recorded use is as "Mohogeny" in Ogilby's *America*, in 1671. Various spellings were subsequently used—mohogony, mohogany, muhagnee, mehogeny, mehogenny, mahagoni, mahoginy, and mahogany, the last mentioned appearing for the first time about 1724. The French name for mahogany is acajou, and this apparently owes its origin to the early practice of coating the ends of the logs with resin from the acajou or cashew tree (*Anacardium occidentale* L.).

The earliest mention of mahogany ("Mohagony wood") in an English newspaper appears to be in an advertisement in the *London Gazette*, February 22–25, 1702, regarding the sale of the cargoes of two prize ships. The first reference in the statistics of imports filed at the Public Records Office is for the year "Xmas 1699 to Xmas 1700" and pertains to a small lot of "Mohogony wood" from Jamaica. In an authoritative paper on "Early Imports of Mahogany for Furniture" (*The Connoisseur*, London, October and December 1934), R. W. Symonds says the following:

"Taking into consideration all

the available evidence, I think it is permissible to state that Mahogany was employed in England from 1715 onwards for the making of tables, sometimes of gatelegged construction, but usually with straight round legs terminating in club feet or with the plain cabriole-shaped legs. Tables such as these were made in considerable numbers by many firms of London joiners and cabinetmakers and also by provincial furniture makers who lived in towns where a supply of imported Mahogany was available. Previous to 1715, Mahogany tables were only made sporadically owing to the cabinet-makers not being able to obtain a regular supply of the wood. . . .

"Mahogany overcame the difficulty of making table tops, owing to the large widths of the planks of this wood in comparison to Walnut. It was for this reason that Mahogany became at once popular with cabinet-makers. On its introduction, numerous new types of tables were designed, the construction of which would not have been possible in Walnut. These tables were not only made for the wealthy classes, but large numbers were produced of a plain character for the less well-to-do householder. Evidence in support of this last statement is to be found in the very large quantity of flap and tripod tables of a plain design that have survived. The number of the latter, however, has considerably decreased within recent years owing to the obnoxious habit of the furniture faker of carving up the plain example so that he can pass it off to the unwary collector, at a high rate of profit, as a period piece with the claw-and-ball feet. . . .

"It would appear from the contemporary information, cited from the statistics of imports, Sheraton's *Cabinet Dictionary*, and the *History of Jamaica*, that the first Mahogany to be imported into England in the early eighteenth century was Jamaican and, afterwards, Cuban. In the third quarter of the same century, Honduras Mahogany was imported. The reason for the cessation of any particular variety of Mahogany was because the trees near the coast having been felled, the traders sought another supply which was cheaper, owing to its being more easily procurable. It was not so much a question of seeking wood of fine quality, otherwise exporters would have gone to the trouble and expense of transporting the better quality timber from the interior."

It was during the middle of the 1800's that many of the sailing vessels with their cargoes of West Indian and Central American mahoganies would be consigned directly to the yards of Constantine & Company, at Seventh Street and the East River, New York, to await their turn to unload.

In the *History of Jamaica*, we note the following: "In felling these trees, the most beautiful part is commonly left behind. The Negro workmen raise a scaffolding, of four or five feet elevation above the ground, and hack off the trunk, which they cut up into balks. The part below, extending to the root, is not only of the largest diameter, but of closer texture than the other parts, most elegantly diversified with shades or clouds, or dotted, like ermine, with black spots; it takes the highest polish, with a singular lustre, so firm as even to reflect objects like a mirror. This part is only to be come at by digging below the spur to the depth of two or three feet and cutting it through; which is so laborious an operation that few attempt it, except they are uncommonly curious in their choice of the wood, or to serve a particular order. Yet I apprehend it might be found to answer the trouble and expense, if sent for a trial to the British market, as it could not fail of being approved of beyond any other wood, or even tortoise-shell which it most resembles."

Sheraton gives an account of Jamaican mahogany in his *Cabinet Dictionary* (1803), and is chiefly concerned with three types, designated as Cuba, Spanish, and Honduras mahogany. Cuba wood is "a kind of Mahogany somewhat harder than Honduras wood, but with no figure in the grain. It is inferior to Spanish wood, though probably the Cuba and Spanish Mahogany are the same, as the island of Cuba is a Spanish colony. . . . That, however, which is generally distinguished by Spanish Mahogany is finer than that called Cuba, which is pale, straight-grained, and some of it only a bastard kind of Mahogany. It is generally used for chair wood, for which some of it will do very well." Regarding the Honduras variety, he says: "From this province is imported the principal kind of Mahogany in use amongst cabinetmakers, which generally bears the name of Honduras Mahogany, and sometimes Bay-wood, from the bay or arm of the sea which runs up to it. The difference between Honduras and Spanish wood is easily perceived by judges, but not by others unskilled in wood."

The comparatively recent discovery of commercial quantities of *Swietenia* in the upper Amazon region is of great importance to the industry, as it opens up a vast, though still undetermined, area of virgin forest containing mahogany.

The known and probable distribution of mahogany in South America is approximately as follows: in Venezuela, it extends from eastern Miranda westward to Calabozo and Guanare, around the northern end of Cordillera Mérida to the Lake Maracaibo region, avoiding the dry coastal zone and elevations above 3,000 ft. In Colombia, it is mostly in the upper valleys of the Magdalena and Cauca rivers. *Swietenia* is also a component of the virgin forests in northwestern Ecuador. In Peru, mahogany occurs east of the divide at elevations of 400 to 4,500 ft. and is in a belt of forest varying in width up to several hundred miles and extending from southern Ecuador through the Ucayali basin to the headwaters of the Tambo and Urubamba rivers in the south. Eastward across the border in Brazil, there are commercial stands of mahogany in the upper reaches of the Juruá and Purús rivers, and large quantities of logs are floated down to Manáos for export, either in the round or after manufacture into lumber. There are indications of a separate mahogany timber belt of unknown extent along certain tributaries of the upper Madeira River in eastern Bolivia. Apparently there is no genuine mahogany in any part of the basins of the Rio Negro and Putumayo, or in the lower portions of the Juruá and Purús, or below the falls of the Madeira. The reputed discovery above the waterfalls of the Tapajoz and Xingu rivers of old Indian canoes made of mahogany implies an extension of the Bolivian belt across Matto Grosso, Brazil. While from the foregoing it appears that only fragmentary knowledge of the range of *Swietenia* in South America exists, enough is known to reassure anyone who fears that the supply of genuine, first-growth mahogany timber is nearing exhaustion.

MAHOGANY, PHILIPPINE

THE PHILIPPINE ISLANDS are the source of a great variety of hardwoods, few of which are imported into the United States. The greatest volume of the latter compose a group of timbers marketed as "Philippine mahogany." However,

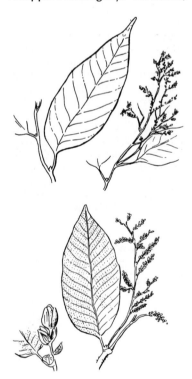

these are in no way, botanically or otherwise, related to the true or classical mahoganies which belong to the plant family *Meliaceae*. The "Philippine mahoganies" are members of a plant family called *Dipterocarpaceae*.

Philippine mahoganies are quite varied in color and texture and are divided into two classes:

Class I. Red Lauans
  (a) Red lauan (*Shorea negrosensis*)
  (b) Tangile (*Shorea polysperma*)
  (c) Tiaong (*Shorea teysmanniana*)
Class II. White Lauans
  (a) Almon (*Shorea eximia*)
  (b) White lauan (*Pentacme* spp.)
  (c) Bagtikan (*Parashorea* spp.)

In general, all of these woods, as compared with the tropical American and African mahoganies (*Meliaceae*), are of coarser texture. They require a greater amount of sanding to produce a finished surface and are much less stable under atmospheric changes. Their color varies from fairly light shades to red and brown. As a rule, these woods are employed in lower-quality furniture, doors and cabinetwork. The Philippine mahoganies are available in quartered, sliced and rotary veneers and as lumber.

MAHOGANY, ROSE *Dysoxylon fraseranum* (Dys/o/xylon—hardwood; fraseranum—after Fraser)
  This is known also as AUSTRALIAN MAHOGANY and sometimes as PICK WOOD.
  Rose mahogany emanates from Malaya and is fairly heavy, weighing 50 lbs. per cubic foot. It re-

Selective logging of lauan in a mixed forest, Philippines.

Quarter-sliced white lauan, formerly marketed as Philippine mahogany. Pale pink and brown color and mild, straight grain.

Maidou burl, two-piece match.

sembles Honduras mahogany in color and is also similar to the strong reddish brown color of Koko, making it hard to distinguish these two woods. The wood has a fragrant rose odor when freshly cut, but it does not in any way resemble the rosewood family.

MAIDOU *Pterocarpus pedatus* (Ptero/carpus—winged fruit; pedatus—footed)

It is known also as MADOU and MAI TADU and sometimes is mistaken for Burmese padauk.

This tree is found in French Indochina and resembles Amboyna very closely. Maidou varies from a pale straw color to brownish and scarlet shades, has a satiny finish and a ribbon stripe. Only rarely does it come in the form of burls and crotches.

MAKORÉ *Mimusops heckelii* (Mimusops—monkey face; heckelii—after Heckel)

It is known also as AFRICAN CHERRY, AGANOKWE, BAKU and MAKARU.

Coming from the west coast of Africa, this tree is large and produces logs up to 5 ft. in diameter. It is somewhat similar to close-grained mahogany, but with growth lines and pores more similar to cherry. It is heavy in handling, weighing 40 lbs. per cubic foot. The logs which are exported are short in length, being crosscut and then cut again to make them easier to transport. The wood is dense and hard, firm-textured, heavier than mahogany, and while some logs are straight-grained, others have a very striking mottled figure.

There is a luster to the wood and it glues well but is difficult to

Makoré. This wood is known commonly as African cherry.

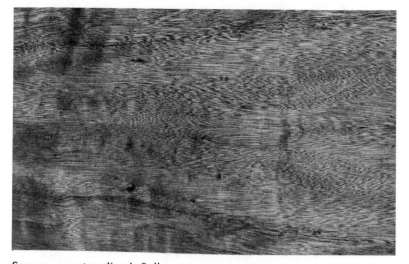

Sonora, quarter-sliced. Full name: manggasinora.

work, as the timber contains silica which rapidly dulls the tools. It is often cut into veneers, which is much easier than sawing.

MANGGASINORA *Shorea philippinensis* (Shorea—in honor of Lord Teignmouth, John Shore, Governor of Bengal; philippinensis—of the Philippines)

This species is known also as SONORA.

Emanating from the Philippines, this wood has a yellow-white to pale brown color and a texture like almond. It is hard and heavy and the veneer is available in quartered form.

MAÑIO *Podocarpus nubigens* (Podo/carpus—foot fruit; nubi/gens—cloudy race)

This emanates from southern Chile, in the Andes Mountains. It is a tree that would be difficult to recognize in the woods as being a conifer or evergreen, because it has straight, stiff, leathery leaves and cones which do not look like cones. It is a relative of the yellow wood of South Africa and the podos of east Africa, with similar straight grain, and fine, uniform yellowish wood.

Before drying, the wood twists and warps badly, but after careful seasoning, which can be accomplished without any trouble, it works well and is stable. The average weight is around 35 lbs. per cubic foot.

In South America mañio is used in the manufacture of furniture and general cabinetwork, as it has a very pleasing appearance; and because of the well-shaped logs and size of the tree, it could be suitable for the manufacture of veneers. However, very little has been exported to foreign markets because the supply is not too plentiful and the transportation charges would be exceedingly high.

MANSONIA *Mansonia altissima* (Mansonia—after Manson; altissima—of the highest)

It is known also as AFRICAN BLACK WALNUT, APRONO, BÉTÉ and OFUN.

This small tree comes from the Gold and Ivory Coasts of Africa and has a diameter from 16 to 24 in. The heartwood is yellowish brown to greenish and purplish brown, but the rich colors, apparent when first manufactured, generally fade when exposed to the light and the wood assumes more of a uniform dark purple-brown.

Mansonia dries quickly with little warping and weighs about 37 lbs. per cubic foot. It is similar to walnut, especially when sliced or quarter-sliced, and is usually straight-grained and fine-textured, but it is harder than American walnut. However, its strength properties are close to walnut's.

The tree is very resistant to decay, but the sapwood may be attacked by pinhole borers. The wood works easily and glues well, finishing nicely. The better-colored timber may be used as an alternative to walnut in quality furniture and cabinetmaking, in interior decoration and in items such as piano cases.

MAPLE, JAPANESE *Acer palmatum* (Acer—the classical Latin name of maple; palmatum—shaped like one's palm, a reference to the palmlike nature of the leaf)

In Japan it is known as KAEDE and grows in the forests of Honshushikoku and Kayushu, along with oak, chestnut and beech.

This tree is small, between 30 and 40 ft. in height and with a diameter of 12 in. and upward. The wood is a pinkish brown to pale brown in color with no division in appearance between the sapwood and the heartwood. When dried, the wood weighs about 40 lbs. per cubic foot, but it must be dried slowly, otherwise a large amount of warpage may take place and the shrinkage is quite high. The logs usually are straight-grained or slightly irregular, and occasionally wavy grain is found. It has a fine texture, a lustrous surface and is a hard timber, about equal to our rock maple.

While Japanese maple is a wood that bends poorly, it is much used in the furniture industry, as it takes a good finish. In addition, it is used in Japan for flooring, in some decorative woodwork, and in the manufacture of agricultural equipment.

MAPLE, QUEENSLAND *Flindersia brayleyana* (Flindersia—in honor of the English captain, M. Flinders; brayleyana—probably after Brayley)

This tree, known also as AUSTRALIAN MAPLE, MAPLE SILKWOOD and WARRI, is not of our maple (Acer) family.

It grows in Queensland and New South Wales in Australia. The color is light red, similar to African mahogany, with a wavy, curly grain, from plain to stripe figure. It has a silken luster but is light in weight though tough and moderately elastic. The bending strength is poor. It has a hard, close grain.

Queensland maple works easily, stains readily and is one of the finest Australian cabinet woods used in making quality furniture, for decorative interiors, boat interiors and for planking and propellers. It is not often used here.

MAPLE, RED *Acer rubrum* (Acer —the classical Latin name of maple; rubrum—red, in reference to the red autumn foliage, the red flowers and red leaf stalks)

It is the state tree of Rhode Island and is known in various states as SCARLET MAPLE, SHOE-PET MAPLE, SOFT MAPLE, SWAMP MAPLE and WATER MAPLE.

This maple, one of the most valuable of the soft maples, grows in about the same states as the sugar maple but as a rule is found in lowlands, swamps and along river banks. Well named "red" maple, it displays something red all year. In winter the buds, in spring the early flowers and the young leaves, also the seeds, shine in red. The young reddish twigs show a brilliance as summer comes, and the autumn foliage is the most striking of the red colors. Red maple grows rapidly and is especially desired in landscaping.

The early colonists, before mahogany was imported, used red maple for most of their furniture pieces.

The wood of the red maple resembles that of the sugar maple, being close-grained, but it is much softer in texture and lacks the figure that the sugar maple has, although it has an attractive plain grain. It is not as costly as hard maple and is generally used in cheaper furniture and all types of general woodwork. A curl figure is quite common in soft maple, but a soft maple with a very strong bird's-eye figure is rare.

MAPLE, SILVER *Acer saccharinum* (saccharinum—sugary or sweet in reference to the sap)

Silver maple belongs to the soft maple group and is very similar

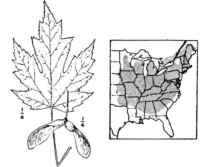

to the red maple in respect to its growing conditions and the texture of the wood. But it is easily distinguished from the red maple because of the difference in the leaves, which have five lobes with deep fissures. They have a light green surface and are silvery white on the underside. Silver maple lacks the bright coloring of the red maple in the fall, and the leaves turn to a pale yellow.

MAPLE, SUGAR *Acer saccharum* (saccharum—sugary, in reference to the sweet sap from which maple sugar is made)

This species is known also as BLACK MAPLE, HARD MAPLE, ROCK MAPLE, SUGAR-TREE MAPLE, SWEET MAPLE and WHITE MAPLE.

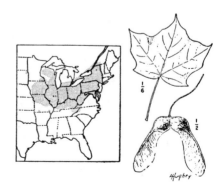

Left: Red maple is second largest lumber producer in maple family. Sugar maple comes first. Right: Silver maple yields softer wood usually identified by its dark streaks.

Sugar maple grows throughout most states east of the Rocky Mountains, but the largest quantity is found in the New England states and the states along the Great Lakes. It grows from 70 to 120 ft. tall and from 20 to 38 in. in diameter. Sugar maple is the state tree of Vermont, New York, West Virginia and Wisconsin. It is easily recognized by its leaves, which are five-lobed and pointed. They turn to gorgeous red and yellow colors in the fall. The brilliant orange and red colors of this species are responsible for making our mountainsides so beautiful in the fall.

The heartwood is a very light tan, sometimes reddish brown, and the sapwood is really white. It is a heavy, strong wood and has an even texture.

The maple family is divided between hard maple and soft maple. In the United States over 20 different species of maple may be found, such as black, broadleaved, fig leaf, hard, Oregon, red, rock, river, rough, scarlet, silver, soft and sugar. Of the many species of maple, sugar maple is the

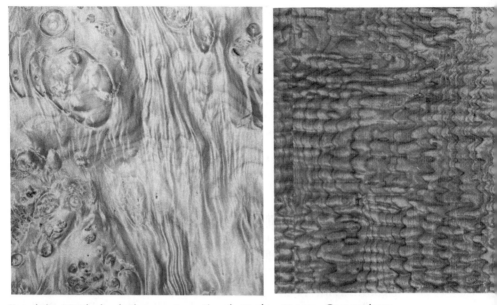

Top left: Maple burl, the most exotic of maple veneers. Comes from sugar maple and inherits the color of its fall leaves—red and gold. Top right: Quilted figure hard maple. Bottom left: Rotary cut hard maple, called "white" maple. Bottom right: Curly sugar maple. Pale gold with wavy figure.

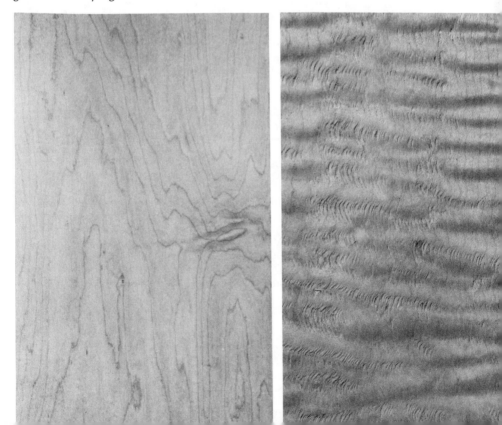

most abundant and important of the maples found in the United States.

This maple is named sugar maple because of the delicious maple sugar and maple syrup obtained in the spring by processing the sap from the trees. A tree will produce as many as twelve gallons of sap a year and it takes thirty-five to forty gallons of sap to distill one gallon of the pure syrup. The production of this syrup is confined principally to the states of Wisconsin, Vermont, New York and other northern states, and the business amounts to many millions of dollars a year.

Various types of figures are obtained in the maple trees, like curly—often called a fiddleback figure because of being used on the backs of violins—bird's-eye maple, maple burl, leaf figure and straight-grained maple. All these are available in the veneer form for craftsmen's use.

As sugar maple has a hard texture, is easy to work and is excellent for turning, taking a high polish, the finest dance floors, bowling alleys and bowling pins are made of this wood. It is also used in one of the most vital parts of piano construction, the manufacture of the pin plank—the part into which the pins for the strings of the piano are driven.

MARÍA *Calophyllum brasiliense* (Calo/phyllum—beautiful leaf; brasiliense—of Brazil)

This wood is known also as ACA, BARA, BARE, BALSAMARIA, CALABA, CRABWOOD, GACAREUBA, OCUJE, SANTA MARÍA, WILD CALABASH and by other names.

Small quantities of this wood

have been imported into the United States from time to time, but it has no definite commercial value. The heartwood is brick-red to pink in color, and when cut into rotary veneers, attractive figures are obtained. This wood requires special attention when kiln-drying. Locally it has been used for furniture, shipbuilding and general construction work.

MĚNGKULANG *Tarrietia simplicifolia* (Tarrietia—probably a personal name; simplici/folia—simple leaved)

This tree grows throughout the forests of Malaya, but the growth averages only one tree in every four or five acres. It reaches a very large size, however, often exceeding 120 ft., and exceptional trees have been recorded as high as 140 ft. with diameters ranging from 18 to 36 in. The wood is coarse-grained and when seasoned properly gives little trouble.

Only small quantities of this wood are exported. It is used locally for various types of furniture, interior cabinetwork and the making of boxes.

MĚRBAU *Intsia bakeri* (Intsia—a native name in Madagascar; bakeri—after J. G. Baker, English botanist of late nineteenth century)

This large tree grows throughout Malaya, but sparsely, so no large quantities are available. The heartwood is of an attractive dark brown and reddish brown color and is of fine texture. Some pores contain a yellow deposit which at times is extracted for use in making a dye.

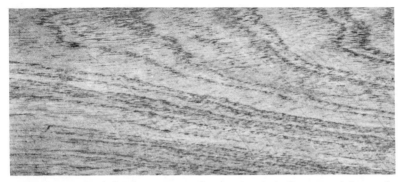

Mesquite, one of the few recent discoveries as a fine wood for craft-workers, is hard with a wavy figure and a rich brownish red color.

As měrbau is extremely resistant to decay, it is highly valued in the East for house building, construction and bridge work, and is exported in limited quantities only. It is also used in the manufacture of frames for billiard tables. Selected wood makes very attractive paneling for rooms.

MESQUITE, HONEY *Prosopis glandulosa*

The mesquite grows wild, in the open, on the plains chiefly in Arizona, Texas and Oklahoma, where it is known as IRONWOOD, a name given to woods of many families of trees. It is small to medium sized with a short trunk and crooked limbs which account for the narrow widths of lumber it produces.

Mesquite is hard and heavy, averaging 55 lbs. per cubic foot. The color is rich milk-chocolate with a reddish cast, and the figure is straight to wavy. Flowers of the mesquite are a source of honey, the bean pods are eaten by cattle and the wood is now directed away from the sheepherder's fire toward the lumber market.

MESUA *Mesua ferrea* (Mesua—after the Arabic physician Mesuach of the tenth century; ferrea—iron in reference to the hard wood)

Native to India, Burma, Ceylon and the Andaman Islands, this wood is called INDIAN ROSE-CHESTNUT and IRONWOOD in India.

The wood is of a bright, rose-red color which darkens upon exposure. It is very hard and heavy—weighing about 70 lbs. per cubic foot—and it is little used because of the difficulties in dragging it. It is very strong and used locally in its native country for gunstocks, for tool handles and in the construction of bridges and buildings, but none of it is used commercially in the United States.

MONKEY POD *Pithecolobium samán** (Pithec/o/lobium—monkey pod; samán—after a native Central American name, samán)

Other common names for the monkey pod include RAIN TREE,

* This species may be referred to as *Samanea samán*.

This large plank of beautifully grained rain tree wood, cut from a huge monkey pod tree in the Philippines, is being sanded to prepare it for use as a free-form coffee table.

ALGARROBO, SAMÁN and CARRETA.

The monkey pod is commonly distributed as an ornamental plant throughout the tropics and may be found in the Hawaiian Islands in great abundance. It has become naturalized in some areas. Mature trees in the Magdalena River Valley in Colombia may attain heights of 100 ft. or more and reach diameters of 4 to 6 ft. Even though it is one of the most beautiful of neotropical trees, the timber is of little commercial importance. Forest-grown trees are scarce and others are too useful for shade. Young trees grow rapidly and produce a light and soft, easily worked, brown wood. However, later growth is slower, and the wood formed is comparatively hard and heavy, very dark in color, fibrous, tough and somewhat refractory. The wood has little resistance to decay. It is used in the manufacture of novelties to some extent, and selected pieces may exhibit an attractive figure. Locally the wood of the monkey pod is used for dugout canoes, split posts and construction.

The name rain tree is probably derived from the falling liquid excreta of *Cicadeae* insects, which inhabit the trees in Central America. Carreta is a Spanish name referring to wagon or cart and probably owes its use to the fact that cross sections of the trunk of *Pithecolobium samán* are employed in some areas as wagon wheels. The monkey pod yields a dark-colored gum of poor quality and the pulp of the pods is said to be edible.

MULBERRY, BLACK *Morus nigra* (Morus—classical Latin name of mulberry; nigra—black)

Black mulberry, weighing about 40 lbs. per cubic foot, grows in the United States and is native to western Asia. It has a brilliant yellow color, becoming a golden, rich brown, and has a firm grain. This is an excellent wood for chair work.

MULBERRY, EAST AFRICAN *Morus lactea*

Locally this tree is known also as KIZULEVULE, MUKIMBU and NYAKATOMA.

The tree generally reaches a height of 60 ft. with diameters from 12 to 18 in. However, the trunk is seldom straight, which prevents obtaining long-length lumber.

When first cut, the wood has a very striking bright yellow heartwood and almost a pure white sapwood. In time, with exposure to light and air, the heartwood continues to darken, going through shades of a golden-brown to a warm brown color.

The wood is not durable if exposed to the ground or to the weather, but it is a most satisfactory wood for general cabinet-work, interior woodwork and wooden articles, its use being limited by the lack of suitable logs.

MUNINGA *Pterocarpus angolensis* (Ptero/carpus—winged fruit; angolensis—from Angola)

It is known also as BLOOD-WOOD, KEJAAT, KEJATENHOUT, SEALING-WAX TREE and TRANS-VAAL TEAK.

The growth of this tree is confined to eastern Transvaal. The heartwood has a wide variation in color from a dark reddish brown with purple markings to a light uniform brown color. It is of medium weight, averaging 40 lbs. per cubic foot, and the wood has an attractive figure.

There is no difficulty encountered in seasoning, and the wood is free from warpage and shrinkage. It works a little harder than teak, but it glues easily and takes a fine polish.

This is a very popular wood and much in demand in Africa as a fine wood for furniture and quality cabinets. A good example of its use is the railroad station in Johannesburg, which is entirely paneled in this wood, as well as all the furniture in it.

MUSIZI *Maesopsis eminii* (Maesopsis—origin unknown; eminii —probably after Emin)

Musizi is known also as AWU-RU, ESENGE and MUHUNYA.

Growing in east Africa, this tree is generally found on land from which the original trees have been removed, or along the edges of large forests. It reaches heights from 40 to 110 ft., occasionally a little more. The wood is in the lighter class of woods, averaging about 30 lbs. per cubic foot, of a medium to fairly coarse grain, which is generally straight.

The bark is distinctive, inasmuch as it is deeply grooved and a dirty white color. The sapwood is whitish and distinctly different from the colored heartwood, which when first cut can best be described as greenish yellow. Upon exposure it darkens through several shades of yellow-brown, sometimes reaching a rich brown.

The wood seasons very easily, without warping or twisting, and works easily with either power or hand tools. After a careful filling of the pores, it will take a fine polish either in varnish or lacquer. It may also be painted.

It can be described as a useful, general-purpose wood for all types of interior work, but is not suitable for use outdoors or in wet conditions, as it is not resistant to decay. However, this condition can be easily overcome, as the wood is particularly receptive to treatment with wood preservatives.

MYRTLE *Umbellularia californica*

This species is known also as ACACIA BURL, CALIFORNIA LAUREL, CALIFORNIA OLIVE, MOUNTAIN LAUREL, PEPPERWOOD and SPICE-TREE.

It grows along the western coast of the United States and particularly in southern Oregon and northern California. This is an evergreen tree, distinguished from the others by a strong, aromatic odor when the leaves are crushed. The leaves have been used as a substitute for bay leaves in flavoring meats and soups.

The wood is rich golden brown and yellowish green with a wide range of color from light to dark. It is a mixture of plain wood, mottle and cluster burls. Also, a stump and burl figure will be found with a scattering of dark purple blotches. The myrtle that grows in Oregon is the most beautiful for varied types of figure and coloring.

Great care is necessary in the seasoning of the green wood, as it will check and warp if not prop-

Myrtle burl cluster, two-piece match.

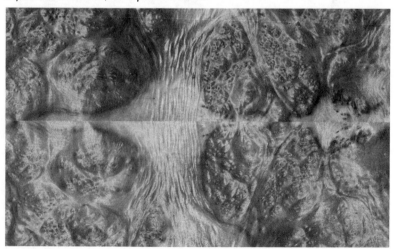

erly handled. The wood is hard and strong and furnishes a magnificent, highly figured veneer that takes an excellent polish. It is used in decorative panels and furniture and is prized by wood turners for making bowls, candlesticks and other items. Oregon myrtle burl, when manufactured in the veneer form, is a favorite wood of the finest cabinetmakers.

MYRTLE, BEECH *Nothofagus cunninghamii* (Notho/fagus—bastard beech, *Fagus;* cunninghamii—after Cunningham)

This attractive evergreen tree is known also as RED MYRTLE and TASMANIAN MYRTLE.

The beech myrtle grows on the island of Tasmania and the most southerly part of Victoria. The finest species are found on moist soils in sheltered areas, but it will grow on mountain slopes up to elevations of 3,500 ft. and higher—however, the higher up, the smaller the tree until it becomes just a shrub. In the most desirable conditions trees can be found as high as 100 ft. and 24 in. or more in diameter.

It has lovely coloring, with a range from a light pale color in the sapwood through shades of pinkish brown to reddish brown and brown heartwood. Because the lighter-colored wood has a tendency to dry much more quickly than the darker shades of heartwood, considerable care is required in drying. Unless it is first treated with a proper preservative, this wood is unsuitable for use in circumstances that would be favorable for the development of wood rotting, as it has a low resistance to decay.

The use of this hardwood is somewhat limited because of the lack of suitable logs, but it is much used in Tasmania for furniture, turning, general interior woodwork, carving and other purposes for which beech is used.

NAINGON *Tarrietia utilis* (Tarrietia—probably a personal name; utilis—useful)

This wood grows in Ghana, Africa, along the Ivory Coast and northward to Sierra Leone, and is considered a medium-sized tree for this area, generally averaging around 70 ft., occasionally growing to 100 ft., and from 24 to 30 in. in diameter. It often is found in marshy grounds.

A casual glance at the wood shows a resemblance in color to some species of African mahogany, but upon closer examination one finds the texture coarser and the weight a little heavier, averaging around 40 lbs. per cubic foot. When growing, the tree looks somewhat like the mangrove because of the large buttresses, which have a tendency to develop large roots.

The wood contains an unusual amount of resin, which is in sufficient quantity to make polishing difficult at times and presents a problem in making glued joints, but it is not enough to prevent working with tools. The wood is suitable for all lower grades of furniture and parts of interior woodworking.

NARRA (See AMBOYNA)

NÉDUN *Pericopsis mooniana* (Pericopsis—having a round appearance; mooniana—probably after Moon)

Growing in the low forest regions of the island of Ceylon between the sea level and up to 1,000 ft., this tree is becoming increasingly scarce, as large sections of this type of forest have been logged to make room for rubber plantations. The tree can be recognized by the unusual pale, pinkish brown color of its smooth bark. The wood is an attractive warm brown or orange color with darker streaks at regular intervals, all the colors becoming softer with age. Nédun is fairly heavy, weighing from 50 to 60 lbs. per cubic foot.

Formerly, a good deal of the wood was used in cabinetmaking and in the furniture industry, and today some logs are being manufactured into quarter-sliced veneers.

NEPORA *Caryota* sp. (Caryota—pertaining to a walnut, probably a reference to the fruit)

Emanating from Ceylon, this wood has a cubic weight per foot of 45 lbs. It is black in color with brown streaks. The wood is used for water conduits and baskets. The leaves, which are very strong, are made into rope, brushes, brooms and other articles.

OAKS

BOTANISTS have classified more than 60 species of oaks growing in the United States. They vary a great deal in size, shape and appearance. Some of the woods are extremely valuable commercially and others have little value except for the appearance of the tree. Only a few of the most important ones will be described here. However, these have a number of names, like other woods, known by different names in different states.

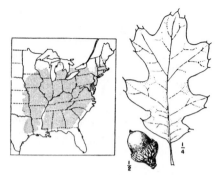

All oaks, regardless of where they grow, are divided into two general groups—the white oaks and the red oaks, the latter sometimes referred to as the black oaks. Those in the white-oak classification have by far the most important commercial value, but there are many more species and trees in the red oak family.

OAK, BLACK *Quercus velutina* (Quercus—the classical Latin name for oak; velutina—velvety, a reference to the downy young leaves)

Black oak, which grows in the eastern part of the United States, is known also as BLACK JACK, BYER'S OAK, JACK OAK, PANBARK OAK, QUERCIPRON OAK and YELLOWBARK, according to the state it grows in.

The name black oak was given to the tree because of the color of the bark. It is probably the most prevalent of the oaks growing in the eastern section. The acorns take two years to ripen, as do all acorns in the black oak family, in contrast to one year to ripen in the white oak family. However, this black oak produces one of the poorest-quality timbers of the more prevalent oaks. It is used in general construction work and in connection with the manufacture of cheaper furniture.

OAK, BUR *Quercus macrocarpa* (Quercus—the classical Latin name for oak; macro/carpa—large fruit)

In various states this oak is known also as BLUE OAK, MOSSY-CUP, OVERCUP OAK and SCRUB OAK.

This tree grows in southern Canada and throughout the eastern half of the United States, and is the state tree of Illinois. The largest trees are found in rich bottomlands, and the valley of the Wabash River is considered one of the best spots. Bur oak is one of the largest of all oaks but it is not as beautiful or impressive as the white oak.

The leaves are larger than any of the other oaks, 6 to 10 in. long and half the length in width, having five to seven irregularly shaped lobes and a wedge-shaped face. They are dark green on the top and a silvery green on the underside and are on the tree in great profusion. Also, larger acorns are produced by this species than by any other oaks. The kernels have a white meat which is sweet and edible.

Bur oak produces very fine

wood. When made into veneers and lumber, it has an appearance similar to white oak. It is particularly desired in the quarter-sawed form because of the handsome figure.

OAK, CALIFORNIA LIVE *Quercus agrifolia* (agrifolia—probably an error for *aquifolia*, meaning holly-leaf, or *acrifolia*, meaning sharp-leaved, although literally it means field-leaved)

Originally this oak was known as the HOLLY-LEAVED OAK, as the leaves resemble the large evergreen holly. It is known in California as the COAST LIVE OAK and the EVERGREEN OAK.

This tree is found in southern California and northward to San Francisco in the valleys and along the coastal mountains. It is fairly tall, from 55 to 65 ft., and the limbs are crooked, thick and long. The wood warps and checks to a great extent during drying and it has little or no commercial value.

OAK, CHINKAPIN *Quercus muehlenbergii*

This species of oak is sometimes incorrectly called chestnut oak. Best stands are in and flanking the Ohio Valley, where it becomes larger than its usual 40 ft. The wood is heavy, close-grained and durable. While the tree is attractive, the lumber goes chiefly into heavy construction use.

OAK, ENGLISH *Quercus robur* (robur—strong)

This oak is often referred to as EUROPEAN OAK or POLLARDO.

It varies in color from a light tan to a deep brown with occa-

English oak. Light tan with deep brown stripes sometimes with black spots that make it resemble tortoise shell.

sional black spots. It produces burls and swirls which are very brittle and fragile, but beautiful work can be obtained with their use. English oak is considered one of the finest woods in use today.

OAK, HOLM Quercus ilex (ilex—the genus of the holly, Ilex)

Holm oak has long been a native of the countries bordering on the Mediterranean Sea and was first brought into cultivation in England over three hundred years ago. It is a large evergreen tree, reaching a height of 70 to 90 ft. The large crown often measures as much in diameter as the height.

The wood is reddish brown in color, hard and heavy. Because of this heavy density and hardness, it requires extra care in drying to prevent warpage and also care in working with tools to prevent splitting. When manufactured on the quarter, it has a flashy figure which might be considered too prominent to suit the taste of many.

Little of this timber has been used in industry, except in the countries it grows in, where it has been converted into furniture and used for other similar purposes.

OAK, JAPANESE Quercus mongolica (mongolica—from Mongolia)

Originating in Japan, this oak is the hardest and heaviest of all the timbers produced there, weighing 40 lbs. per cubic foot. Some of this wood is used in house building, but its principal use is in the making of charcoal.

OAK, LIVE Quercus virginiana (virginiana—of Virginia)

Live oak grows in the southeastern part of the United States from Virginia and westward along the coast as far as Texas and Mexico. It is short in height, from 45 to 50 ft., and often two or three times

Right: A massive live oak known in New Orleans Audubon Park as the "George Washington" live oak stands 62 feet high, has a crown spread of 103 feet and a trunk diameter (taken at official "breast height") of 9 feet, 4.6 inches. It is still growing.

as broad as it is high. It is the state tree of Georgia and received its name of live oak because the leaves remain on the tree the entire year, gradually being replaced by new leaves in about thirteen months. The leaves have rounded edges and tips, of a shiny, dark green color and whitish on the underside. It is one of the most beautiful of the oaks, with a short trunk and tremendous spreading limbs.

The wood is tough and heavy. Unfortunately, there is very little commercial value to this wood, owing to the fact that the trunk is so short it produces little lumber. When available, however, the wood has a very fine figure and will take a high polish. Along the Gulf states it is generally covered with Spanish moss.

For many years so-called "knees" obtained from the section where the large roots join the trunk have been used in shipbuilding. Live oak has a historical connection with our Navy. The *Constitution,* commonly known as "Old Ironsides," was made from live oak grown in Georgia.

OAK, NORTHERN RED *Quercus rubra* (rubra—red)

Northern red oak is known also as CANADIAN RED OAK, GRAY OAK and RED OAK.

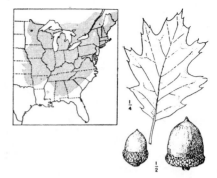

This tree grows across the mid-eastern part of southern Canada and the eastern section of the United States as far south as Alabama and Arkansas, and it is the state tree of New Jersey. It reaches an average height of 65 ft., though a height of 145 ft. has been recorded. It is probably the fastest growing of our native oaks. As a young tree it may add 2 in. to the diameter in a year and 12 in. to the height. It has a short trunk that divides into many heavy branches and is a broad, well-shaped tree. The bark varies from gray to brown in color, and the leaves, from 4 to 9 in. long, are dark green in color. The heartwood, of a light reddish brown color, is more coarse-grained than the white oak and is considered inferior to the white oak.

The wood is used for many purposes in furniture and flooring and takes a satisfactory finish, though all oaks, because of the open pores, should be filled before finishing or painting.

The red oak has become one of the most popular North American oaks used in Europe. It was introduced into France and England during the early part of the eighteenth century and today there are many fine buildings of this oak in France, Belgium and Germany.

Typical live oak forest. Sparsely leafed branches draped with Spanish moss. Jekyll Island, Georgia.

Oregon white oak. The short trunk of this species yields low lumber footage per tree but the wood is high grade, excellent for cabinetwork.

It is estimated that there are over eighty billion feet of oak in this country and over 50 percent of this is the red oak.

OAK, OREGON WHITE *Quercus garryana* (garryana—after Nicholas Garry, secretary of the Hudson Bay Company, who aided David Douglas in his botanical explorations in northwestern United States)

It is known also as GARRY'S OAK, PACIFIC WHITE OAK, PRAIRIE OAK and WESTERN WHITE OAK.

This oak grows in a small, definitely located area from central California northward through Oregon, Washington and British Columbia. The short-length trunk produces a good quality of yellowish brown heartwood that is strong, hard and fine-grained. There is a large shrinkage in drying, but the wood is easy to work with tools and will take a fine

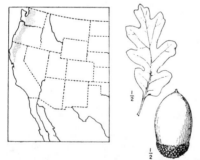

polish. It is used in flooring, all types of cabinetwork and in the manufacture of higher-grade furniture.

OAK, SOUTHERN RED *Quercus falcata* (falcata—sickle-shaped)

Growing from Florida westward to Oklahoma and north through

Illinois and New Jersey, this oak is known also as FINGER OAK, HILL RED OAK, SPANISH OAK, SPOTTED OAK and TURKEY RED OAK.

The leaves of this tree are shiny green on top and dull green on the bottom, having either three, five or seven sharply pointed lobes. It is a hard and heavy, fairly strong but coarse-grained wood and is difficult to dry, as it checks badly. It deteriorates quickly when exposed to the ground. This oak is used in general construction work and will take a fine painted surface providing the wood has first been filled.

OAK, WHITE *Quercus alba* (alba —white)

It is known also as FORKED-LEAF WHITE OAK and STAVE OAK.

White oak is native to the eastern part of Canada and the United States, south to Florida and the Gulf states. It is the state tree of Maryland and Connecticut and is the tree which produces the finest oak lumber and veneers, as well as the largest quantity of lumber.

The heartwood is light tan in color, and in the fall the tree produces beautiful coloring in red

Oak is a large family. Fifty-five species are native to North America. It takes 100 years for red oak and white oak to reach minimum harvestable size. Top left: Red oak. Top right: White oak. Bottom left: A budding bur oak. Bottom right: The less familiar chinkapin oak.

White oak. Light brown, broken pin stripes. Example, called rift-sawed, shows marked comb grain effect created by quarter sawing.

and bright yellow leaves, later turning to a pale brown. The leaves cling to the tree all during the winter. The tree has a large, high, straight trunk and is considered one of the most beautiful of hardwoods. The acorns of the white oak are large, about ¾ in. long, and edible—the Indians made use of them. They are eaten in a number of different ways— baked in muffins, boiled or roasted. The birds, deer, squirrels and other animals are particularly fond of the acorns, which decreases the chance of germination.

This is one of the heaviest, strongest and hardest of all the oaks. It may be worked easily with any type of tool and when properly finished will take a fine polish. Large quantities of white oak are manufactured into veneers, cut either on the quarter to obtain the flake figure, or what is known as "rift cut" to obtain the fine straight lines very popular in mod-

ern furniture. It is a favorite wood for the paneling of fine rooms.

The lumber is largely used in the manufacture of containers for liquids and a good deal is used in the manufacture of barrels for liquors. It is particularly desirable for this purpose, as the pores of the wood are filled with a substance known as tyloses, which does not permit liquids to penetrate.

OGEA *Daniellia ogea* (Daniellia— after Samuel Daniell, 1777–1811, English painter; ogea—after the native Nigerian name)

Ogea is known also as DANIELLIA, GUM COPAL and OZIYA.

Ogea originates in west Africa and is generally found in the heavy rain forests of Nigeria. It comes from the same genus of trees which produces the west African gum copal. It is a fairly straight tree and has a smooth bark until the tree ages, when the bark becomes very scaly. The age of this tree can be determined by studying the bark.

The tree produces wood of a pale white or pinkish brown color without much character and with large pores that produce the lines in the wood. It is of medium weight and strength and does not present any difficulty in working with tools. It takes a good stain, but for a high polish the pores have to be filled first. It is exported only in limited quantities.

OKWEN *Brachystegia spiciformis* (Brachy/stegia—short covering; spiciformis—pointed)

Okwen is a large tree growing in the dense forests in tropical Africa, including Zambia and western Africa. It varies greatly in size, as some trees are slender and unusual in height and others are much shorter with unusual diameters.

The heartwood has a background of light brown with variable darker brown stripes of irregular width. It is a heavy wood, averaging 47 lbs. per cubic foot, and is hard and resistant to decay. With experienced handling the wood seasons well in the dry kilns and is suitable for all types of interior work and construction. Se-

lected logs will produce a good quality of rotary-cut veneer.

OLIVE, EAST AFRICAN *Olea hochstetteri* (Olea—ancient Latin plant name, *oleum*, meaning oil; hochstetteri—after C. F. Hochstetter, a German professor)

This tree, found in the forests of Kenya and also in Abyssinia, reaches a height of 80 ft. or more with diameters around 3 ft. It has an unusually fine texture, heavier than average, around 60 lbs. per cubic foot, and a pleasing brownish, sort of olive color, with attractive markings. The tree bears a small white flower and the fruit is similar to the olives growing on the olive trees in Italy—probably why this tree is so named.

East African olive has unusual strength and is an excellent wood for columns and heavy construction work. Because of its wide variation in color, it is also suitable for paneling, veneering, decorative work and bandings on cabinets.

OLIVE, EUROPEAN *Olea europea* (Olea—Greek name for the olive; europea—from Europe)

Native to southern Europe and particularly Italy, this tree some-

Olive burl, also called olive ash burl.

what resembles the willow but belongs to the same family as the ash. The wood, which is yellowish brown in color, streaked with dark brown pigment lines, is hard and heavy, close-grained and slow-growing. Occasionally veneers are available—at high prices—and at times burls and swirls may be obtained.

OLIVILLO *Aextoxicon punctatum* (Aex/toxicon—goat poison; punctatum—dotted)

Emanating from Chile, this is a medium-sized tree, similar to red gum or satin walnut, and it grows in stands so thick and close that it kills the smaller vegetation.

The wood has a brownish background without much variation in color and is of medium weight and hardness, but with a very fine, even texture and straight grain. Small quantities have been exported in the last ten years to commercial markets where it has been used for miscellaneous work and in the construction of furniture. In Chile it is used for all types of general carpentry, joining and staves for casks.

OMU *Entandrophragma candollei* (Ent/andro/phragma—within the male membrane; candollei—after de Candolle, a family of Swiss botanists)

Growing throughout west Africa, this is a large tree, known as KOSIPO in the French territories, and weighing about 45 lbs. per cubic foot. The heartwood is reddish brown, which darkens upon exposure, and it is especially difficult to season, particularly when kiln-dried.

Selected logs are suitable for furniture, and the heavier species are used in large construction and naval work. The principal interest in this wood is that occasional figured logs will produce a very beautiful veneer, though little of it is available on the market.

OPEPE *Sarcocephalus diderrichii* (Sarco/cephalus—fleshy head; diderrichii—after Diderrich)

This tree grows in southern Nigeria and the Gold Coast in Africa. It is a gray-white to yellowish pink in color. The heartwood is nearly an orange color and has a pattern somewhat like mahogany.

ORANGE, OSAGE *Maclura pomifera* (Maclura—after William Maclure, 1743–1840, American geologist; pom/ifera—apple bearing)

Osage orange grows in the southwestern United States, and the logs obtained are in lengths from 6 to 8 ft. and 12 to 16 in. in diameter. The wood has a greenish yellow color, very close grain somewhat like locust, and is hard and strong. It is seldom cut into lumber or veneers, but when it is, the principal uses are for archery bows and for wheels. It also is used as a dyewood for extracting dyes. Decorative mottles are obtained from selected logs.

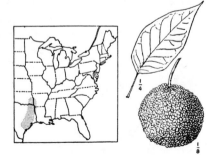

ORANGE, SOUR *Citrus aurantium* (Citrus—from Greek, citron used for the citron tree, *Citrus medica*; aurantium—orange)

This tree grows in India, southern Europe, Africa and tropical America. It is a yellowish white wood, hard, close-grained, weighing about 49 lbs. per cubic foot, and has a tough surface after being planed. It is used all over the world for making small articles of turnery, fancy boxes, novelties, inlays, and particularly for manicure sticks.

PADAUK, ANDAMAN *Pterocarpus dalbergioides* (Ptero/carpus—winged fruit; dalbergioides—appearing like *Dalbergia*)

Padauk, while emanating from Africa, is secured principally from the Andaman Islands, a group of islands in the Bay of Bengal about 650 miles southeast of Calcutta. Most of the settlements here are penal colonies and a great portion of this timber is logged by convict labor. The padauk tree is one of the most common in these islands. The trees do not grow in groups, but are scattered throughout the forest. They are large, growing to 15 ft. in circumference at the stump and 60 ft. high to the first branch.

Because of the brilliant red color of some of the wood, the name vermilion has been given to it. Among old cabinetmakers it is often referred to as East Indian mahogany and Indian redwood. It comes in both a stripe and a mottled effect. Much use

Striped padauk. Predominantly violet red and golden brown alternating narrow stripes. Some examples have mottle. Its color has given it the alternate name of vermilion.

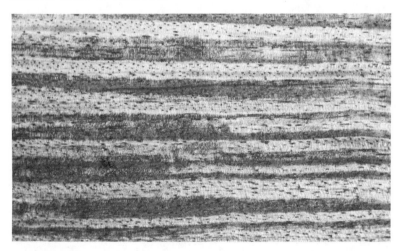

has been made of it by the Pull-man Company for trim in dining, smoking and sleeping compart-ments. Craftsmen find it an excel-lent wood for various small pieces of furniture, turned articles and certain musical instruments.

The padauk from Africa is gen-erally inferior to that described above because of its open grain and softer texture. It is used ex-tensively in the making of dyes. In using this wood one must avoid application of water to the un-finished surface.

PALDAO *Dracontomelum dao* (Draconto—a kind of bird; melum —origin unknown; dao—a native name in the Philippines)

Paldao grows in the East Indies, Indochina and the Philippines. It has a grayish to reddish brown color, varied grain effects, usually with irregular stripes and occa-sionally some very dark stripes. At times a crotch or swirl will de-velop. It is a fairly hard wood, available in quartered veneers, half-round, and lumber, and is used for building and furniture.

Semifigured paldao, two-piece match.

New Guinea wood. Same family as paldao. Yellowish with strongly contrasting and irregular brown stripes. Faint greenish undertone. Comes from New Guinea and Philippines.

PALMS

THE PALM TREE is another of our biblical woods from which, as we all know, Palm Sunday is named. However, what is not generally realized is that if all species of palms were counted there would be nearly twelve hundred, classified under the name *Palmaceae*.

Practically all of them grow in tropical lands and the greatest number have a cylindrical trunk with a crown of leaves, either fan-shaped or featherlike, and having polygamous flowers. The most valuable in commerce are the coconut palm (*Cocos*) and the date palm (*Phoenix*).

Some of the others often seen are the Washingtonia palm (*Washingtonia rabusta*), native to lower California and Mexico; the royal palm (*Roystonea regia*), native to Cuba and south Florida, which is one of the most striking in appearance, growing to 100 ft. in height with a whitish trunk; the fishtail palm (*Caryota urens*), the most widely known of the nine species from Asia and Australia; the king palm (*Archontophoenis alexandrae*), native of New South Wales and Queensland; the pygmy-date palm (*Phoenix roebelenin*), native to Africa and tropical Asia, though also widely grown in Florida for landscaping, and the palm often found in our northern states as potted house plants. Then there is the African oil palm (*Elaeis guineensis*), native of tropical Africa and the East Indies, which is cultivated commercially for "palm oil" used in cooking, ointments and the making of soap.

Palms have considerable interest to botanists for study, and commercially for the fruit, oil and other products derived from them. However, the palm has little interest to the craftsman because it does not provide wood suitable for working with tools.

PALMETTO, CABBAGE *Sabal palmetto* (Sabal—an unexplained name; palmetto—from the Spanish, palmito, for little palm)

This palm is known also as CAROLINA PALM and SWAMP CABBAGE and is the state tree of Florida and South Carolina.

This tree grows to an average height of 30 to 50 ft., with diameters of 16 to 24 in., and is native

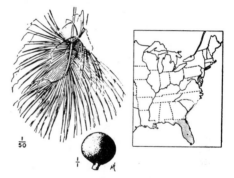

to the southeastern United States from North Carolina southward. It obtains its common name from the fact that the leaf bud or "heart" at the top of the trunk is a delicacy with a fine cabbage flavor when cooked as a vegetable would be cooked. The early Florida Indians used it as one of their principal foods and today it is stocked in some stores, pre-cooked, in cans. However, the tree generally dies when the tender bud is cut away.

This is the palm that is used in churches on Palm Sunday and it also has a historical background.

The state seal of South Carolina shows the cabbage palmetto, commemorating the fact that during the Revolution the South Carolinians built a stockade from logs of the cabbage palm, and in Charleston Harbor on Sullivan Island, on June 28, 1776, General William Moultrie defeated the ships of the British.

Cross sections from large trunks of palmetto trees can be polished to make unusually attractive table tops. It is fairly light and soft wood and locally is used for making fences and telegraph poles.

PARTRIDGE WOOD *Andira inermis* (Andira—from the Brazilian name; inermis—unarmed, without spines)

Emanating from Venezuela and Colombia, this tree averages about 6 ft. in height and 1 to 2 ft. in diameter. The heartwood is deep, purplish brown or chocolate-brown, with the positions of the pores marked with a lighter-colored line of soft tissues. The wood is named from the figure produced by these soft tissues on plain surfaces, as it is somewhat similar to the markings on a partridge wing.

Partridge wood is very heavy, about 75 lbs. per cubic foot, occasionally more, and extremely hard. It has strength and high resistance to rot, which is one of the reasons it is used locally for outdoor construction work. It is suitable principally for turning, as it is extremely hard to work, either in wet or dry form, but it takes a very smooth polish. A small quantity of this wood is imported into the United States and used principally for turned work, fancy articles and walking sticks.

PAU d'ARCO *Tabebuia serratifolia* (Tabebuia—a Brazilian plant name; serrati/folia—saw-toothed leaf, referring to the notched margins of the leaflets)

Native to Brazil, this tree is known there as the IRON TREE and IRONWOOD. It is known also as BASTARD, GREENHEART, LIGNUM VITAE and SURINAM, and in the southern part of Brazil as IPÉ.

This tree is described as one of the tallest in the Amazon region, with a height of from 180 to 200 ft. It has a lustrous brown color with a slightly greenish tinge, somewhat resembling a dark greenheart but with a much closer and finer grain. Some of the logs are highly figured with a small broken roe and mottle, and veneers have been obtained which give the appearance of a dark, golden brown Ceylon satinwood. These have been used for high-class decorative work in both England and America. Other uses of this wood are in general construction and for piling and harbor work.

All of the different varieties have astringent qualities and are reported to have medicinal value.

PAU FERRO *Libidibia sclerocarpa* (Libidibia—probably pleasure bird from *libid ibid*; sclero/carpa—hard fruit)

This wood is native to the Guianas, Brazil and other parts of tropical South America. Its texture resembles African blackwood for smoothness and marblelike appearance. This is another wood known as IRONWOOD. It is a deep, purplish brown in color, merging almost into a black, and weighs 69 lbs. per cubic foot.

Locally it is used for building docks, piling, etc., but there is no known use of it commercially in this country.

PAWPAW *Asimina triloba* (Asimina—from the American Indian name; tri/loba—three-lobed, referring to the three-parted flower)

This tree grows from western New York through Nebraska and southward through the Middle Atlantic states to Texas and Florida. The fruit resembles a short banana in shape, from which it receives its common name.

The wood has little commercial value except for fuel, and its principal use is for ornamental planting. However, it works well with tools and where locally obtainable it offers possibilities to the craftsman for various types of turned work.

PEAR WOOD *Pyrus communis* (Pyrus—pear; communis—common)

This also is called PEAR TREE and grows in the United States, Germany and France.

The wood is rosy pink in color, with shadings on a light cream background. It has a moderate, leafy grained figure, sometimes with a mottle figure, and is fine

and close-grained. It is very suitable for reproducing flesh colors. It is used in mechanical-drawing instruments and rulers, and a great portion of it in marquetry work. The most sought-after for veneers is the pear wood from Europe.

PECAN WOOD *Carya illinoensis* (Carya—from the Greek name for nut; illinoensis—from Illinois)

Pecan is a species of the hickory tree found in the southern part of the United States, east of the Mississippi, and is the state tree of Texas. It was named after the Algonquin Indian, Peccan. For many years the Indians believed that this tree was a part of the Great Spirit himself.

Both wild and cultivated pecan trees are highly regarded for their edible long, oval-shaped nuts.

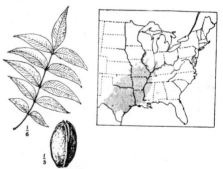

Pecan, sliced, reddish brown with darker streaks.

These trees also yield valuable lumber. Veneers are quite plentiful, lumber is available but not plentiful because of the short trunk and forked and twisted branches. The wood is close-grained, hard and strong, reddish brown with darker streaks.

In lumber form pecan wood is often used for office chairs. Veneers go into furniture and wall paneling.

Another use for pecan wood is for the smoking of meats, it being considered especially desirable for this purpose.

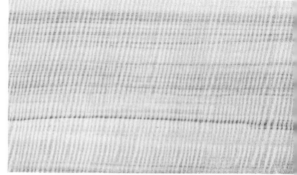

Rosa peroba, fiddleback.

PEROBA, ROSA *Aspidosperma peroba* (Aspido/sperma—shield seed, referring to the waferlike shape of the seed; peroba—a native name)

Other names by which this tree are known are AMARILLO, PALO and ROSA.

This large tree, with well-formed trunk, grows in southeastern Brazil and attains a height of 125 ft. and 4 or 5 ft. in diameter. The trees are slender, with sparse foliage and a wrinkled bark, but they stand out in the landscape clearly because of their majestic appearance. The heartwood is rose-red to yellowish, often variegated or streaked with purple or brown, and the surface becomes brownish yellow to dark brown upon exposure. It is not sharply demarcated from the sapwood. Being hard and moderately strong, the wood weighs 46 lbs. per cubic foot.

It has a low to medium luster. The odor is not distinctive, but

Left: The Pecan State Champion and state tree of Texas at Weatherford, Texas.

the wood has a very bitter taste. It has good working qualities, with a fine, uniform texture and a grain which runs from straight to very irregular. Rosa peroba is one of the highly important group of Brazilian timbers, comparable in general utility to the oak of the United States. It is used in great abundance in all kinds of building construction.

Other colors of peroba are indicated by their names, as follows: Peroba preta, with conspicuous black streaks; peroba miuda, which is red with darker patches; peroba poca, a white wood; peroba rajada, light red with large black patches; peroba tremida, yellow with lighter patches, almost golden; peroba revesa, having a figure similar to bird's eye maple. Veneers are available in the peroba species.

PERSIMMON, COMMON *Diospyros virginiana* (Diospyros—fruit or wheat of the gods; virginiana—of Virginia)

It is known also as BARA-BARA, BOA-WOOD, BUTTERWOOD, CYLIL DATE PLUM, and POSSUM WOOD.

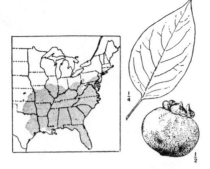

Growing in the southern part of the United States, this wood is known as the ebony of America and has a cubic weight of 59 lbs. per cubic foot. This is usually a small or medium-sized tree, but it has reached heights of 100 ft. and more, with a diameter of 20 to 30 in. The heartwood is black, brown or variegated; when freshly cut, the sapwood is white. The sapwood is strong and tough, of medium to fine texture with fairly straight grain, and finishes very smoothly.

Persimmon sapwood is used for the heads of golf clubs and the manufacture of shuttles, in which form it will withstand 1,000 hours of work without any need of replacement.

PERSIMMON, KAKI *Diospyros kaki* (Diospyros—fruit of the gods; kaki—probably from a native name)

This wood comes from Japan, where it is used extensively. It weighs about 49 lbs. per cubic foot and has a marblelike coldness to the touch. The color of the wood is dense black with beautiful streaks of orange, yellow, gray and brown, but it has a very disagreeable scent.

PIMENTO *Pimenta officinalis* (Pimenta—from the Spanish pimento; officinalis—referring to use in medicine)

Growing in the West Indies, this wood is firm, hard and close-textured, and varies in color from a light salmon to dark salmon. It has a very limited use, practically the entire output being used in making canes.

PINES

BELONGING to the softwood group of the forest trees in the United States, the pines include thirty-five different species. A brief description is given of a few of them, as well as several important foreign pines.

PINE, CHILEAN *Araucaria araucana* (Araucaria—after the Chilean province of Arauco; araucana—of Arauco)

This species of pine has been known in England for many years as MONKEY PUZZLE.

Growing in a very limited area of southwest Argentina and a small section of Chile, the wood was first discovered many years ago in the province of Arauco, which explains how its scientific name was derived. The height is from 80 to 120 ft. and occasionally trees are found considerably taller than this, with diameters anywhere from 30 to 48 in. An interesting thing about this tree is its seeds, which are large and often number 100 or more in each ripe cone. They are generally about an inch long. In Chile they are collected for food and when served in roasted form are considered a rare delicacy.

The wood is of a yellowish or gray color and has a tendency to darken slightly with age. It is of fine texture, straight-grained, and like many pines, without any distinctive odor. Chilean pine secretes a valuable resin or gum and it gives up its moisture so slowly and so unevenly in drying that considerable care is necessary.

This wood has been exported for 150 years or more, with considerable quantities going to Great Britain, but as most of the finer trees are in mountainous regions and difficult to get at, only limited amounts are exported today. The tree is often seen in English gardens under the name, as mentioned above, of monkey puzzle.

The wood is suitable for interior work, doors, and was especially used in airplane construction and propellers.

PINE, EASTERN WHITE *Pinus strobus* (Pinus—the classical Latin name; strobus—a Latin word for pine cone)

This tree is known also by other common names, such as NORTHERN WHITE PINE, BALSAM PINE and CANADIAN WHITE PINE; in Michigan it is known as CORK PINE, SPRUCE PINE and WHITE PINE.

This is the king of all pines in the eastern part of our country and the state tree of Maine. The height of a virgin growth of these trees has been known to reach from 100 to 200 ft., with diameters up to 6 ft. The heartwood is a very light creamy brown, sometimes tan, and tinged with red. It has a dark gray bark that is deeply furrowed in long ridges and bluish green needles, from 3 to 5 in. long, which grow in bundles of five. The cones are from 5 to 10 in. long and usually curve; they mature at the end of the second season.

It is the favorite wood of carpenters, as it works easily and finishes well. It has been used for a long time for patternmaking and for general interior trim.

For over three hundred years early Americans used this wood to build their homes, churches and mills. The colonies' flag, which was flown in the American Revolution on all colonial ships, carried a reproduction of the white pine tree, and the state of Massachusetts in the seventeenth century honored the tree by having its image on a coin.

Many things have reduced the large stand of white pine that was in America at the time of the white man's arrival. As far as can be estimated, the original amount was better than three-quarters of a trillion square feet; today's figures indicate that about fifteen billion feet have been left growing. White pine in its natural state may have a lifetime of four hundred years.

PINE, JACK *Pinus banksiana* (banksiana—after Sir Joseph Banks, 1743–1820, benefactor of one of Cook's voyages to Australia, and naturalist)

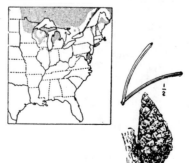

Top left: Shortleaf pine. Top right: Longleaf pine.

Bottom left: Eastern white pine. Bottom right: Slash pine.

Quarter-sawed Liberian pine.

This pine is known also as BLACK PINE, GRAY PINE, HUDSON BAY PINE and SCRUB PINE.

Jack pine, considered one of the poorest of the species, grows in eastern Canada, the provinces of Nova Scotia and Quebec, throughout northern New England and northeastern United States, through the Great Lakes states of Indiana, Illinois, Michigan and Wisconsin.

The tree grows to a height of 20 to 65 ft. and the trunks are from 6 to 24 in. in diameter. It may be recognized by the needles, which grow in pairs, only 1 in. long; they are narrow, flat, twisted and sharply pointed, dark gray-green in color. The cones are oblong and curved with thick scales. The tree has a dull, dark red-brown, thin bark with narrow, shallow ridges.

The most important use of this wood is in the manufacture of paper pulp. However, an increasing quantity is being used each year for the manufacture of furniture and plywood and for paneling rooms because of the attractiveness of the knots. It is known as "knotty pine."

PINE, LIBERIAN *Tetraberlinia tubmaniana* (Tetra—Latin, meaning fourth; berlinia—generic name of the Ekop group of the *Leguminoseae* family, or the fourth division; *tubmaniana*—in honor of William V. S. Tubman, President of the Republic of Liberia)

This is a large, very straight, tall tree with diameters up to 4 ft., the most common diameters being between 2 and 3 ft. It grows along the coastal region of Liberia, and in a number of places is found in such concentration that large quantities are available for export to the various wood markets of the world. Leaves, fruit and wood specimens were collected in 1954 by E. W. Fobes of the United States Forest Products Laboratory.

The wood has a pleasing grain with a light to medium reddish brown color. It is a wood of average weight—40 lbs. per cubic foot when oven-dried. It seasons without difficulty and no special care is required in drying other than procedures normally used with hardwoods. It works well with either power or hand tools and can be compared with yellow poplar for planing; in a lathe it does not turn quite as well as American black walnut. However, it shapes much better than American walnut, although not quite as well as Honduras mahogany.

The raw wood has an oily feel but it takes a fine finish. In Denmark it has been sliced into veneers without difficulty and used in the commercial manufacture of furniture. In Liberia it has been used extensively for home building and construction and also in the manufacture of furniture.

PINE, LOBLOLLY *Pinus taeda* (taeda—ancient name of resinous pines)

This is known also as BASSETT PINE, BLACK PINE, FOXTAIL PINE, INDIAN PINE, LONGLEAF PINE, SWAMP PINE and YELLOW PINE.

Loblolly pine grows in the southeastern part of the United States along the Atlantic coast from Delaware to northern Florida and westward to Texas. It may be recognized by its thin bark, deeply furrowed by long, large scales, and its red-brown color. The needles are pale green, sharp-pointed, 5 to 9 in. long, and three in a bundle. The heartwood is light tan or yellowish brown. It is a strong, moderately hard wood, used in the manufacture of commercial veneers, boxes, in general construction, and large quantities for paper pulp.

PINE, LODGEPOLE *Pinus contorta* (contorta—contorted or twisted, alluding to the irregular crown of the typical, scrubby shore pine of the coast)

Other common names are BLACK PINE, SCRUB PINE, SHORE PINE, COAST PINE, TAMARACK PINE.

The common name of this tree was given because of its tall, slender, very light poles which were used by Indians of the region in the structure of their lodges. Poles 15 ft. long and 2 in. in diameter were selected, set in a circle, the tops bent together and tied, and the frame covered with skins or bark.

Lodgepole pine has often been called a "fire tree"—a very appropriate name—as it profits by severe burning, as some other trees of the United States do. The sealed cones are opened by fire, which softens the resin; and after the fire has passed, the seeds are liberated to wing their flight wherever the wind carries them. The passing fire may be severe enough to kill the parent tree without destroying or bringing down the cones. The seeds soon fall on the bared soil where they germinate by thousands. More than 100,000 small seedling trees may occupy a single acre. Most lodgepole pines never reach large size.

The tree is one of the slowest in growing; possibly 3 ft. is the limit in diameter. However it does grow tall and slender. A hundred years will scarcely produce a saw log of the smallest size. The wood is about the same weight as eastern pine, light in color, rather weak and brittle. The wood is characterized by numerous small knots.

Lodgepole pine has long and widely been used as ranch timber, serving as poles and rails in fences and for sheds, barns, corrals, pens and small bridges.

If fires cease among the western mountains, with more efficient methods of patrol and stricter enforcement of laws against starting fires, the spread of lodgepole pine will come to a standstill and existing forests will grow old without much extension of their borders.

PINE, LONGLEAF *Pinus palustris* (palustris—of the marsh)

This species is known also as FLORIDA PINE, GEORGIA HARD PINE, NORTH CAROLINA PITCH PINE, TEXAS LONGLEAVED PINE and TURPENTINE PINE.

This pine grows in the southeastern states, extending westward to Alabama (of which state it is the official tree), Mississippi, Louisiana and Texas. It bears one of the longest needles—6 to 20 in.—of a dark green color, shiny, flexible, growing three in a cluster. They drop off every two years. The tree's name comes from these very long needles. The bark is of an orange-brown color, slightly marked into broad scales. The brownish cones also are long—5 to 10 in.—and grow in clusters of several cones.

This tree has no heartwood until it is about eighteen years old; then the heartwood is light orange, yellow and red, while the sapwood is practically white.

Longleaf pine provides large quantities of turpentine, resin and pine oil, for the manufacture of cosmetics and perfumes. The wood is used in the manufacture of pulpwood and craft paper and also for railroad ties, piles, heavy construction work and shipbuilding.

PINE, PINYON *Pinus edulis* (edulis—edible, referring to the large edible seeds commonly called Indian nuts, pine nuts or piñones)

This species is known also as NUT PINE, PITCH PINE and SCRUB PINE.

This is a very slow-growing tree and its life span may reach 350 years or more. It has a short trunk and often is no higher than 8 or 10 ft., twisted and crooked. At times it may reach 50 ft. and is from 10 to 24 in. in diameter. The tree grows in mountainous areas at elevations of 5,000 ft. and upward and is found in the western part of the country from Wyoming through Colorado and into northern Mexico and Texas. It is the state tree of Nevada and New Mexico.

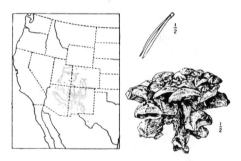

This tree is mostly prized for its pine nuts, which are delicious and edible. These nuts are generally baked shortly after being gathered to retain their rich flavor. They are the most valuable product of the tree, and the annual crops of nuts range from one million to as high as eight million pounds.

As the tree is very knotty, because of the many limbs, the wood is generally used locally for general construction and in the manufacture of charcoal. It is a favorite wood for telephone poles.

PINE, PONDEROSA *Pinus ponderosa* (ponderosa—ponderous or heavy, in reference to the heavy timber)

This species is known also as BIG PINE, BIRD'S-EYE PINE, KNOTTY PINE, LODGEPOLE PINE, OREGON PINE, PITCH PINE, POLE PINE and PRICKLY PINE.

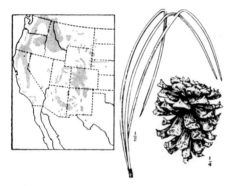

Ponderosa pine is the state tree of Montana.

It grows along the extreme western part of the continent from Alaska down through California and through most of the Rocky Mountains, up to elevations of 10,000 and 12,000 ft. It is one of the most beautiful pines, with diameters up to 7 ft. It may be recognized because of the thick, scaly, irregular bark of a pale brown or grayish color. The needles generally are in bundles of three, from 5 to 10 in. long with a gray-green to deep yellow-green color.

The town of Flagstaff, Arizona, was so named because of this tree. On the Fourth of July in 1876, lumberjacks selected one of the tallest trees, and as it grew, stripped it of all its branches to fly the American flag from its top. It is said that this is the only American wood whose name has been under consideration by the U.S. Supreme Court. It issued a ruling in 1934 preventing the sale of the wood as California white pine. It is estimated that over 185 billion feet are growing, over 3 billion feet being logged annually.

Sometimes a bird's-eye figure, the same as in maple, is found in this pine. It provides a large quantity of lumber for cabinetwork, general millwork, sash, doors and moldings, and it is used as knotty pine for interior trim. Also it is used for various types of poles, fence posts, paper pulp and other articles.

PINE, RED *Pinus resinosa* (resinosa —resinous)

This pine at times is known also as NORWAY PINE. It acquired this name because originally large quantities of these trees were located in the village of Norway, Maine.

Top left: Stand of Ponderosa pine in Sequoia National Forest, California. Top right: Closeup of Ponderosa trees in southern Oregon.

Bottom left: Loblolly pine in Francis Marion National Forest, South Carolina. Bottom right: Old pinyon pine and seedlings.

The average red pine grows to a height of 65 to 80 ft. with diameters of 2 to 3 ft. and it is estimated there are over a quarter million acres of red pine in Minnesota. U.S. figures show that there are a little less than three billion board feet, most of it in the northeast with the balance divided between Wisconsin, Michigan and Minnesota. Red pine is the state tree of Minnesota.

This pine is a light, close-grained wood of average softness and produces better lumber for building purposes than the eastern pine because of its extra weight and strength. It is an excellent tree for piling because it has a high penetration with creosote.

The early colonists found that this wood was best suited for the deckings, masts and spars of their sailing boats. Today there is a great demand for the red pine logs for building summer cabins.

PINE, SCOTCH *Pinus sylvestris*
(sylvestris—of the woods)

This pine emanates from Europe, particularly Great Britain, and is generally known abroad as RED WOOD.

It weighs about 26 lbs. per cubic foot, is even and straight in grain, tough and elastic. It is easily worked and is famous for use as heavy timbering and in general construction work.

PINE, SHORTLEAF *Pinus echinata*
(echinata—spiny, describing the cones)

This species of pine is known also as CAROLINA PINE, NORTHERN CAROLINA PINE, PITCH PINE and YELLOW PINE.

It is the official state tree of Arkansas and grows from New York southward to most of the southeastern states as far as Florida, and the eastern sections of Oklahoma, Texas and Arkansas. It

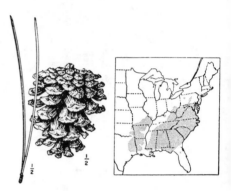

is recognized by the blue-green, slender needles, 3 to 5 in. long, in bundles of two that remain on the tree from two to five years. The cones are a dull brown, only 1 to 2 in. long, and of prickly egg shape.

The name *echinata* was given to this pine in 1768 by Philip Miller, the British botanist, as coming from the Latin word for hedgehog, probably suggested by the cones and needles. Before the days of the steamship, it was one of the most prized woods in ship construction and was used for the masts in all naval vessels of the United States and Great Britain. Early in the 1700's the wood was proclaimed by Great Britain as the property of the British Crown for the masts of the Royal Navy.

It is now used in building construction and interior trim as knotty pine. It is so rapid in growing that it is being used in increasing quantities for paper pulp.

PINE, SLASH *Pinus elliottii* (elliottii—after its discoverer, Stephen Elliott, 1771–1830, botanist and banker of South Carolina)

This species of pine is known also as MEADOW PINE, SALT WATER PINE, SPRUCE PINE, SHE PITCH PINE and SWAMP PINE.

Growing in lowlands and swamps, called "slashes," from which it is named, this pine is found in the southeastern states from the Atlantic seaboard to Mississippi and Louisiana. The needles are a dark lustrous green, 8 to 12 in. long, two or three in a bundle, growing in clusters at the end of the twigs. The cones are a glossy brown, egg-shaped, 3 to 6 in. long, with short spines at the end of each scale of the cone, which is a distinguishing feature of the slash pine.

This is the pine largely used along roadsides and for home planting because of its fine appearance. It also outranks all others in the production of pine oils, resins, etc.

PINE, SUGAR *Pinus lambertiana* (lambertiana—in honor of Aylmer Bourke Lambert, 1761–1842, English specialist in pines)

It is known also as BIG PINE, GIGANTIC PINE, GREAT SUGAR

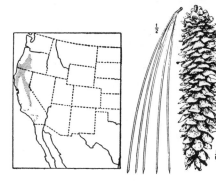

PINE, SHADE PINE and other names.

This tree grows in the regions of southern Oregon to lower California and Mexico, generally at higher altitudes. It reaches a height of up to 150 ft. and is from 4 to 8 ft. in diameter, though species have been found as high as 240 ft. and diameters up to 18 ft. Sugar pine has been described as the finest of all pines for size and is similar in color to the eastern and western pines, although of a little lighter shade.

PINE, WESTERN WHITE *Pinus monticola* (monticola—of the mountains)

Other names of this species are IDAHO WHITE PINE, MOUNTAIN PINE, WHITE PINE and SILVER PINE.

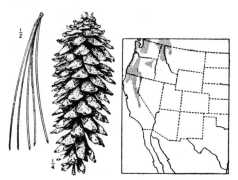

This is the pine of the northwest and is similar in character to the wood of the eastern pine but very different in appearance. This wood grows from the southern region of British Columbia southward along the Cascade Mountains and the Sierra Nevadas, through Washington and Oregon to central California, and it is also the state tree of Idaho.

The wood is very light cream to

light reddish brown in color, darkening somewhat upon exposure. Its chief characteristic is its knots.

Western white pine has a remarkable resistance to weather, growing both in very dry lands and in moist lands, in temperature anywhere from 25 degrees below zero to 100 degrees above. It is a long-lived tree, sometimes up to five hundred years, and it is estimated that over sixteen billion board feet of this pine exists in the United States today, with more than two-thirds of it growing in Idaho.

This pine was discovered around 1830 by a Scottish plant explorer, Davis Douglas, who sent some of the seeds to England. However, it was many years before the tree was cultivated, and more of it can be found in Ireland and Scotland than in England.

The wood is used for the same purpose as the eastern white pine, particularly for interior trim in the lumber form, but it is also available in veneers for the manufacture of plywood.

PINYON, SINGLELEAF *Pinus monophylla* (mono/phylla—one leaf, in allusion to the solitary needles)

This is the state tree of Nevada and grows in parts of Idaho, western Utah, Nevada and parts of Arizona and southern California. Singleleaf pinyon is one of the hardiest of trees, going undamaged through long periods without any moisture and subject to changes in temperature from well below zero to over 120 degrees.

The Indians have received the greatest benefit from these trees, as the nuts which they produce are still an important part of their food. They have a period of feasting and dancing at the time of harvesting the nuts. Each Indian may gather as many as thirty-five bushels of nuts a year. Much of the ill feeling and the resultant bloodshed stemmed from the destruction of this tree by the white man in the southwestern part of our country.

This wood has little commercial value, with the exception that it is preferred for the manufacture of charcoal and is used for firewood.

PLANE, EUROPEAN *Platanus acerifolia* (Platanus—from the classical Latin name for the oriental plane tree; acerifolia—with leaves like maple, *Acer*)

Of the various kinds of plane

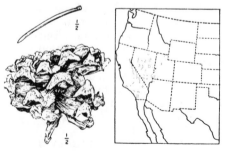

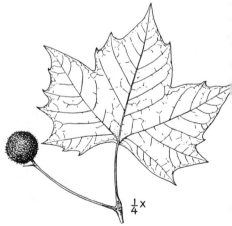

European planetree, in same family as American sycamore, has pinkish brown coloration. Tiny flecked figuration resembles lacewood.

tree, the London plane tree, as cultivated in Great Britain, is one of the most common. It is a rapidly growing tree and apparently thrives well in the dusty and smoky air of large cities.

The wood is of very fine texture, with a straight grain, and when cut across the heart resembles beech, except that it is a little grayer in color. It averages about 40 lbs. per cubic foot, and unless the lumber is quarter-sawed, requires considerable care in drying to prevent warpage. However, it has good strength and is an easy wood to work. At times the quartered wood has been sold as a substitute for lacewood. The wood is used in inlaying and also in cabinetmaking.

PODO *Podocarpus gracilior* (Podo/carpus—foot fruit; gracilior—slender)

In east Africa this wood is known as MUSENGERA WOOD.

Podo is a large evergreen tree growing in several countries of east Africa, including Kenya, Uganda, Abyssinia and parts of Transvaal and Tanganyika territories.

The wood varies in color from a pale yellow to a pale brown and often there is no difference in appearance between the heartwood and the sapwood. It is of fine, uniform texture with a straight grain and weighs a little more than 30 lbs. per cubic foot.

Podo is similar in strength to other foreign softwoods and while slightly harder, does not have the strength of those woods to sustain heavy loads. It is a good all-around wood for the cheap, unseen parts of furniture, such as drawer bottoms and shelves, and also would be suitable for cutting into veneers for the making of plywood.

POON *Calophyllum tomentosum* (Calo/phyllum—beautiful leaf; tomentosum—hairy)

This large tree, sometimes reaching a height of 150 ft., with diameters up to 48 in., is found in the heavy evergreen rain forests on the western side of the peninsula of India, in various altitudes up to 5,000 ft. It is found also on the island of Ceylon.

Because of the color, at first glance the wood seems similar to mahogany or more like the andiroba from South America with its darker wavy streaks of reddish brown lines. With care the wood may be properly seasoned despite its tendency to warp, which is more marked in wood that has great irregularity of grain. However, it works well with saws sharpened and set properly to prevent burning in sawing. The wood has fine strength for its weight of approximately 35 lbs. per cubic foot and is much sought after in the East for the masts and spars of boats.

Choice logs have been converted successfully into attractive veneers. The extracted oil from the seeds of these trees is used for burning lamps.

POPLAR, BALSAM *Populus balsamifera* (Populus—the classical Latin name for the poplar; balsamifera—balsam bearing)

This wood is known also as BALSAM, BALM-OF-GILEAD POPLAR and TACAMAHAC and is one of the thirteen species of COTTONWOOD.

Poplar burl, one of the exotic veneers, highly favored for its pleasant green color and fascinating figure of interlaced swirls.

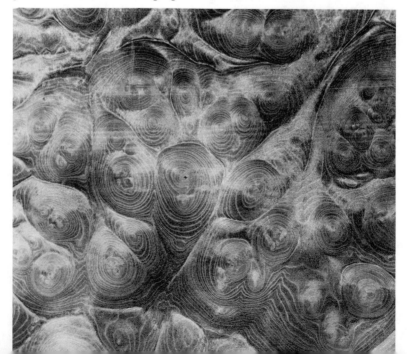

Left: Balsam poplar in a crowded forest, relative of cottonwood. Right: Tuliptree, largest hardwood of eastern United States. Botanically it is not a poplar, although its wood is sold as yellow poplar. The tall, straight trunk is a lumberman's dream. This specimen is in Yorktown, N.Y.

This tree may be found almost across the entire northern part of the United States from the Atlantic coast to the Rocky Mountains, and also in Canada and Alaska. It is the state tree of Wyoming.

Its leaves tremble in the breeze like those of the aspen, but the difference is easily noticed because of the pale green, lustrous leaves, the underside of which is a bright, rusty brown. It is a tall, straight tree which grows up to 100 ft. in height, with a diameter of 2 to 3 ft.

Great care has to be taken in drying this wood or it will warp badly. One of the principal uses is for making boxes and crates, as the wood is light in weight, strong, nails easily without splitting and its appearance is suitable for stenciling or printing. Other uses are for butter and lard pails, matches, excelsior and rough lumber work.

According to records, standing timber in the United States is over 500 million feet, and each year a little over twelve million board feet is cut. The wood itself is light grayish and straight-grained. It always requires wet, moist land. In

Yellow poplar comes from the tuliptree, no relation to Brazilian tulip-wood. The wood is canary yellow, often with a greenish tinge. It has straight grain of even texture.

the West it is one of the principal woods used for shade in city streets.

POPLAR, YELLOW *Liriodendron tulipifera*

This tree also is called CANARY WOOD and CANOE WOOD and the lumber is known as POPLAR, TULIPTREE and WHITEWOOD.

It grows throughout the eastern part of the United States, usually in damp locations, such as along the banks of streams. It is also found in southern Ontario. It is the state tree of three states: Indiana, Kentucky and Tennessee. It grows singly, out in the open, generally 100 ft. or less in height, but it has been known to reach 200 ft. with a trunk of 8 to 10 ft. in diameter. About three-quarters of the remaining first growth of timber is in the southeastern Appalachians. With good reason, it is regarded as one of the most valuable hardwood trees in the eastern United States.

The flowers are very sweet and the mature tree will yield as much as 7 or 8 lbs. of nectar a year, from which the bees produce up to 4 lbs. of one of the most strongly flavored honeys.

The heartwood is a yellowish or grayish color, occasionally with a slight greenish cast or dark streaks. It sometimes turns to a dark purple or blue. The second growth of this timber has a very thick, white sapwood.

Yellow poplar is manufactured into veneers, furniture and musical instruments and is used in general cabinetwork such as sash, doors and shelving and for painted interior trim. It makes good hat blocks in the hat industry, because it does not absorb the moisture present during the steaming process. In the veneer form, this wood is generally used for cross-banding and backs, and the soft yellow poplar growing in the mountain regions is considered the most desirable wood for cross-banding.

It works very easily with all kinds of tools, being suitable also for carving and painting.

PRIMAVERA *Tabebuia donnell-smithii* (Tabebuia—a native name; donnell-smithii—after Donnell-Smith, a botanist)

Primavera is found growing along the west coast of Mexico and Nicaragua in rich, damp soil. However, trees growing in the uplands are stronger and produce a more beautiful figure.

Although it resembles white mahogany and is often erroneously called "white mahogany," it does not come from the botanical classification which produces the true mahogany (*Swietenia*). It perhaps is a good name, however, as it is similar in all respects to mahogany except for the color. When first cut, it is a pale yellow or cream color, which darkens with exposure to air and light, changing to a yellowish rose color, resembling Ceylon satinwood, with streaks of red, orange and brown. The principal defect is that many of the logs contain small pinholes caused by insects.

One of the little-known facts about this tree is that the sap of these trees in the tropics rises and falls with the phases of the moon instead of in the spring and winter as it does in temperate zones. This has an important effect upon the value and marketability of the timber—according to when it was felled. It should be cut in the "dark of the moon." The reason for this is that when the sap is down and the logs are cut, little of it exudes from the ends of the log. On the other hand, if the trees are felled when the moon is on the increase, there will be a large amount of sap in the trees and greater quantities will exude from the ends of the cut logs, attracting quantities of insects and causing damage to the trees before they are taken to the mill and converted into timber or veneers.

Primavera averages about 35 to 38 lbs. per cubic foot, works easily and finishes nicely and is very suitable for craftsmen, either in the thin lumber or veneer form, for producing individual effects.

While primavera is well known in the United States, it is little used in the United Kingdom.

Striped primavera with mild figure.

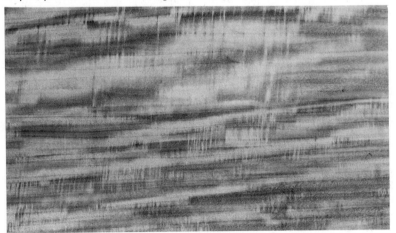

Purpleheart. The figure is a mildly accented stripe, but the color is startling. Upon exposure to air, after cutting, it turns purple and continues to color as it ages.

PURPLEHEART *Peltogyne paniculata* and other species (Peltogyne—with the female organs shield-shaped; paniculata—referring to the flower cluster)

Purpleheart is known also as AMARANTH and VIOLET WOOD. Locally, in British Guiana, it is called SUCUPIRA.

This tree attains a top height of 125 ft., with diameters up to 4 ft. It is a well-formed tree covered with smooth, grayish black bark, and often clear of branches up to 50 ft. The heartwood is a dull brown in color, but when freshly cut it turns deep purple upon exposure to air. It is used in the lumber form, one of its main uses being for making butts of billiard cues. When cut into 1/28 in. veneer, it is used for decorative work and in general cabinetmaking.

PYINKADO *Xylia xylocarpa* (Xylia—wood; xylocarpa—woody fruit)

Pyinkado grows in India and Burma and is known as the IRON WOOD OF BURMA.

The wood is reddish brown in color, hard and heavy, weighing about 70 to 81 lbs. per cubic foot, and is very strong and rigid. Its pores are filled with a thick, glutinous, oily substance which gives a sticky feeling to the touch and is still noticeable after a great many years of exposure to the weather. As the logs are too heavy to float, transportation of them is not only difficult but very costly.

When the tree is freshly cut, it works with some difficulty, but after long exposure it becomes practically impossible for any woodworking tool to work it. Locally, the main use of the wood is for the Burma railways. It is an excellent wood for paving blocks, having successfully served this purpose in Rangoon.

QUEBRACHO *Schinopsis* spp. (Schinopsis—having the appearance of *Schinus*)

Native to Argentina, this wood

also is known there as BREAK-AXE, IRONWOOD and RED LIGNUM VITAE. It is a heavy wood, weighing about 70 to 80 lbs. per cubic foot.

QUEENSLAND WALNUT *Endiandra palmerstoni* (En/di/andra —in two stamens; palmerstoni— after Palmerston)

This wood is known also as AUSTRALIAN LAUREL, AUSTRALIAN WALNUT, ORIENTAL WALNUT and ORIENTAL WOOD.

It grows only along the coast of Queensland in Australia and is a rich, decorative wood resembling in color the American and European walnut. While it is not related to the genuine walnut, it is a beautiful and striking wood.

In this country the greatest quantity is manufactured into veneers and originally was called oriental walnut, so named by those who imported it so that others might not learn of its origin and true identity. Throughout the United Kingdom it is known as Australian or Queensland walnut.

The color varies from a pinkish gray to brown with a figure somewhat like walnut but with much darker stripes. It is a fairly heavy wood, averaging around 45 lbs. per cubic foot, has a highly figured grain and emits a most objectionable odor when freshly sawed. This, however, is not apparent after manufacture and drying into veneers.

The wood is difficult to season, requiring great care to prevent warpage and shrinkage when used in the solid wood. It also splits easily and is difficult to work with hand or power tools. When the wood is completely dry, the amount of silica in it quickly dulls knives and teeth of machine tools. For this reason the wood is much more suitable when used in the veneer form. However, it turns and polishes well, being firm and hard.

The wood is said to have more than fifty times greater insulating resistance to electric current than most other woods, so it is particularly desirable in work that involves electrical appliances.

Quarter-sliced Queensland walnut or oriental wood, mottle figure, two-piece match.

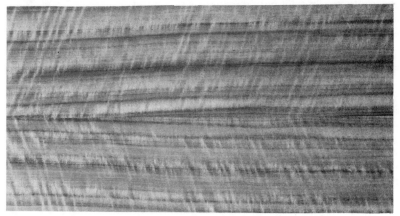

This is one of the very popular woods in Australia, where it is used in cabinetwork, in the manufacture of pianos and, as just mentioned, in various types of electrical equipment because of its insulating value.

RANIA *Alseodaphne semecarpifolia* (Alseodaphne—grove laurel; semecarpifolia—naked with leaf-like fruits)

The growth of this tree in its natural state is strictly limited to two places, western Ghats in India and what is known as the dry zone in the northern part of the island of Ceylon, in which place it grows on the mountainsides up to an elevation of 4,000 or 5,000 ft.

The wood, which has a very pleasing brownish appearance, is moderately heavy, averaging 45 to 60 lbs. per cubic foot, is hard and in Ceylon is considered one of the best timbers. It is unusual that it is so little known in other countries.

While the wood is more or less straight-grained, some of the logs produce a very beautiful broken mottle figure which should find a good market in the furniture centers of the world if more of it were exported. In Ceylon it is used for the finest cabinetwork, in furniture manufacture and house construction and decoration.

REDBUD, EASTERN *Cercis canadensis* (Cercis—the classical Greek name of *Cercis siliquastrum*, of southern Europe and western Asia; canadensis—of Canada, erroneous as the center of distribution is more southern)

Eastern redbud, the state tree of Oklahoma, is a small tree, growing from Connecticut to northern Florida and westward to the Mississippi, from 20 to 30 ft. in height and from 12 to 18 in. in diameter. A large number of these trees may be found on the grounds of Mt. Vernon, in Virginia, planted by George Washington and Thomas Jefferson.

This is a strong, hard wood of a brownish color, variegated with darker streaks. One of its main values is for ornamentation, but in some southern sections of the country the blossoms and buds are eaten in salads, and fritters are made from the young pods. In Mexico, fried redbud flowers are a delicacy and the bark of the redbud is used in medicine. Refer to the chapter on "Woods of the Bible" for the legend of the redbud tree.

There is little value to the lumber it produces, but it has been used in some degree for small cabinetwork and turning.

REDWOOD *Sequoia sempervirens* (Sequoia—after the Cherokee Indian, Sequoyah, 1770?–1843; semper/virens—always green) Stephen Endlicher, well-known Austrian botanist, in 1947 gave the botanical name to this tree.

Redwood trees grow along or near the coast of California in a narrow strip not more than thirty-five miles wide and about five hundred miles long, extending from one hundred miles south of San Francisco to a little above the Oregon border. Single acres of redwood have been found that contained over one million board feet of lumber. Redwood is the state tree of California.

A record-size redwood tree that

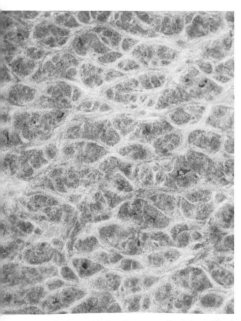

Redwood burl is easily identified by its rich, dark, mahogany-red color with an ever-changing velvety sheen and small-eye clusters of tight burls.

was felled 7 ft. above the ground had a diameter of 26 ft., was 261 ft. to the lowest branch, and measured 380 ft. in height. When sawed into lumber, it produced 344,000 board feet.

One of the loftiest redwoods is in the Humboldt State National Park in California—368 ft. in height and still growing. How-

The General Sherman Bigtree in the Sequoia National Park, California

ever, the size of these trees is not an accurate determination of their age. A giant sequoia that was felled had a diameter of 27 ft. but was only 1,244 years old, whereas another of only 11½ ft. in diameter was over 2,000 years old. The availability of sunlight, condition of the soil and amount of water determine to a great extent the size of the trees. The Indians considered these trees immortal because of their long life.

The heartwood is usually a uniform deep reddish brown. The wood is without resin canals and has no distinctive odor, taste or feel. A typical redwood is moderately light in weight, averaging 20 lbs. per cubic foot, and is moderately hard.

Over half of the redwood lumber produced is used in the form of planks, dimension boards, joists and posts. A large part of this material goes into framing for houses and industrial buildings, bridge trestles and other heavy construction. Some of the finer boards, and particularly the burls, are cut into veneers and used for decorative work on fine furniture.

ROSEWOOD, BRAZILIAN *Dalbergia* spp. (Dalbergia—after the Swedish physician, N. Dalberg, 1735–1820)

This species is known also as JACARANDA and PALISANDER WOOD.

Coming from the ports of Bahia and Rio, in Brazil, this rosewood is one of the most beautiful of cabinet woods. At one time many of the finest pianos were made of Brazilian rosewood and some may still be seen today. The wood has been popular for well over 100 years. A great amount of rosewood was used during the Empire Period, in the early days of Queen Victoria's reign.

There is a wide variation in

Brazilian rosewood, cream to tan with chocolate brown and jet black streaks usually in a wild pattern.

color from almost a cream to a light brown with streaks of jet black, and some pieces of lumber will contain a number of variegated irregular streaks which form a stripe pattern. Some of the wood, when manufactured into veneers and cut on the quarter, produces a straight stripe and other logs, cut half round, produce wild effects and wider sheets. The lumber may be obtained in squares of 1 x 1 in., 2 x 2 in. and other thicknesses, which are excellent for turning purposes.

Rosewood has a very fragrant odor when cut and even when it is burned, and it is said that from this odor the name of Brazilian rosewood was derived.

One can obtain an exceedingly smooth and highly polished surface with the use of this wood. It is employed in the veneer form for decorative and inlay effects in cabinetwork.

ROSEWOOD, HONDURAS *Dalbergia stevensonii* (stevensonii—after Stevenson)

The rosewood of British Honduras has been exported for over a century, the first record being a shipment of 188 pieces in 1841. It is a tree which obtains a height of 50 to 100 ft. and the trunk, which is often fluted, commonly forks at about 20 or 25 ft. from the ground.

Growing in damp places in Central America and concentrated for the most part along rivers, it is lighter in color than the Brazilian wood, more pinkish brown or purplish, with darker and lighter bands. When freshly cut, the bark and sapwood have a distinctive odor, suggesting stored apples, and the taste is slightly bitter.

It is a coarse-textured wood, hard and heavy, weighing from 60 to 70 lbs. per cubic foot when thoroughly dried. It does not take a high natural polish very well. The supplies are fairly scarce, but when available the wood is used in cabinetwork and marquetry, but it is chiefly employed for the bars of the marimbas and xylophones manufactured in the United States.

ROSEWOOD, INDIAN *Dalbergia latifolia* (Dalbergia—after the Swedish physician, N. Dalberg, 1735–1820; lati/folia—broadleaved)

Emanating from India and Ceylon, this wood, after teak, is considered one of the most valuable produced there. The logs are mostly cut on the quarter to obtain a straight stripe effect. The

Indian rosewood, also called East Indian rosewood, dark purple to ebony with somewhat regular streaks of red or yellow.

color runs from a very light yellow or light rose, with light and dark streaks, to logs that are almost black in color. The wood weighs about 53 lbs. per cubic foot and experiments show that it has an unusual quality of not shrinking either way of the grain, retaining exact measurements after being cut. It is therefore very useful where definite measurements must be secured.

In India it is one of the most important woods in the manufacture of furniture, and in this country and throughout Europe, quantities of this rosewood have been used for a number of years in the lumber form and in veneers for fine cabinetwork and paneling.

ROSEWOOD, MADAGASCAR
Dalbergia greveana

This wood comes from the forests of Madagascar and often is called FRENCH ROSEWOOD and also MADAGASCAR PALISANDER.

It is a very hard wood, light rose-pink and sometimes of darker shades, with pronounced lines of a darker shade of red. It is generally available in veneers in the quartered-cut form.

RUBBER TREE *Hevea brasiliensis*

Other names are PARÁ RUBBER TREE in England, ÁRBOL DE CAUCHO in Venezuela and SERINGA in Peru.

This is the principal rubber tree. On occasion it grows to a height of over 100 ft., with a well-developed trunk more than 12 ft. in circumference. The usual height on plantations is from 60 to 80 ft. The structure of what is popularly known as the bark is of considerable importance in this tree because it contains the latex vessels which are the chief source of the world's rubber supply. The trunk of the tree may be divided roughly into an inner portion of wood and an outer portion of bark. The tree originally grew in the Amazon Valley.

The *brasiliensis* tree produces the purest and best para rubber. At one time there was no other source except in the Amazon Valley, but as long ago as 1834 Thomas Hancock, the English discoverer of vulcanization and a rubber manufacturer, called attention to the possibility of growing it in the East. The *hevea* trees were established in Ceylon and many are now growing in plantations in Malaya and the Dutch East Indies. Smaller amounts are grown in India, Sarawak, French Indochina, Thailand, and parts of Africa. The tree thrives on many types of soils with the exception of swampy, undrained, exposed land. It grows better in altitudes under 2,000 ft. than over.

Hevea brasiliensis is the most important genus of the *Euphorbiaceae*, as its latex is the source of nearly all the world's supply of rubber. Twelve species grow in the Amazon basin, but only the *hevea brasiliensis* is cultivated on plantations. Some trees in Brazil at times attain heights from 100 to 125 ft. They have a large cylindrical trunk, with or without buttresses.

Hevea wood is pale brown in color, light in weight, medium coarse-textured and brittle. It stains easily and is perishable when exposed to a humid climate, so has few if any commercial uses.

The plantations are thinned out, leaving about ninety trees per acre. Most trees on an estate yield 4 to 5 lbs. of rubber per year, but a few yield as much as 30 lbs., sometimes growing alongside others which yield only 2 lbs. The trees are ready for tapping for latex when about five years old, but the yield of latex and the quality of rubber obtained is not as good as when the trees are a few years older. Tapping is a delicate and important operation, consisting of the removal or the shaving of the bark with a sharp knife. For perfect tapping it is necessary to cut within 1/25 in. of the wood, an operation requiring practice.

During Christopher Columbus' second visit to South America, he was astonished to see native Indians amusing themselves with a heavy black ball made from a vegetable gum. Later explorers were equally impressed by these balls and a historian of the time reported that they rebounded so much that they appeared alive. Three centuries elapsed before the material was brought into commercial use in Europe, not marketed for its elastic properties but to rub out lead-pencil marks; hence the name India rubber or rubber.

SABICU *Lysiloma latisiliqua* (Lysiloma—to loose the border, in reference to the separation of the pods at the borders at maturity; lati/siliqua—broad pods)

Sabicu grows in the West Indies and the wood is generally exported as square logs from 8 to 10 ft. and longer, with widths of 12 to 30 in. and occasionally larger. The wood is a dull brown color but has a bright luster. A large number of the logs are highly figured, containing not only straight and broken roe but a mottle. Fine examples of crotches are also produced.

The wood seasons slowly, does not split and shrinks but little during this process. It stands exposure to weather like teak, not being affected in any degree and not requiring the protection of paint or varnish. It is a hard, strong, tough wood with exceedingly close, smooth, firm grain, weighing 60 lbs. per cubic foot. In this connection it is said to have a peculiarity similar to greenheart in that the wood shows no sign of yielding as additional weight is added when tested for crushing force, but suddenly at a certain point it gives way, leaving nothing but a mass of shapeless fibers.

This wood works well in the timber form and was used extensively for many years in the works of the Adam brothers, Sheraton and others of that period. It is most attractive when used in conjunction with satinwood, developing a mellow tone which improves with years of exposure. In fact, much of the wood used by these cabinetmakers which was considered mahogany has been later found upon examination to be sabicu.

SANTA MARÍA *Calophyllum brasiliense* var. *rekoi*

Growing all through Central and South America, this species of wood is known also as HARI, LECHE MARÍA and PALO MARÍA.

The wood is of pinkish color to a deep red, usually developing a dark stripe and bearing a resemblance to mahogany. It has to season very slowly, and the greatest danger in splitting is toward the

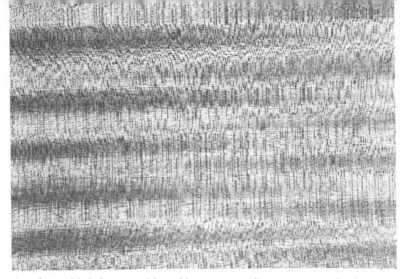

Sapele, reddish brown ribbon-like stripes reflect a constantly changing luster. Harder than African mahogany, which it resembles somewhat.

end of the seasoning period. It is a fairly heavy wood, weighing around 45 lbs. per cubic foot, and moderately hard.

Santa María is easy to work with and is generally produced in veneers for drawer bottoms. In the countries where it grows, it is used for carpentry, bridge work, boat building and bridges.

SAPELE *Entandrophragma cylindricum* (Ent/andro/phragma—within the male membrane; cylindricum—cylindrical)

This species is known also as ABOUDIKROU, SAPELE MAHOGANY, SIPO and TIAMA.

Sapele grows in Nigeria and along the African Ivory Coast. It is a large tree and logs are often as much as 72 in. in diameter, though the usual range in the market is from 30 to 36 in. The color of the wood is a dark reddish brown with a very strong stripe and at times the grain is very irregular. This irregularity causes the plum pudding and blister figures so highly prized in the veneer field.

The wood is very fine in texture and care has to be taken in the seasoning, as it warps badly. Sometimes it is mistaken for African mahogany and used as such; however, it is harder and heavier, weighing from 35 to 40 lbs. per cubic foot, and the stripe is much more pronounced. Sapele is superior to either African or American mahogany in strength and is somewhat similar to the strength of our American oak.

Sapele is used for interior paneling and also in general furniture work.

SAPODILLA *Achras zapota* (Achras—ancient Greek name for ancestor of the common pear; zapota—from the Mexican Indian name, sapote)

Sapodilla is an evergreen tree growing throughout British Honduras, Guatemala, Venezuela and down into Brazil, and also found in the West Indies. This tree is known for its remarkably long life and it provides three separate products. One is a very tasty fruit, similar in appearance to plums,

and it is reported that this sapodilla plum is considered one of
the best of the tropical American
fruits.

Secondly, the bark of this tree,
reddish brown in color, contains
a large amount of latex, which
ranges from a white to a purple
color. This is gathered and used
commercially as a basis for chewing gum. This latex is the most
valuable product of the tree and
large plantations have been
planted for this purpose alone.

Thirdly, the tree is useful in that
the wood is fine-textured, heavy,
averaging 65 lbs. per cubic foot,
and produces straight-grained
wood which turns well and is
used, among other purposes, in
the manufacture of tool handles.
A very fine polish can be obtained
with this wood.

SASSAFRAS *Sassafras albidum*
(Sassafras—a Spanish name, possibly of American Indian origin;
albidum—whitish)

This species is known also as
CINNAMON-WOOD and RED
SASSAFRAS.

This tree grows in an area from
Massachusetts to Iowa and Kansas, and south to Florida and
Texas. In the northern limit of its
range it is generally small, often
of brush size, but further south it
becomes a tree which sometimes
exceeds 100 ft. in height and 3 or
4 ft. in diameter. The best development of the species is in
Arkansas and Missouri.

This wood bears a considerable
resemblance to ash in color and
in grain, but is lighter in weight,
about 31 lbs. per cubic foot, and
has a slightly aromatic scent. It is
inclined to check in drying and
has less strength than ash, but is

very durable when exposed to
dampness.

The tree has had a peculiar history. It was once supposed to possess miraculous healing powers
and people believed that it would
renew the youth of the human
race. Bedsteads made of sassafras
were supposed to drive away certain nightly visitors which disturbed slumber, and the belief
was that a bed made of sassafras
would help the individual sleep
more soundly.

The production of sassafras oil
is perhaps the largest industry dependent upon this tree. Roots are
grubbed by the ton and are sub-
jected to distillation. The oil obtained is used in flavoring medicines and candies, and also in
perfuming soap. The early settlers
dyed their homespun articles with
the orange color obtained from
the bark.

Another product of the sassafras is tea made from the flowers
or bark of the roots. It is relished
in early spring and is popular in
most regions where the tree is
known. This bark is tied in small
bundles and retailed in drug
stores and groceries in various
parts of the country.

Most of the sassafras manufactured by sawmills is used in furniture and listed as ash, generally
losing its name.

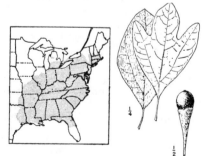

SATINAY *Syncarpia hillii* (Syn/carpia—fused fruits; hillii—after Hill)

This large tree grows on Fraser Island, off the coast of Queensland in Australia. It is a hard wood, averaging 50 lbs. per cubic foot, and at times the logs produce a fiddleback figure for which there is an active demand in fine cabinetwork. The heartwood is very attractive, of a pleasing reddish color like that of tropical mahogany.

It is used for interior paneling, but to prevent deterioration in quality, the stock first must have a considerable period in which to air-dry before it is kiln-dried.

SATINE *Brosimum paraense* (Brosimum—edible; paraense—from Para, a Brazilian state)

This wood is known also as MUIRATIRANGA, SATINA and principally as SATINÉ RUBANNE.

Emanating from South America, the wood has a rich red coloring, is of medium texture, is an easy wood to work with and takes a fine polish.

SATINWOOD, BRAZILIAN *Euxylophora paraensis* (Euxylophora—true bearer of wood; paraensis—from Para, a Brazilian state)

Also known as PAU AMARILLO and SATINA, this wood from Brazil at times is used as a substitute for Ceylon and Santo Domingo mahogany. However, it is of coarser grain and the figure and mottle are lacking. It has a rich, bright, warm golden yellow color and can be obtained in good widths and lengths.

SATINWOOD, EAST INDIAN *Chloroxylon swietenia* (Chloroxylon—yellowish green wood; swietenia—after Baron Gerald von Swieten, 1700–1772, Dutch physician and founder of the Vienna botanical garden)

This satinwood grows in Ceylon and India, and an important trade has been carried on with the island of Ceylon for a great many years. Logs running in size from 12 to 30 in. and of good lengths, from 5 to 20 ft. and longer, are obtained.

Nearly all of the timber is more or less figured, the plain log being an exception. The figure ranges from a plain light- and dark-colored stripe to the finest mottle (a very fine sized mottle being especially desirable in the inlay and furniture trade) and what is known as a bee's-wing mottle. It varies considerably in color from a light, bright yellow to a dark brown. As a rule, the lighter and brighter colors are the most sought after. In the form of veneer, the wood has long been used for furniture and by marquetry manufacturers. Entire suites have been made of satinwood veneer. In the solid form it is usually confined to brush and mirror backs.

In India the wood has been used for many purposes, including wharf piling and agricultural implements. The well-known bridge at Peradeniya in Ceylon was constructed almost entirely of satinwood. It contained a single arch of over a 200-ft. span, but this bridge was taken down some years ago.

In this country the wood commands a high price, based upon the indication of the figure, size and soundness of the log. The big

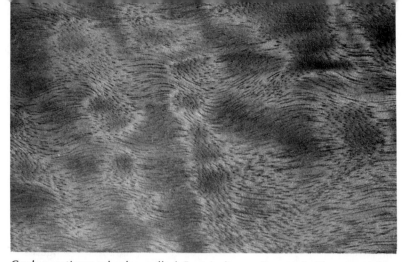

Ceylon satinwood, also called East Indian satinwood. The wood is a beautiful pale gold. Figures vary widely. Top: Rippled figure. Bottom: Bee's wing mottled, a striking pattern.

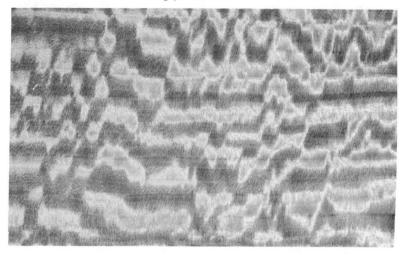

problem in the handling of these logs is what are known as cup shapes and gum rings. They may be seen upon careful examination on the butt ends—thin lines following the annual growth. Defects of this kind at times can render almost worthless an otherwise valuable tree when manufactured. On one occasion it is reported that one log was bought at a price of $5,000 for the purpose of converting it into veneers.

A peculiarity of the wood is that while it burns in an open fireplace very well and with a fragrant restful odor, inducing slumber in many who sit before it, the smoke of this satinwood will kill canaries.

SATINWOOD, WEST INDIES Zanthoxylum flavum (Zanth/oxylum —yellow wood; flavum—yellow)
Coming from the West Indies,

this is the finest satinwood known, not only for quality but also for color. The best wood comes from Santo Domingo. However, the supplies have been so exhausted that no logs have been imported into this country for many years.

The logs that did come in ranged from 6 to 22 in. in diameter and were generally manufactured into oblong pieces with square edges. The average probably ranged from about 8 to 10 in. Logs could not be kept for long before manufacturing, as they split badly, but when once manufactured, this wood splits less than the East Indian satinwood.

This satinwood has a strong, pleasant scent, sometimes associated with that of coconut oil. It is this satinwood that you find on old pieces of furniture—the Sheratons and Hepplewhites. The wood is a lovely golden yellow and has a bright sheen like satin, an effect which cannot be equaled by any other wood or obtained by artificial means. Pieces that were made 100 to 150 years ago have matured to a lovely tint that even the old masters did not realize would result. The finest furniture was sometimes made with West Indian satinwood combined with mahogany.

Nearly all of this wood was converted into veneers for highly decorative work, and prize veneers from good logs commanded high prices, sometimes as high as one dollar per square foot for the log.

SEN Kalopanax ricinifolium (Kalo/panax—beautiful Panax; ricinifolium—with castor, Ricinus, leaves)

Growing in the mountainous districts of central Japan, this tree is known also as CASTOR ARABIA.

The heartwood is a pale greenish brown color, somewhat like our native ash, and is of medium hardness and weight. The lumber seasons easily but with a high shrinkage. When the wood is dry, it always presents danger of warping and shrinking or swelling with the change of moisture content. Notwithstanding this, it is widely used in Japan for such purposes as chests, furniture, passenger coaches, baseball bats. It has the advantage of working well with all types of tools. When converted into veneer, it is used for the manufacture of plywood, and quantities of the plywood have been exported to various countries.

SEQUOIA, GIANT Sequoia gigantea (Sequoia—after Sequoyah, or George Guess, 1770?–1843, American Indian inventor of the Cherokee alphabet; gigantea—gigantic)

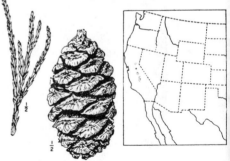

Right: Giant sequoia is the lone survivor of the last logging operation on this mountain in Sequoia National Forest. Known as the Frank Boole big tree, it stands 269 feet high and measures more than 35 feet in diameter.

This tree is known also as BIG-TREE, MAMMOTH-TREE and the SEQUOIA.

The sequoia grows in higher altitudes than the redwood and is limited more or less to some thirty groves, varying from a few trees to over a thousand. These are located only in the Sierra Nevadas of California, in Sequoia National Forest and in Tahoe National Forest. These trees are the oldest and largest of all living things, the largest sequoia and largest tree in the world being in Sequoia National Park. It was reported to have a diameter at the base of 36½ ft., and an 18½-ft. diameter 100 ft. above the ground, with a height of 273 ft. Its bark is over 4 ft. thick. If the tree were converted into lumber, it would provide over 600,000 board feet. It is estimated to be somewhere between three thousand and four thousand years old.

The wood is a dull, purplish red-brown when exposed to the light, similar but lighter in color than redwood.

There is very little use for this wood. Inasmuch as the supply is so limited, plans having been made to preserve these trees for posterity.

SERVICEBERRY, DOWNY *Amelanchier arborea* (Amelanchier—the common name of a European species; arborea—treelike)

This tree, which grows in the eastern part of Canada and through all of the eastern states west of the Mississippi in the United States, is known by a number of different names in the various states, as CURRANT TREE, JUNE-BERRY, MAY-CHERRY, SERVICEBERRY, SHADBERRY, SUGAR PLUM and WILD INDIAN PEAR. The wood is also marketed as LANCE-WOOD.

Downy serviceberry is a small, attractively shaped tree and an excellent one for landscaping. The tree blossoms in the early spring, when the shad travels upstream, which is why the tree is sometimes referred to as shad-berry or shad-bush. The small, mealy, black berry, which ripens in June or July, according to where the tree is located, is sweet, edible and a favorite with the birds. This tree is generally found along brooks or bordering on the edge of woods.

The wood is very hard, heavy and close-grained but has excellent bending qualities. Because of its toughness and flexibility, it is used in the manufacture of fly rods. It is easy to work with all types of tools and takes a fine finish. Outside of the manufacture of fly rods, large quantities of it are used for making all types of handles and various turned work.

SISSOO *Dalbergia sissoo* (Dalbergia—after N. Dalberg, Swedish physician; sissoo—a native name)

Sissoo often is called the SHISHAM WOOD of British India. It is an extremely hard-textured wood, rich brown in color, often having a pronounced stripe and attractive mottle figure which is caused by deeper shades of gold and brown. The figure is essentially striped with some mottle.

Sissoo, or Sisso as often called, is not difficult to work, in spite of its hard texture. It is used for furniture and parquet flooring, and in India is highly favored for making delicate, handmade earrings.

Downy serviceberry, displaying white blossoms of spring, is significant as a lumber producer mainly because it is one of the important woods for fly rods.

Sissoo from India. Rich, warm brown with darker brown stripes and sometimes mildly mottled. A favorite for handmade earrings.

Snakewood.

SMOKETREE, AMERICAN *Cotinus obovatus* (Cotinus—from the Greek for oleaster or wild olive, although the origin is confused; obovatus—the shape of the leaf is ob-ovate)

This tree is referred to in the Bible as SHITTIM WOOD or SMOKETREE.

The tree is rare in this country, even more so in Europe, and is found in the eastern United States, in parts of Tennessee, northern Georgia, southwestern Missouri and the northern part of Arkansas. Smoketree is small in size and is a bright, clear, rich orange color with thin, nearly white sapwood. It is so named probably because the small yellow and purplish flowers, which appear in clusters, have the look of a puff of smoke or a thin film spreading over the foliage when they turn to a rosy haze.

Commercially, the wood is rare and the only use that is made of the tree is for obtaining a dye from the rich orange heartwood. In localities where the tree is grown, it is used for fence posts, because of its high durability in contact with the soil.

If desired, it can be used in the lumber form for craftwork, but should always be finished in its natural color so as to preserve the beautiful coloring, which would be altered by most finishing materials.

SNAKEWOOD *Piratinera guianensis* (Piratinera—sea pirate; guianensis—from Guiana)

Commonly known as snakewood, doubtless because of its markings, this wood is known to some as LEOPARD WOOD, LETTERWOOD and SPECKLED WOOD.

It is native to British Guiana and South America and has a deep bright red color, darkening upon exposure. The wood turns very well, though it does not slice well. It takes a high polish and is available in 1/24 in. sawed veneers and also in 1 x 1 in. squares.

Snakewood is prized for the handles of fine parasols, violin bows and umbrellas, and for the butts of choice fishing poles. A cane made of snakewood is considered the aristocrat of canes.

SOURWOOD *Oxydendrum arboreum* (Oxy/dendrum—sour tree; arboreum—treelike)

This species also is known as ARROW-WOOD, ELK TREE, LILY OF THE VALLEY TREE, SORREL GUM, SORREL TREE and TITI TREE.

The trees are found along the coast from New Jersey down to Florida and westward from Kentucky to Louisiana. The greatest value of this tree is its handsome foliage and it is planted for decoration in landscaping. It has little value commercially. The wood is heavy, hard, strong and close-grained, making it fairly difficult to work with tools, except for turning purposes.

Certain extracts from the sap of this tree are used in medicine for the treatment of fevers. Otherwise, sourwood is only of ornamental value.

SPRUCE, BLACK HILLS *Picea glauca* var. *densata* or *Picea glauca* (Picea—the ancient Latin name from *pix* or *picis*, meaning pitch; glauca—a blue-green covering; densata—dense or compact, probably referring to the crowded needles)

Locally, in South Dakota where this tree is found, it is often called WHITE SPRUCE.

French explorers were the first white men to visit the little-known Black Hills in the land of South Dakota. The Black Hills spruce is now the state tree of South Dakota. This spruce varies from the eastern variety of white spruce in that it is a much slower-growing tree and the foliage is a very bright green.

SPRUCE, BLUE *Picea pungens* (pungens—sharp-pointed, referring to the needles)

Locally it often is known as COLORADO SPRUCE and SILVER SPRUCE.

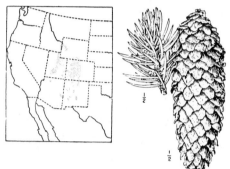

This spruce is called the pride of the Rocky Mountains and it is the state tree of Colorado and Utah. It is a very hardy tree and grows in mountainous elevations up to 11,000 ft., sometimes in pure stands. It is one of the slowest-growing spruces, having a height of no more than 10 to 20 in. after five years and only 3 to 8 ft. after ten years' growth.

Blue spruce was first discovered on Pikes Peak in the middle 1800's. It is one of the most widely used trees for landscaping because of the silver-blue color and symmetrical shape. The wood is soft and weak and its only value commercially is in landscaping.

SPRUCE, ENGELMANN *Picea engelmannii* (engelmannii—after George Engelmann, 1809–1884, German-born physician and botanist of St. Louis, who was the first

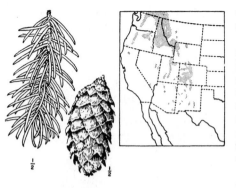

to identify and clarify this spruce species about the year 1862)

This spruce grows in the high mountains of the West at elevations of 4,000 to 12,000 ft., ranging from British Columbia southward through the western states into Arizona, Colorado and New Mexico. The trunk is straight and is identified by the bark—a dark, purplish brown with small, overlapping scales. The deep blue-green needles are about 1 in. long, soft, flexible, four-angled, and with a tendency to curve forward.

Some of this spruce has been used in aircraft-glider work because of its extreme lightness combined with strength. Quantities have been used in construction work and sheathing. It also makes some of the finest-quality paper.

SPRUCE, NORWAY *Picea abies*

This large, conical evergreen is a native of central and northern Europe, where it grows abundantly and is used for paper pulp and lumber. It grows readily in the cool, moist climates of the northeastern United States, across the upper Rocky Mountain regions and west to the Pacific coast. It is widely planted in these areas as a forestry crop.

The distinguishing characteristics of the Norway spruce are its laterally spreading branches, drooping twigs, pyramidal shape, tall growth to 150 ft., and unusually long cones measuring up to 6 in. Dark green needles are four-sided, 3/8 to 1 in. long. An injured trunk exudes excessive amounts of whitish pitch.

The tall, straight trunk of Norway spruce, averaging 2½ ft. in diameter, has a good lumber yield, which is used for a wide range of purposes from musical-instrument cases to house frames.

SPRUCE, SITKA *Picea sitchensis* (sitchensis—of Sitka Island in southeastern Alaska)

This species is known also as SEQUOIA SILVER SPRUCE, SILVER SPRUCE, WESTERN SPRUCE and WEST COAST SPRUCE.

Sitka spruce grows along the Pacific coast from Alaska to northern California. It is found in a very narrow strip at elevations up to 3,000 ft. and never more than fifty miles inland from the coast. It is the largest species of spruce, ranging to 150 ft. or more in height with diameters up to 7 ft. The largest tree known at present is one growing in the state of

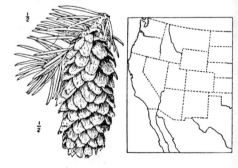

Engelmann spruce.

Blue spruce.

Washington with a recorded height of 240 ft. and 14 ft. in diameter. Most of the trees in dense forests grow from 40 to 70 ft. high.

The wood is light pink to tan and it darkens to light brown upon exposure. The needles stand at right angles to the tree and are stiff, pointed, and grow all around it.

Some Sitka is used for making musical instruments, but the white spruce is preferred for this purpose. Sitka spruce is one of the favorites for making high-quality paper.

SPRUCE, WHITE *Picea glauca* (glauca—blue-green in reference to the foliage)

This species is known also as ADIRONDACK SPRUCE, BLUE SPRUCE and SKUNK SPRUCE.

The white spruce trees grow across Canada from Newfoundland to Alaska and southward into British Columbia, Montana, Minnesota, Wisconsin and Michigan, up through the northeastern states and upper New York State. It is a tree of many branches, drooping downward from the trunk and then turning up to form a beauti-

fully shaped tree, tapering to a long, sharp crown. Its needles are dark blue-green and if injured give off an unpleasant odor that has resulted in the tree being called a cat spruce or skunk spruce. The needles are four-angled, sharp-pointed, and grow in great profusion along the twigs.

White spruce is one of the most sought-after woods for the manufacture of paper pulp because of the extra-long, fine quality of the fibers. Also it is a wood that piano manufacturers buy for making the best sounding boards. In addition, the wood is used for many of the usual purposes, as interior finishing and furniture, and for the manufacture of lightweight oars and canoe paddles.

STINKWOOD   *Ocotea   bullata* (Ocotea—a Guayana plant name; bullata—inflated)
    This species is known also as STINKHOUT, CAPE LAUREL and UMNUKANE in South Africa.

Left: White spruce.

Stinkwood is closely related botanically to East African camphorwood (*Ocotea usambarensis*) but the tree and wood are appreciably different in their commercial aspects. The tree is from 60 to 80 ft. high with a clean, straight bole from 3 to 5 ft. in diameter. The species grows in South Africa, predominantly in the forested country of the Cape Peninsula northward to Natal and eastern Transvaal.

The wood varies in color from an even straw shade through various shades of gray-brown to almost black. The straw-colored wood does not appreciably darken on exposure, but the brown wood darkens noticeably under oil and exposure. The wood is moderately hard and heavy to very heavy, varying in specific gravity according to color. Light-colored portions have an average specific gravity of 0.67; black portions may have an average specific gravity of 0.80.

The dark portions of the wood air-season and kiln-season rather poorly with a marked tendency to distort and honeycomb. The light-colored wood dries more rapidly with much less degrade.

The wood is stronger in proportion to its specific gravity than eastern African camphorwood. Stinkwood compares favorably with domestic hardwoods of similar specific gravity. The seasoned wood of stinkwood may be compared to that of rock elm (*Ulmus thomasii*) of somewhat greater specific gravity.

The shrinkage of the wood is exceptionally great, being 8.0 percent tangentially and 4.2 percent radially. These values are in the order of those for blue gum (*Eucalyptus globulus*) and are associated with the tendency of the wood to distort and collapse in drying.

The wood works well with hand and machine tools, but is hard and severe on the tools. The best surface appears to be obtained by scraping and an excellent finish is easily secured in this manner. Smooth surfaces can also be obtained by sanding.

In spite of its drawbacks, stinkwood is reported to be one of the most prized furniture woods in Africa and is largely used for furniture, paneling, framing and high-class millwork. Supplies of the wood are becoming increasingly scarce and it brings a greater price than any other furniture wood. There are no reports of this species being exported from Africa.

STRAWBERRY   TREE   *Arbutus unedo* (Arbutus—the classical Latin name of this species; unedo —Latin name for the fruit of this tree)

The original home of the strawberry tree was in southwestern France along the Mediterranean and in Ireland. It is still fairly abundant in the Killarney and Kerry districts. In England it is cultivated as an ornamental tree because of the fine appearance when in full bloom or flowering in the late autumn. A small tree, it seldom grows higher than 25 ft. It produces fruits which are orange-red to a bright scarlet color, round in shape and rough on the outside with tiny grains.

The wood is available only in small sizes. However, it is of fine texture, fairly hard and weighs about 45 lbs. per cubic foot. Sometimes the figure is so irregular as to give it almost the appearance of burl, and veneers cut from this tree at times are hard to distinguish from the madrona burls that grow on the Pacific coast. It is closely related to these trees (*Arbutus menziesii*), though they may grow three or four times the height of the strawberry tree.

The wood seasons satisfactorily and works with little difficulty, though it has a tendency at times to check. This species makes very attractive veneers for fine cabinetmaking.

SWEETGUM *Liquidambar styraciflua* (Liquid/ambar—liquid amber in reference to the fragrant resin; styraciflua—old generic name meaning styrax or storax, in allusion to the production of medicinal storax from *L. orientalis* of western Asia)

This wood is known also as ALLIGATOR-TREE, ALLIGATOR WOOD (because of the warty excrescences on the bark of some

of the trees), HAZEL PINE, INCENSE TREE, LIQUIDAMBAR, SATIN WALNUT and STAR-LEAVED GUM. Sweetgum is sold on the market as RED GUM or SAPGUM.

Sweetgum, or red gum, grows in the United States and extends from Connecticut to Texas and as far northwest of the Alleghenies as Missouri and Illinois. It reaches the largest size in the lower Mississippi region. The largest examples exceed a height of 120 ft. and a diameter of 4 ft., but logs from 20 to 34 in. are the usual

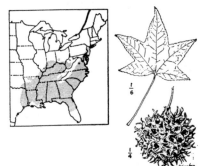

Sweetgum, more often called red gum, though the color is not so much red as it is light brown with dark brown streaks. When highly figured it is a favorite of marquetry picture craftsmen who use it to represent mountainous terrain.

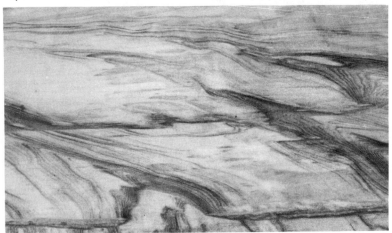

Virgin stand of red gum, same species as sweetgum, near Holly Bluff, Miss.

size. It grows well on land which is never covered with water, but it needs plenty of moisture.

This tree is in the witch hazel family. It does not belong to the same group as black gum and tupelo, which are in the dogwood family.

Green red gum is so heavy that it scarcely floats. The trees are often girdled and left standing for a year to partly season them. It is only moderately strong and stiff and is a poor competitor of hickory, ash, maple and oak for strength and elasticity. The wood weighs about 37 lbs. per cubic foot; a large percentage of it is figured; and the tree has green seed balls, more commonly known as burrs, that hang by long, threadlike stems for about two years.

The description "red" does not refer to the color of the wood, but originally referred to the color of the autumn leaves. The resin, which is sometimes used in France and probably elsewhere to perfume gloves, has a pleasant odor, and therefore the name "sweetgum" was derived.

The wood is often painted or stained to look like oak, cherry, maple or mahogany, and this species of gum is used more in the veneer form than any other species.

SYCAMORE, AMERICAN *Platanus occidentalis* (Platanus—the classical Latin name for the Oriental plane tree; occidentalis—western)

This species is known also as AMERICAN PLANETREE, BUTTONBALL, BUTTONWOOD, PLANETREE and WATER BEECH. It also is

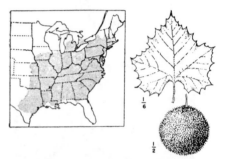

Rotary-cut American sycamore.

called the GHOST TREE of the woods because of its white bark, which is mottled with various shades of green and brown.

American sycamore grows singly or in scattered groups from southern Maine westward to Nebraska and southward to eastern Texas and northern Florida. It is a very large tree, up to 120 ft. high, with wide-spreading branches and a large trunk. The best species are found on flatlands where there is a good supply of ground water and along the edges of streams, lakes and swamps.

The heartwood is reddish brown or flesh-brown in color and it is moderately heavy, averaging 34 lbs. per cubic foot. Large shrinkage is encountered in drying, and the wood is inclined to warp, being somewhat difficult to season. Sycamore wood does not impart taste, odor or stain to a substance that comes in contact with it.

The principal use of this wood is in the manufacture of lumber and veneer for decorative surfaces, but it is used also for railroad ties, fence posts and fuel. Because of its toughness, it is the favorite wood for butchers' blocks.

TAMARACK *Larix laricina* (Larix —the classical name of the European larch; laricina—like a larch)

This tree is known also as HACKMATACK, JUNIPER and LARCH.

The tamarack is an eastern wood found all through eastern Pennsylvania, southeast from Maine to Maryland and into Minnesota. It generally grows in swampy locations. The limbs, which start close to the ground, are horizontal and curve slightly upward. The needles give a feath-

ery appearance and are bright green in color. They grow in clusters all along the small branches, about 1 in. in length. In the fall they turn yellowish or brown and then drop off.

The heartwood is yellowish to brown in color. The timber is generally used for rough construction such as railroad ties, flagpoles, telephone poles and some paper pulp. Boat builders use the lower portion of the trunk and the larger roots to cut out "ship knees" for keels of wooden hulls.

TAMBOOTIE *Spirostachys africanus*

This tree grows in the forests of Zululand and Transvaal in eastern Africa. The logs secured from this species are from 6 to 8 ft. long, seldom averaging more than 12 in. in diameter. The wood is dark brown with black streaks that create beautiful markings. It is a hard wood, averaging about 65 lbs. per cubic foot, and has a very pleasant scent, sweeter than that of sandalwood. This pleasant odor will last a long time after the wood is cut. A piece of furniture made of it can scent a large room for a long time.

Because of the limited quantities, and the defectiveness of the tree, it is a rare wood, and therefore much sought for small fancy articles and high-grade furniture. Although the wood seasons easily, it is fairly difficult to work, but not quite so difficult as other woods of the same hardness, owing to the unusual oily nature of the wood.

TAMO *Fraxinus mandshurica* (Fraxinus—classical Latin name

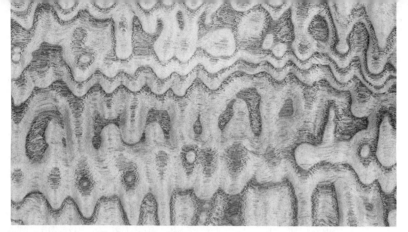

Tamo with so-called peanut figure.

Tamo, leaf figure, yellowish tan with wild, brown swirls. Tamo is also called Japanese ash.

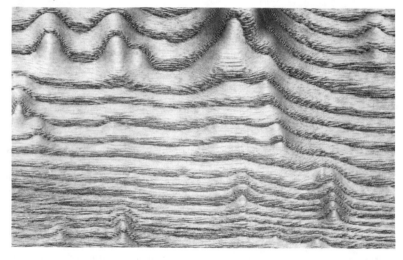

for ash; mandshurica—of Manchuria)

This is known also as JAPANESE ASH.

This tree grows in the mountainous regions of Japan and is obtained only with great difficulty. Often the logs are carried and dragged out by human labor. The first export shipments were made from Japan about 1908, records seem to indicate, and since then it has been exported in steadily increasing amounts.

The wood varies in color from a light straw-yellow to a bright brown, with intermediate shadings, and the color is permanent. It does not dim with age and retains depth and richness in the finished product. The figured logs are eagerly sought in this country. The prize figure is known as "peanut" because of the resemblance to this product. The wood, either in the veneer or lumber form, is easily glued and makes a hard, flat surface.

A peculiarity of the wood is that half of the tree is figured and half is plain. The trees are split in the forests and the plain half generally is left because it has little commercial value.

Craftsmen find this wood particularly fine for producing bizarre effects in matching for table tops and small articles of furniture.

TAWA *Beilschmiedia tawa* (Beilschmiedia—after Beilschmied; tawa—a native name)

Tawa grows in the northeastern area of South Island and all of North Island, both of New Zealand. The average size tree is from 60 to 70 ft. with diameters from 9 to 18 in. It grows at sea level and up to altitudes of no more than 1,000 ft.

This species comes from the family of trees known as *Lauraccae*, from which such timbers as aromatic camphorwood, Queensland walnut, black stinkwood and greenheart are obtained. It is an attractive wood, even-colored, yellowish to grayish brown with occasionally streaks of darker brown. It is medium heavy, averaging around 40 lbs. per cubic foot, with strength in proportion to the weight, of fine texture and a good straight grain.

A considerable amount of this wood is used in New Zealand for decorative woodwork, interior trim and furniture. A good quantity is also used in the manufacture of staves in the cooperage industry. Selected logs are converted into rotary-cut veneers from which attractive plywood may be manufactured. Because of the distance of New Zealand from many of the major wood markets and the high cost of transporta-tion, not too much of this wood is used elsewhere.

TAWENNA *Cryptocarya membranacea* (Crypto/carya—hidden nut; membranacea—parchment-like, probably a reference to the leaves)

This tree grows only in the rain forests of Ceylon, along the coast, up to elevations of around 2,500 ft. The wood, when freshly cut, is a dull yellow color, but with exposure often turns to a dark reddish brown. It is a moderately heavy wood, weighing about 45 lbs. per cubic foot, and of fine texture and straight grain. The small pores are partially filled with a chalklike white deposit and the wood is easy to work with sharp tools.

In Ceylon it is used in heavy construction such as bridges, but a limited quantity is produced in sliced-veneer form, which gives a very attractive appearance.

TEAK *Tectona grandis* (Tectona—after a Malayan plant name, tekku; grandis—great or large)

Teak grows in India, Burma, Thailand and Java and often attains a height of from 70 to 100 ft. or more, with a circumference of 5 to 12 ft. Samples of one of the largest logs secured weighed over 12 tons.

Because of its tremendous weight and the difficulty in getting it out of the forest, an original method is used in forestry. The trees to be felled are first girdled —that is, cut completely around from the bark into the heartwood. In this condition the trees soon die and in three years they become light enough to float down

Teak, flat-cut, stripe, yellow and brown.

Teak, flat-cut, figured.

and buffaloes. A good-sized, well-trained elephant will cost several thousand dollars and because of the great difficulty and labor, an elephant may handle only thirty to forty teak trees a year. Local firms engaged in this work will employ several thousand elephants to carry on the work of transportation. Today it takes from two to eight years for a log to arrive after cutting, because of the girdling process and the labor of getting the trees out of the woods.

the river; otherwise the wood would be so heavy it would sink. Transportation to streams is carried on with the aid of elephants

Teak wood varies from a yellow or strawlike color to a rich deep brown when first cut and darkens with exposure to the air. Some wood will have streaks almost black in color. It has an oily surface and when first cut, feels very sticky to the hand.

There is little shrinkage in drying and the wood is moderately hard (comparable to oak), strong, of straight grain and easily worked. It may come in a straight stripe to an occasional mottle, which is much sought after in the cabinet trade.

Teak has a peculiar scent of its own, which, while agreeable to some, is unpleasant to others and is not unlike that of old shoe leather. Occasionally parcels of teak have a much stronger and more unpleasant odor than the majority of the wood.

The teak tree has the largest leaves of any tree, running from 10 to 20 in. in length and 7 to 14 in. wide, of an oblong shape. They are so rough that the natives use them as an abrasive, just as a modern worker uses sandpaper, because they have a peculiar tough and coarse surface.

Few people know this interesting fact.

An immense quantity of teak goes into shipbuilding, as for decks of liners and warships. Also, a good percentage of this wood is used in the paneling of fine homes and offices and in the construction of all types of furniture. It is obtainable by the craftsmen in both the lumber and the veneer form.

THUYA BURL *Tetraclinis articulata* (Tetra/clinis—four slopes or angles; articulata—jointed)

Thuya, which grows along the Mediterranean in northern Africa, is also found on the island of Malta and has been planted in Cyprus. It is always used in the burl form, the burls growing underneath the ground and having to be dug out. The cause of burls is still a subject of scientific study and speculation, and craftsmen often make inquiry as to the knowledge and full history of these.

Thuya burl, golden brown, highly figured, aromatic, highly prized.

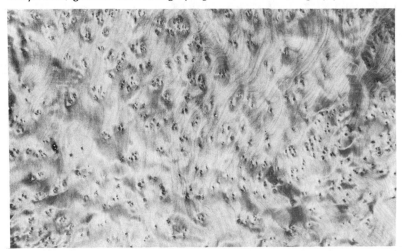

The wood has a figure and color similar to the American redwood burls and is very similar to Amboyna burl, except that it is considerably harder. It is yellowish brown in color with various shades of red, and can be identified by its aromatic scent. It is much more suitable to work with in the veneer form than the redwood burl, owing to a better and more solid texture. Thuya wood was one of the woods used in the earlier-known cabinetwork. During the time of the Roman Empire it was greatly sought after for fine tables.

TOTARA   *Podocarpus*   *totara* (Podo/carpus—foot fruit; totara—a native name)

Totara is principally found only in the islands of New Zealand. The largest trees recorded have been a little in excess of 150 ft. in height and as much as 5 and 6 ft. in diameter, though the great majority are considerably smaller than this. It is a tree that grows in dry valleys but occasionally may be found on the sides of mountains, up to an altitude of 2,500 ft.

The wood has a very uniform coloring of a dull pinkish or reddish brown, is of medium weight, around 35 lbs. per cubic foot, and has an unusually fine, uniform texture with a straight grain. The heartwood is quite resistant to decay, which makes it suitable for many purposes. It works very easily and because of its fine, even texture it is a good wood for cutting into veneer for the manufacture of furniture and plywood. In New Zealand large quantities are used in the planking of boats, building of barges and pontoons, the making of vats, and in exterior work.

TULIPWOOD *Dalbergia variabilis* (Dalbergia—after N. Dalberg, Swedish physician; variabilis—variable)

Emanating from Brazil, this timber is exported from the port of Bahia in the form of round logs.

Tulipwood from Brazil. Light yellowish background streaked with rose red and yellow. Made into veneer and lumber, but neither is plentiful.

Most of these are under 6 ft., although occasionally longer ones are found, and the diameters are from 2 to 12 in. without sapwood.

It is a beautiful wood when freshly manufactured, but in time gradually fades and loses some of its original attractiveness. It is irregularly striped, the prevailing colors being yellow, red rose and violet. It also has a mild, fragrant scent when worked. The wood is heavy, averaging about 60 lbs. per cubic foot, strong and hard, and is not particularly easy to work, being inclined to splinter, but it takes a high natural polish.

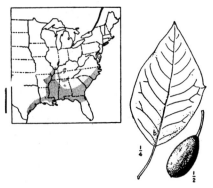

TUPELO, WATER Nyssa aquatica
(Nyssa—a water nymph; aquatica —of the water)

This species is known by many different names, some of the most prominent being BAY POPLAR, GUM, GRAY GUM, HAZEL PINE, OLIVETREE, PAW PAW GUM, SOUR GUM, SWAMP TUPELO, SWAMP GUM, TUPELO, TUPELO GUM, WHITE GUM and YELLOW GUM.

This tupelo grows in a long, narrow belt around one hundred miles wide, running down from southern Illinois through the Mississippi Valley to Texas, across the Gulf states and up along the Atlantic coast as far north as Virginia. The name of this wood stems from the fact that it grows best in freshwater swamps, along the edges of lakes and streams. Generally it is a fairly small tree— 50 to 75 ft. in height with an average diameter of around 2½ ft.

The heartwood is a light brownish gray to a yellowish brown and sometimes nearly white in color. The bark is roughened by small scales, furrowed longitudinally and of a dark brown color. This wood has to be worked with care, as it is difficult to produce lumber that will stay flat. It has a natural tendency to twist and requires unusual attention in drying.

Water tupelo is a weak wood, soft and light in weight. It is a poor wood for craftsmen to work with, as it glues very poorly and has to be worked with considerable care. This wood is used for paper pulp, caskets, cheaper furniture and veneers. It is a favorite veneer for the manufacture of tobacco or cigar boxes, tupelo serving as a core with a thin veneer of cedar on either side.

TURPENTINE Syncarpia procera
(Syn/carpia—fused fruits; procera —high)

This large tree grows in the coastal districts and the Blue Mountains of New South Wales. The wood in appearance and characteristics is very closely related to the red satiné. The sapwood is pale pink and the heartwood a color like brown mahogany. The wood is heavy, averaging 60 lbs. per cubic foot, and is considered about 100 percent harder than oak.

An important feature in handling this lumber is that it has to be air-dried well before it is kiln-dried, otherwise a state of collapse will take place. Its most valuable characteristic is probably its resistance to attack by marine life. It will stand, without ill effects, many years of life in saltwater and is resistant to all decay, especially when the logs are used as piling with the bark still attached.

Turpentine wood is used principally for heavy construction and beams, so it is not of particular importance that it does not work well with hand tools and also rather poorly with power tools, in that it rapidly dulls the edges of saw teeth and cutters.

UTILE   *Entandrophragma   utile* (Ent/andro/phragma—within the male membrane; utile—useful)

In Ghana the wood is usually known as CEDAR or UTILE, and in Uganda it is known as MU-FUMBI. It also has been called SIPO.

Utile grows along a large part of west Africa, extending inland to Uganda. It is an unusually large tree and logs are exported at times with diameters of 6 ft. The wood weighs about 35 to 45 lbs. per cubic foot and closely resembles sapele, except that it is a little darker in color and the cedar scent noticeable in sapele is missing. Also it is not as plentiful as sapele.

Utile requires considerable care in seasoning, as it has a strong tendency to warp and twist. It is not a particularly difficult wood to work with, but being harder and having a more irregular grain, is more difficult to work than mahogany.

This wood is suitable for the manufacture of furniture and interior fittings. It has a limited use in boat building and also is a satisfactory wood for converting into veneers.

WALNUT, BLACK *Juglans nigra* (Juglans—the classical Latin name for walnut, meaning Jupiter's nut; nigra—black)

Black walnut has long been considered one of the most desirable woods of this country, not only because of the beautiful wood of various figures that the tree produces, but also for the food value in the black walnuts—a delicacy used in candies, bread and ice cream.

The bark of the tree is dark and deeply grooved. This bark, in addition to the husks of the nuts, is used in manufacturing a yellow dye. The leaves of the black walnut are as long as 1 and 2 ft. and have many narrow, sharp, slender-pointed leaflets, as many as 23.

After being seasoned, the wood shrinks and expands very little and is a good wood for craftsmen to use. The wood saws, planes and finishes excellently. It has long been used for gunstocks, being superior to all other woods because it keeps its shape, is fairly light in weight and helps take up the recoil better than any other wood. In the veneer form the figures obtained are butts, crotches, burls, fiddleback, leaf and straight stripe.

American black walnut, a beautiful tree typically light-foliaged with exposed branches, has been associated with American history from Colonial times as an abundant source of fine cabinet woods and walnuts.

American black walnut, plain half-round figure.

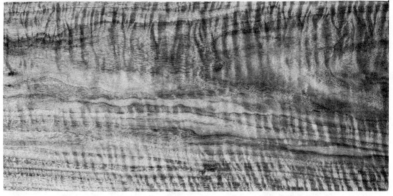

Sliced black walnut, cross figure with wild heart.

Claro walnut from southern Oregon and northern California. Color is tannish with dark brown. Prominent stripes, wavy grain. Available only as quarter-cut veneer.

Circassian walnut.

French walnut, lighter in color than American walnut, grain not as wild as Circassian.

WALNUT, CIRCASSIAN or EUROPEAN *Juglans regia* (regia—royal)

This walnut is obtained from Circassia, in the Caucasus, at the Black Sea, and is the original of all species of European walnut. The wood, which was prized by the Romans and Greeks for its fine nuts, was heavily planted and the species extended to other European countries. The difference in the color and texture between Italian, French, English, Spanish and Circassian walnut is due to the varied climate and the different soils it grows in, which affect the color and marking of the wood. It resembles most closely our American black walnut, but it has a closer grain with distinct color shadings from a light brown to dark, with occasional black streaks in some of the logs.

The walnut from England is naturally limited in quantity because of the size of the British Isles, but it has long been used in its native country. The color and texture vary considerably and the wood is somewhat harder and considerably darker than the French walnut. In the seventeenth

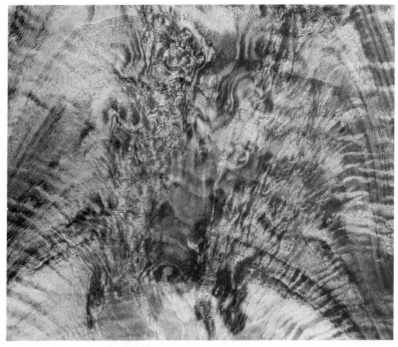

Walnut crotch, golden brown sunburst.

Walnut burl, intertwined swirls of dark brown.

century a portion of the finer furniture was made of this wood, but because of the early supremacy of the English oak, it was only in later years that it was used more extensively.

The major portion of French walnut is consumed in the French market and only a relatively smaller portion is exported to the United States and other countries for special cabinetwork, interior paneling and trim. This wood is known by its light color of gray or grayish brown. Architects occasionally specify French walnut for their finest work. This walnut works and handles very much like our own American walnut.

WALNUT, HINDS *Juglans hindsii* (hindsii—after Richard B. Hinds, English botanist aboard the ship *Sulphur* in a voyage around the world, 1836–1842)

It is known also as CALIFORNIA WALNUT, but there is considerable confusion as to the exact species of *Juglans* that produces this walnut.

This is a fast-growing walnut, found in the southern Oregon and northern California coastal areas. It has an ivy grain, prominent light stripes and sometimes resembles Circassian walnut. Hinds walnut is seldom available in the lumber form and only small quantities are manufactured into veneers.

WALNUT, JAPANESE *Juglans cordiformis* (cordi/formis—heart-shaped)

In Japan this species is known as KURUMI and is one of that country's more valuable hardwoods.

The tree grows in quantities in the forests of Hokkaido from 50 to 65 ft. high with diameters of around 24 to 30 in. This walnut is rather similar in appearance to the European and American walnut with the exception that the overall color is of a golden hue instead of brownish or grayish. It weighs between 35 and 40 lbs. per cubic foot. It has the same characteristics of seasoning well, is free from warpage and stays in place with a minimum of shrinkage and expansion after the proper seasoning. The wood works easily and smoothly with sharp tools.

This Japanese walnut was brought into Great Britain some time in the 1860s, but the climate did not lend to good growth. In Japan the kernels of this nut are used as a food.

WALNUT, MANCHURIAN *Juglans mandshurica* (mandshurica—of Manchuria)

Growing in Korea, this walnut resembles the European species but is generally milder and straighter in grain. The wood weighs about 32 lbs. per cubic foot and the trees are small in girth, providing only narrow widths. As a result, it has very little value commercially.

WALNUT, NEW GUINEA *Dracontomelum mangiferum* (Draconto—a kind of bird; melum—origin unknown; mang—the mango, a tropical fruit; iferum—to bear)

This is a tall tree, growing in New Guinea and the Philippines, and often reaches a height of 125 ft. and with diameters of 30 in.

The color is similar to paldao and it runs very heavily to a contrasting stripe and some mottled figure. Being a rather hard cabinet wood, very much like paldao, it is often mistaken for it. The average weight is 45 lbs. per cubic foot.

The lumber can be dried without difficulty and may be worked easily with hand and power tools. When cut on the quarter, it produces very attractive veneers which command a good price, and it is used in architectural front panels and in furniture.

WALNUT, SOUTH AMERICAN

WALNUTS of different kinds grow in Ecuador, in Peru on the western Andean slopes and in Argentina. These trees are of the *Juglans* species and vary slightly from each other, but in most ways the wood is similar to the American walnut.

WALNUT OF ARGENTINA *Juglans australia* These trees seldom grow more than 60 ft. in height and generally are considerably shorter, but have a very thick trunk, at times more than 3 ft. in diameter. They grow in fair-sized quantities in Salta, Estero and Jujuy. The wood is very similar to American walnut for color and general characteristics, with the exception that it is lighter in weight. All other properties of seasoning, workability and stability are the same as the American species.

Walnut also grows in the Cordilleras of Colombia and one species produces a rich brown wood of a beautiful satiny luster, similar in many ways to Spanish cedar, which explains why it is commonly known as Cedro, Negro and occasionally as Cedro Nogal.

WALNUT OF PERU *Juglans neotropica* This tree often attains a height of from 45 to 60 ft. and a diameter up to 36 in., occasionally more, with a straight, well-formed trunk, at times 20 to 30 ft. above the ground before the first branches occur. The tree grows in sandy valleys at elevations of 5,000 to 8,000 ft.

While sharing many of the fine characteristics of our American walnut, this wood is little known because of the inaccessibility of the countryside where it grows. One way is to raft the logs through hazardous rapids, involving great danger, to the town of Iquitos. A safer and more tedious method is to transport small lots over the western Andean range on pack mules to the town of Celendin—a six-day trip—and then by road and railroad to the nearest port on the Pacific Ocean.

A product of the fruit, leaves and bark is used for dyeing. The lumber locally is used for cabinetmaking, furniture manufacture and musical instruments. It is highly prized for these purposes.

WANDOO *Eucalyptus redunca* (Eu/calyptus—true cover; redunca —curved backward)

Wandoo grows in an area of some 10,000 square miles throughout western Australia, the trees reaching a height of 110 ft. or more with a diameter of some 30 in. It is one of the twelve or more eucalyptus which are classed as red gums.

The wood is plain-colored, of

fine, dense texture, the color varying from a rich reddish brown to a light yellow-brown color, the color darkening after exposure to air and light. Wandoo is heavy and hard, weighing about 70 lbs. per cubic foot, and is seldom exported from Australia because its extreme hardness and weight limit its usefulness in most industries.

This wood is very difficult to work with hand tools, but power tools do a satisfactory job. It is not a wood that is used in fine cabinetmaking. The large timbers are generally used for decking, wharves, girders, joists and bridge timbers. It is also a good wood for railroad ties because of its high resistance to decay and some have been reported as being in good condition after serving for thirty-five years or more.

WELI-PENNA *Anisophyllea cinnamomoides* (Aniso/phyllea—unequal leaves; cinnamomoides—like *Cinnamomum*)

This wood emanates from the lowlands of Ceylon and produces a dark, heavy wood, about 50 lbs. per cubic foot, very similar in color and grain to the silver grain of oak. It is a very attractive wood in appearance, and veneers are generally cut on the quarter to show the grain. Only very limited quantities of this timber are exported.

WHITEBEAM *Sorbus aria* (Sorbus —classical Latin name; aria— goodness)

This tree grows in Great Britain and throughout the larger portion of Europe. It is a slow-growing tree, rarely reaching a height of more than 70 ft. and a diameter of 1 to 2 ft. It is a handsome tree, valuable for decorative purposes, and produces very nice timber.

The heartwood is pinkish brown, and the pinkish gray shades have mild markings. It is moderately hard and heavy, about 43 lbs. per cubic foot, of fine texture and straight grain. This wood seasons well, providing the seasoning is done slowly. It is a good wood for carving and turning and suitable for all types of tool handles and heads of mallets.

WILLOW *Salix* (Salix—the classical Latin name)

The well-known species are CRACK WILLOW, CRICKET BAT WILLOW and WHITE WILLOW.

No group of trees grows in a wider range of territory than the willows. They range all the way from the polar regions to tropical countries. There are many species, some of which are more or less shrubs, while others have the dimensions of large trees.

Willow is a straight-grained, white-colored wood and upon exposure it deepens to a pale brownish color. It is soft, light in weight, but extremely tough for its weight. In England this wood is highly prized for the manufacture of bats for playing cricket, which explains why it has names which refer to this use. It is also preferred at times for the manufacture of artificial limbs.

WILLOW, BLACK *Salix nigra* (nigra—black)

This tree grows through practically the entire eastern half of the United States from Canada to the Gulf, with the exception of Florida. Black willow is recognized by

Black willows, with inclined trunks, grow in clumps and attain heights of 80 feet with trunk diameters of 1 to 2 feet.

the long, narrow leaves, pointed at the tip. The top surface is a bright green and the under surface has a hairy appearance and is a little lighter in color. It is considered the most valuable commercially of over one hundred different types of willows that may be found in the United States.

The wood is generally grayish brown with dark streaks, but at other times it is light reddish brown. Working this wood with tools is very difficult. It is of even texture, lightweight but strong, and manufacturers of artificial limbs prefer to use this rather than other woods. Quantities of it are also used in the manufacture of paper pulp and excelsior.

WOMARA *Swartzia leiocalycina* (Swartzia—after Olaf Swartz, 1760–1817, Swedish botanist; leio/calycina—smooth floral leaves)

This large tree grows in British Guiana and is one of the seventy species of the genus *Swartzia*, all of which may be found in tropical America. The tree grows tall and may have a clear trunk up to 60 ft., with a total height at times of 110 ft. or more. There is a large amount of almost pure white sapwood, but the heartwood is in sharp contrast, shading from purple to a dark brown and at times containing a dark green stripe.

The wood is extremely heavy and hard, the weight varying anywhere from 60 to 80 lbs. per cubic foot. In logging, it is advisable to have as little time elapse as possible after the tree is felled before it is sawed into lumber, otherwise there is a great tendency for the wood to split.

A considerable amount of this wood is used in British Guiana for cabinetwork, fancy articles, furniture, inlays, archery bows, and other special items, and this is unusual because the wood is difficult to work, either with hand or power tools. The one exception is that it is an excellent wood for turning on the lathe.

YELLOW STERCULIA *Sterculia oblonga* (Sterculia—from the Latin *Stercus,* referring to the odor of some of these trees and meaning manure; oblonga—oblong)

This species is known as OKOKO in Benin and grows on the west coast of Africa.

The color of this wood is a pleasing yellow with lighter markings, and the wood is hard and heavy, averaging around 55 lbs. per cubic foot. When freshly cut, the wood has a most unpleasant odor, but this disappears almost entirely as it is dried. It dries well when done slowly and it can be worked without trouble with either power or hand tools.

Until recent years this wood was used almost exclusively in the countries in which it grows, but it has lately been exported to Great Britain and other commercial markets in limited quantities.

YEMERI *Vochysia hondurensis* (Vochysia—native name of the plant; hondurensis—from Honduras)

This wood, called QUARUBA in San Juan, grows in southern Mexico and south through British Honduras, in moist soils.

It is a slender tree, often 130 ft.

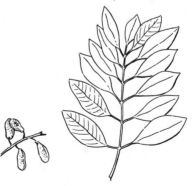

in height, and seldom more than 3 ft. in diameter. The heartwood is a pale, pinkish brown color; it is of straight grain, without any distinctive odor or taste, and light in weight—some 25 to 30 lbs. per cubic foot.

The wood is hard to season, as it has strong tendencies to warp and also has a high shrinkage. It has to be converted fairly quickly after felling, for it will deteriorate rapidly in the forest from attacks by termites and pinhole borers. The manufactured lumber will work fairly easily with either hand or power tools, but quickly takes the edge off them. It is a good all-around, useful timber, suitable for general carpentry work and particularly where the surface is to be painted.

YEW WOOD *Taxus baccata* (Taxus —the classical Latin name; baccata—berrylike, in reference to the red-covered seed)

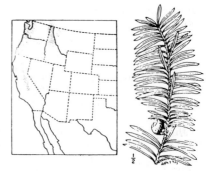

Yew is one of the very few evergreen trees native to Great Britain, but it also grows in many parts of Europe, Asia, Persia, north Africa and in sections of the Himalaya mountain ranges.

The tree is small, from 20 to 60 ft. in height, with a short trunk. At times it is as much as 3 ft. in diameter. The sapwood is white and the heartwood, when first cut, will vary from a bright tan to brown or purple but with exposure to air and light it assumes a uniform, warm brown color.

Yew wood, two-piece match.

It is a heavy wood for a softwood species, tough, hard and strong, and its fine texture will produce a highly polished surface. At times the tree produces burls which are highly prized when manufactured into veneers. They equal the markings and coloring of thuya wood.

For many centuries this wood was manufactured into archery bows and before firearms were invented there was not sufficient yew in some countries to produce the bows required. Today yew is used occasionally in small cabinetwork and in creating unusual pieces of furniture.

YUBA *Castanospermum australe* (Castano / spermum—chestnut-seeded; australe—southern)

Emanating from Australia, this species is known also as BEAN WOOD, BLACK BEAN and MORE-TON BAY CHESTNUT, inasmuch as the tree was first discovered in Moreton Bay near Brisbane, Australia.

The tree is large, reaching a height of over 110 ft. and with diameters up to 3 ft. The wood is attractive in appearance, brown or olive-green in color, deepening nearly to a black, with streaks of lighter shades, like a blending of chestnut and teak. Occasionally it will be highly figured. It is coarse-textured and fairly hard and heavy, weighing 48 lbs. per cubic foot. It has somewhat the feeling of teak to the touch but not as pronounced.

When properly seasoned, it is an excellent wood to work with and is one that is highly prized because of its high electrical insulation properties. The difficulty experienced in the handling and manufacturing of this wood stems from the fact that so many logs contain gum spots, distributed throughout the tree. When it is manufactured, much of the veneer is of little value, as only a

Zebrano or zebra wood.

small percentage of the log will be found absolutely clear and free of this gum.

A fine polish can be secured on this wood. In this country it has been used principally in the veneer form for high-grade paneling and for furniture, although in small quantities.

ZEBRANO *Cynometra*

This wood is known also as ZEBRA WOOD and ZINGANA and is so named because of its similarity to the markings of a zebra with its blackish longitudinal stripes on a light background. The name, however, may be misleading, for there are a number of different species of wood emanating from South America and Africa known as zebra. The zebra illustrated herewith, known throughout this country as zebra, is from the west coast of Africa. It could be better named to distinguish it from the other species known as zebra wood.

The trees grow to large size and owing to their practical inaccessibility, the handling, which is done by native labor, is extremely hazardous and costly. The bark averages a foot in thickness and is always trimmed at the place of felling. It may be used where diamond matching is desired, because of its pronounced lines. Often it is used for borders on furniture, because of the striking effect.

APPENDIX

Terms Commonly Used in Referring to Wood

AIR-DRIED Removing moisture from green wood by exposing to the air, usually in a yard without artificial heat.

BARK A nontechnical term used to cover all the tissues outside the xylem cylinder—the outer layer of a tree, comprising the inner bark, or thin inner living part (see Phloem) and the outer bark, or corky layer composed of dry, dead tissue (Rhytidome).

BUTT DIAMETER The larger cross-sectional measurement of a log, at the end toward the original base of the tree.

CAMBIUM (vascular cambium) The actively dividing layer of cells that lies between, and gives rise to, secondary xylem and phloem or, in other words, the layer of tissue just beneath the bark from which the new wood and bark cells of each year's growth develop.

CELL A chamber or compartment at some time containing a protoplast; a general term for the minute units of wood structure. It includes fibers, vessel segments and other elements of diverse structure and functions.

CELL WALL The limiting membrane of a cell.

CELLULOSE The carbohydrate that is the principal constituent of wood and forms the framework of the cells.

CHECK A separation of the wood, usually extending across the rings of annual growth and commonly resulting from stresses set up in the wood during seasoning.

CLOSE-GRAINED WOOD Wood with narrow and inconspicuous annual rings. The term is sometimes used to designate wood having small and closely spaced pores but in this sense the term "fine-textured" is more correctly used.

COARSE-GRAINED WOOD Wood with wide and conspicuous annual rings; that is, rings in which there is considerable difference between springwood and summerwood. The term is sometimes used to designate wood with large pores such as oak, ash, chestnut and walnut, but in this sense the term "coarse-textured" is more accurate.

COLLAPSE The flattening of single cells or row of cells in hard wood during the drying or pressure treatment of wood, characterized externally by a caved-in or corrugated appearance.

CROSS-BREAK A separation of the wood cells across the grain. Such breaks may be due to internal strain resulting from unequal longitudinal shrinkage or to external forces.

CUP The distortion in a board that deviates flatwise from a straight line across the width of the board.

DENSITY The weight of a body per unit volume. When expressed in the c.g.s. (centimeter-gram-second) system, it is numerically equal to the specific gravity of the same substance.

DRY ROT A term loosely applied to any dry, crumbly rot, but especially to that which, in an advanced stage, permits the wood to be crushed easily to a dry powder. The term is actually a misnomer, since all wood-rotting fungi require considerable moisture for growth.

ELEMENT A general term used for an individual cell.

EPIDERMIS The outermost layer of cells on the primary plant body; often with strongly thickened and cuticularized outer walls; sometimes consisting of more than one layer of cells.

FIBER A general term of convenience in wood anatomy for any long, narrow cell of wood or bast other than vessels and parenchyma.

FIGURE The pattern produced in a wood surface by irregular coloration and by annual growth rings. Rays, knots and such deviations from the regular grain as interlocked and wavy grain also contribute to the design of figure.

GREEN Freshly sawed lumber, or lumber that has received no intentional drying; unseasoned. The term does not apply to lumber that may have become completely wet through waterlogging.

GROWTH LAYER A layer of wood or bark produced apparently during one growing period; frequently, especially in woods of the temperate zones, divisible into early and late wood or bark.

HARDWOOD The botanical group of trees that are broad-leaved and bear flowers. The term has no actual reference to the hardness of the wood. The botanical name for hardwoods is angiosperm. (When "hard wood" has been used in this book as two words, it means that the wood is hard without respect to whether it is botanically a "hardwood" or a "softwood".)

HEARTWOOD The inner layers of wood, extending from the pith to the sapwood, which in the growing tree have ceased to contain living cells and in which the reserve materials (e.g., starch) have been removed or converted into heartwood substances. Heartwood may be infiltrated with gums, resins and other materials which usually make it darker and more decay-resistant than sapwood.

KILN A heated chamber for drying wood. There are two types of kilns: the compartment kiln which keeps the same temperature and relative humidity throughout any given time, and the progressive kiln which provides drying conditions that increase in severity from entrance to exit.

KILN-DRIED Oven-dried.

LAMINATED WOOD A "piece" of wood built up of plies or layers that have been joined, either with glue or mechanical fastenings. The term is most frequently applied where the plies are too thick to be classified as veneer and when the grain of all plies is parallel.

LIGNIN A principal constituent of wood, second in quantity to cellulose. It encrusts the cell walls and cements the cells together.

LONGITUDINAL Generally, the direction along the length of the grain of wood; axial.

MERISTEM A tissue capable of active cell division, thereby adding new cells to the plant body.

MERISTEM, APICAL The meristem at the growing point of shoots and roots.

MOISTURE CONTENT OF WOOD The weight of the water contained in the wood, usually expressed in percentage of the weight of the oven-dry wood.

NAVAL STORES A term applied to the oils, resins, tars and pitches derived from oleoresin contained in, exuded by, or extracted from trees, chiefly of pine species (genus *Pinus*) or from the wood of such trees.

OLD GROWTH Timber growing in, or harvested from, a mature, naturally established forest. When the trees have grown most or all of their individual lives in active competition with their companions for sunlight and moisture, this timber is usually straight with few knots.

PARENCHYMA Tissue composed of cells that are typically brick-shaped or isodiametric, and primarily concerned with the storage and distribution of food materials.

PERFORATION, VESSEL An opening from one vessel member to another.

PHLOEM The principal food-conducting tissue of the vascular plants.

PIT A recess in the secondary wall of a cell.

PITH The small, soft core occurring in the structural center of a tree, consisting chiefly of parenchyma or soft tissue.

PLYWOOD An assembly made of layers (plies) of veneer, or of veneer in combination with a solid core, joined with an adhesive. The grain of adjoining plies is usually laid at right angles, and almost always an odd number of plies are used to obtain balanced construction.

PORE A term of convenience for the cross section of a vessel.

RADIAL Coincident with a radius, from the axis of the tree or log to the circumference. A radial section is a lengthwise section in a plane that extends from pith to bark.

RATE OF GROWTH The speed at which a tree increases in size. This may be measured radially in the trunk, or in the lumber cut from the trunk, or in the dimension of the crown or other tree part. One unit of measure in wood is in number of annual growth rings per inch.

RAY A ribbonlike aggregate of cells formed by the cambium and extending radially in the xylem and phloem.

RAYS Strips of cells extending radially within a tree and varying in height from a few cells in some species to 4 in. or more in oak (*Quercus*). The rays serve primarily to store food and transport food horizontally in the tree.

RESIN CANAL An intercellular canal containing resin.

RING, ANNUAL In wood and bark, a growth layer of one year as seen in cross section.

RING, ANNUAL GROWTH The growth layer added in a single growing year.

RIPPLE MARKS Fine horizontal striations visible on the tangential longitudinal surfaces of certain woods, due to the storied arrangement of the rays or of the axial elements or of both.

SAP All the fluids in a tree except special secretions and excretions, such as oleoresin.

SAPWOOD The portion of the wood that in the living tree contains living cells and reserve materials. The layers of wood next to the bark, usually lighter in color than the heartwood and actively involved in the life processes of the tree. Under most conditions sapwood is more susceptible to decay than heartwood. It is also more permeable to liquids. Sapwood is not essentially weaker or stronger than heartwood of the same species.

SEASONING Removing moisture from green wood in order to improve its serviceability.

SECOND GROWTH Timber that has grown after the removal by any means of all, or a large portion, of the previous stand.

SHRINKAGE When drying or seasoning, timber gives up moisture to the atmosphere and shrinks in size. The amount of shrinkage differs from one timber to another. Within the same piece of timber, the shrinkage varies in different directions and this may cause cracks.

SILICA The chemical compound silicon dioxide which is present in some woods. It imparts a hardness to the wood and dulls the cutting edges of tools used in machining.

SOFTWOOD The botanical group of trees that have needle or scalelike leaves and are evergreen for the most part—cypress, larch and tamarack being exceptions. The term has no reference to the actual hardness of the wood (see note under Hardwood). Softwoods are often referred to as conifers and botanically they are called gymnosperms.

SPECIFIC GRAVITY The ratio of the weight of a body to the weight of an equal volume of water at some standard temperature.

SPRINGWOOD The portion of the annual growth ring that is formed during the early part of the season's growth. It is usually less dense and weaker mechanically than summerwood.

STAIN A discoloration in wood that may be caused by such diverse agencies as microorganisms, metal or chemicals; also, materials used to color wood.

STORIED A term applied to the axial cells and rays in wood when these are arranged in horizontal series on tangential surfaces.

SUMMERWOOD The portion of the annual growth ring that is formed during the latter part of the yearly growth period. It is usually more dense and stronger mechanically than springwood.

TIMBER STANDING Timber still on the stump.

TRACHEARY ELEMENTS The principal water-conducting elements of the xylem, mostly vessel members and tracheids.

TRACHEID An imperforate wood cell with bordered pits.

TREE In common usage a tree is a woody plant that reaches a height of at least 10 ft., has a single stem and a definite crown shape. A shrub usually is less than 10 ft. tall and has several stems without forming a definite crown. Some specimens may take the form of a tree while others of the same species may take the form of a shrub—sumac and willows, for example.

TWIST A distortion caused by the turning or winding of the edge of a board so that the four corners of any face are no longer in the same plane.

VENEER Thin sheets of wood from 1/100 to 1/4 in. thick.

Rotary cut—Veneer cut in a continuous strip by rotating a log against the edge of a knife, in a veneer lathe.

Sawed—Veneer produced by sawing.

Sliced—Veneer sliced off by moving a log, bolt or flitch against a large knife.

VESSEL An axial series of cells that have coalesced to form an articulated tubelike structure of indeterminate length. A union of wood cells which have open ends and are set one above the other, forming continuous tubes. The openings of the vessels on the surface of a piece of wood are usually referred to as pores.

VESSEL MEMBER OR ELEMENT One of the cellular components of a vessel.

VIRGIN GROWTH The original growth of matured trees.

WARP Any variation from a true or plane surface. Warp includes bow, crook, cup and twist or any combination thereof.

WOOD The principal strengthening and water-conducting tissue of stems and roots.

WOOD, COMPRESSION Reaction wood formed typically on the lower sides of branches and leaning or crooked stems of coniferous trees, and characterized anatomically by heavily lignified tracheids that are rounded in transverse section and bear spiral cell-wall checks; zones of compression wood are typically denser and darker than the surrounding tissue.

WOOD, DIFFUSE-POROUS Wood in which the pores are of fairly uniform or only gradually changing size and distribution throughout a growth ring.

WOOD, EARLY The less-dense, larger-celled, first-formed part of a growth ring.

WOOD, LATE The denser, smaller-celled, later-formed part of a growth ring.

WOOD, NON-PORED Wood devoid of pores or vessels; characteristic of conifers.

WOOD, PORED Wood with vessels; typical of woody flowering plants as opposed to conifers.

WOOD PRESERVATIVE Any substance that for a reasonable length of time will prevent the action of wood-destroying fungi, borers of various kinds and similar destructive life when the wood has been properly coated or impregnated.

WOOD, REACTION Wood with more or less distinctive anatomical characters, formed typically in parts of leaning or crooked stems and in branches and tending to restore the original position, if this has been disturbed.

WOOD, RING-POROUS Wood in which the pores of the early wood are distinctly larger than those of the late wood and form a well-defined zone or ring (cf. Wood, diffuse-porous).

WOOD, TENSION Reaction wood formed typically on the upper sides of branches and leaning or crooked stems of dicotyledonous trees and characterized anatomically by lack of cell-wall lignification and often by the presence of an internal gelatinous layer in the fibers.

WORKABILITY The degree of ease and smoothness of cut obtainable with hand or machine tools.

BIBLIOGRAPHY

Audas, J. W. 1952. *Native trees of Australia.* Melbourne: Whitcombe and Tombs Pty.

Benson, L. 1957. *Plant classification.* Boston: D. C. Heath.

Boas, I. H. 1947. *The commercial timbers of Australia.* Melbourne: Government Printer.

Boerhave, B. W. 1964. *Wood dictionary.* Vol. 1: *Commercial and botanical nomenclature of world timbers, sources of supply.* New York: American Elsevier.

Bond, C. W. 1950. *Colonial timbers (British).* London: Isaac Pitman and Sons.

British Standards Institution. 1955. *British standard nomenclature of commercial timbers.* B.S. 881 and 589. London.

Burkill, I. H. 1935. *A dictionary of the economic products of the Malay peninsula.* London: Crown Agents for the Colonies.

Click, A. G. 1967. *Click's veneer tables*. Elkin, N.C.

Craftsman Book Company of America. 1972. *Practical lumber computer*. Paperback. Los Angeles.

Dallimore, W., and Jackson, A. B. 1948. *A handbook of the Coniferae*. London: Edward Arnold and Co.

Dalziel, J. M. 1937. *The useful plants of west tropical Africa*. London: Crown Agents for the Colonies.

Edlin, H. L. 1969. *What wood is that?* New York: Viking.

Fine Hardwoods-American Walnut Association. *Fine hardwoods selectorama*. Paperback. Chicago.

Harlow, W. M. 1970. *Inside wood*. Washington, D.C.: American Forestry Association.

Hartung, R. 1972. *Exploring plywood*. New York: Van Nostrand-Reinhold.

Hill, A. F. 1952. *Economic botany*. New York: McGraw-Hill.

Hough, R. B. 1971. *Hough's encyclopedia of American woods*. 16 vols. New York: Robert Speller and Sons.

Howard, A. L. 1951. *A manual of the timbers of the world*. London: Macmillan.

Jane, F. W. 1956. *The structure of wood*. New York: Macmillan.

Kribs, D. A. 1968. *Commercial foreign woods on the American market*. 2nd ed. New York: Dover.

Lawrence, G. H. M. 1951. *Taxonomy of vascular plants*. New York: Macmillan.

Levin, E. 1972. *The international guide to wood selection*. New York: Drake.

Little, E. L. 1953. *Check list of native and naturalized trees of the United States*. Washington, D.C.: Agriculture Handbook No. 41.

Meyer, H. 1933–1936. *Buch der Holznamen (Book of wood names)*. Hanover: M. Schaper and H. Schaper.

Mitchell, H. L. 1972. *How PEG helps the hobbyist who works with wood. Using chemical PEG to stabilize green wood and prevent checking*. Paperback. Madison, Wisconsin: U.S. Department of Agriculture, Forest Service.

Moldenke, H. N., and Moldenke, A. L. 1952. *Plants of the Bible*. Waltham, Mass.: Chronica Botanica Co.

Panshin, A. J., and DeZeeuw, C. 1970. *Textbook of wood technology.* 3rd ed. New York: McGraw-Hill.

Pearson, R. S., and Brown, H. P. 1932. *Commercial timbers of India.* Calcutta: Central Publication Branch, Government of India.

Penick, S. B. and Co. 1952. *Price list and manual.* New York.

Petro, F. J. 1971. *Felling and bucking hardwoods.* Ottawa, Canada: Pub. No. 1291, Canadian Forestry Service.

Platt, R. H. 1968. *Discover American trees.* New York: Dodd, Mead and Co.

Record, S. J., and Hess, R. W. 1943. *Timbers of the new world.* New Haven, Conn.: Yale University Press.

Rendle, B. J. 1970. *World timbers.* 3 vols. Toronto, Canada: University of Toronto Press.

Reyes, L. J. 1938. *Philippine woods.* Manila: Technical Bulletin 7, Department of Agriculture and Commerce, Commonwealth of the Philippines.

Spalt, H. A., and Stern, W. L. 1956. *Survey of African woods* (A series still in publication). *Tropical Woods* 105 et seq.

Stern, W. L. 1957. *Guide to institutional wood collections. Tropical Woods* 106: 1–29.

U.S. Department of Agriculture. 1949. *Trees, yearbook of agriculture.* Washington, D.C.

U.S. Department of Agriculture. *Wood, colors and kinds.* Agricultural handbook No. 101. Paperback. Washington, D.C.

Villiard, P. 1968. *A manual of veneering.* New York: Van Nostrand.

Wilson, B. F. 1970. *The growing tree.* Amherst, Ma.: University of Massachusetts Press.

A NOTE ABOUT THE TWO INDEXES

WOOD INDEX

This index includes the names of all the woods referred to in the text, indexed under the noun, not adjective—i.e., Spruce, blue. In addition to the approved common name, whenever the wood is often known by other names, these are also given.

Immediately following most of the scientific (botanical) names in the text is an explanation as to why this particular name has been selected . . . who named it, if that is known, or if the person was a recognized authority in his field . . . and what the name means when translated. This is, to our knowledge, the first time this has ever been done.

Scientific names are set in *italics*. Numbers in the index followed by an asterisk * refer to pages giving a detailed description of a wood. If the number and asterisk (161*) follow a name set in *italics*, this indicates an explanation of the derivation of the name of the wood.

GENERAL INDEX

Listed alphabetically are special items of interest referred to in the text, such as the country from which the wood comes (other than the United States), the special products made from each of the woods, the most durable woods, workability of woods, rare woods, those that finish well, odor and taste of woods, exceptionally tall trees, heavier than average woods, woods that are used as substitutes for other woods, figure in woods, poisonous woods.

This cross-indexing makes available at a glance much of the information contained in this volume. For example, if you want to know what woods come from Formosa, India or Turkey, by referring to the listing of the country in the General Index, you will find after each country the page numbers where these woods are discussed. If you want to know the favorite wood used for making baseball bats, archery equipment, artificial limbs or toothpicks, the index directs you.

WOOD INDEX

[343

GENERAL INDEX